"*Varieties of Legal Order* is a fitting tribute to Robert Kagan. It contains an important set of essays by a prominent group of scholars who explore Kagan's seminal distinction between adversarial and bureaucratic legalism in ways that should be of interest to scholars in many of fields."

—Herbert M. Kritzer, Marvin J. Sonosky Chair of Law and Public Policy, University of Minnesota

"This is a rich and diverse overview of the relationship between law, politics, and public policy. Leading scholars examine the political struggles over different forms of law and how those different forms shape social institutions. *Varieties of Legal Order* provides a thoughtful, nuanced introduction to a provocative set of conversations about the profusion of law across the globe."

—Susan S. Silbey, Leon and Anne Goldberg Professor of Sociology and Anthropology, and Professor of Behavioral and Policy Sciences, MIT

Law, Courts and Politics

Edited by Robert M. Howard

Georgia State University

In *Democracy in America*, Alexis de Tocqueville famously noted that "scarcely any political question arises in the United States that is not resolved, sooner or later, into a judicial question." The importance of courts in settling political questions in areas ranging from health care to immigration shows the continuing astuteness of de Tocqueville's observation. To understand how courts resolve these important questions, empirical analyses of law, courts and judges, and the politics and policy influence of law and courts have never been more salient or more essential.

Law, Courts and Politics was developed to analyze these critically important questions. This series presents empirically driven manuscripts in the broad field of judicial politics and public law by scholars in law and social science. It uses the most up to date scholarship and seeks an audience of students, academics, upper division undergraduate and graduate courses in law, political science and sociology, as well as anyone interested in learning more about law, courts and politics.

VARIETIES OF LEGAL ORDER

Across the globe, law in all its variety is becoming more central to politics, public policy, and everyday life. For over four decades, Robert A. Kagan has been a leading scholar of the causes and consequences of the march of law that is characteristic of late 20th and early 21st century governance. In this volume, top sociolegal scholars use Kagan's concepts and methods to examine the politics of litigation and regulation, both in the United States and around the world.

Through studies of civil rights law, tobacco politics, "Eurolegalism," Russian auto accidents, Australian coal mines, and California prisons, these scholars probe the politics of different forms of law, and the complex path by which "law on the books" shapes social life. Like Kagan's scholarship, *Varieties of Legal Order* moves beyond stale debates about litigiousness and overregulation, and invites us to think more imaginatively about how the rise of law and legalism will shape politics and social life in the 21st century.

Thomas F. Burke is Professor of Political Science at Wellesley College. His research focuses on the place of rights and litigation in public policy, and the ways in which organizations respond to rights laws. His most recent books are *How Policy Shapes Politics* (2015), coauthored with Jeb Barnes, and the ninth edition of *Reason in Law* (2016), coauthored with Lief Carter. In a stroke of extraordinary luck, his Ph.D. dissertation, *Litigation and Its Discontents*, was supervised by Robert Kagan. It won the 1996 Edwin S. Corwin Award for best dissertation in public law.

Jeb Barnes is Associate Professor of Political Science at the University of Southern California and a former Robert Wood Johnson Scholar in Health Policy Research. He is the author of five books and numerous peer-reviewed articles on the intersection of law, politics, and public policy and mixed-methods research strategies, most recently *How Policy Shapes Politics* (2015), coauthored with Thomas F. Burke, and *Finding Pathways: Mixed-Method Research for Studying Causal Mechanisms* (2014) coauthored with Nicholas Weller.

VARIETIES OF LEGAL ORDER

The Politics of Adversarial and Bureaucratic Legalism

Edited by Thomas F. Burke and Jeb Barnes

Routledge
Taylor & Francis Group
NEW YORK AND LONDON

First published 2018
by Routledge
711 Third Avenue, New York, NY 10017

and by Routledge
2 Park Square, Milton Park, Abingdon, Oxon, OX14 4RN

Routledge is an imprint of the Taylor & Francis Group, an informa business

Library of Congress Cataloging-in-Publication Data
Names: Barnes, Jeb, editor. | Burke, Thomas Frederick, editor.
Title: Varieties of legal order : the politics of adversarial and bureaucratic legalism / Jeb Barnes and Thomas F. Burke, editors.
Description: Abingdon, Oxon [UK] ; New York : Routledge, 2017. | Series: Law, courts, and politics | Includes bibliographical references and index.
Identifiers: LCCN 2017014263 (print) | LCCN 2017016554 (ebook) | ISBN 9780203095072 (Master) | ISBN 9781136211201 (WebPDF) | ISBN 9781136211195 (ePub) | ISBN 9781136211157 (Mobipocket/Kindle) | ISBN 9780415633383 (hardback : alk. paper) | ISBN 9781138090477 (pbk. : alk. paper)
Subjects: LCSH: Law—Political aspects. | Law (Philosophical concept) | Adversary system (Law) | Law—Philosophy.
Classification: LCC K487.P65 (ebook) | LCC K487.P65 V45 2017 (print) | DDC 340/.115—dc23
LC record available at https://lccn.loc.gov/2017014263

ISBN: 978-0-415-63338-3 (hbk)
ISBN: 978-1-138-09047-7 (pbk)
ISBN: 978-0-203-09507-2 (ebk)

Typeset in Bembo
by Apex CoVantage, LLC

CONTENTS

CONTRIBUTORS

Jeb Barnes is Associate Professor of Political Science at the University of Southern California and a former Robert Wood Johnson Scholar in Health Policy Research. He is the author of five books and numerous peer-reviewed articles on the intersection of law, politics, and public policy and mixed-methods research strategies, most recently *How Policy Shapes Politics* (2015), coauthored with Thomas F. Burke, and *Finding Pathways: Mixed-Method Research for Studying Causal Mechanisms* (2014), coauthored with Nicholas Weller.

Francesca Bignami is Professor of Law at The George Washington University Law School. She has published extensively on comparative administrative and regulatory law, comparative privacy law, and EU law. She is an elected member of the International Association of Comparative Law, and she is on the editorial board of several academic journals, including the American Journal of Comparative Law. She has held visiting professorships at Harvard Law School, the LUISS University (Rome), and the VU University Amsterdam. Among her most recent works is *Comparative Law and Regulation: Understanding the Global Regulatory Process* (2016), which she coedited with David Zaring.

Thomas F. Burke is Professor of Political Science at Wellesley College. His research focuses on the place of rights and litigation in public policy, and the ways in which organizations respond to rights laws. His most recent books are the ninth edition of *Reason in Law* (2016), coauthored with Lief Carter, and *How Policy Shapes Politics* (2015), coauthored with Jeb Barnes. In a stroke of extraordinary luck, his Ph.D. dissertation, *Litigation and Its Discontents*, was supervised by Robert Kagan. It won the 1996 Edwin S. Corwin Award for best dissertation in public law.

Cary Coglianese is the Edward B. Shils Professor of Law and Professor of Political Science at the University of Pennsylvania, where he currently serves as the founding director of the Penn Program on Regulation and has served as the law school's Deputy Dean for Academic Affairs. He specializes in the study of regulation and regulatory processes, with an emphasis on the empirical evaluation of alternative regulatory strategies and the role of public participation, negotiation, and business-government relations in policymaking. His most recent books include: *Achieving Regulatory Excellence* (2017), *Does Regulation Kill Jobs?* (2013), *Regulatory Breakdown: The Crisis of Confidence in U.S. Regulation* (2012), *Import Safety: Regulatory Governance in the Global Economy* (2009), and, with Robert A. Kagan, *Regulation and Regulatory Processes* (2007).

Malcolm M. Feeley is Claire Sanders Clements Dean's Professor of Jurisprudence and Social Policy at Boalt Hall School of Law, University of California at Berkeley. Among his dozen books are *The Process Is the Punishment* (1979), *The Policy Dilemma* (1980) (with Austin Sarat), *Court Reform on Trial* (1983), *Judicial Policy Making and the Modern State* (1998), and *Federalism: Political Identity and Tragic Compromise* (2008) (the last two with Edward Rubin). He has received the ABA's Silver Gavel Award and its Certificate of Merit, the Law and Society Association's Harry Kalven Award, and the Western Society of Criminology's Paul Tappen Award.

Neil Gunningham is a lawyer and social scientist working principally in the areas of safety, health, and environmental law, regulation, and governance. He is a Professor in the Regulatory Institutions Network at the Australian National University. His books include *Smart Regulation* (1998) (with Grabosky), *Regulating Workplace Safety* (1999) (with Johnstone), and *Shades of Green: Business, Regulation and Environment* (2003) (with Kagan and Thornton). He has also consulted to the OECD, the United Nations Environment Programme, and numerous state and federal environmental agencies.

William Haltom is Professor of Politics and Government at the University of Puget Sound, where he teaches courses in U.S. politics and sociolegal studies. Author of *Reporting on the Courts* (1998) and coauthor, with Michael McCann, of *Distorting the Law* (2004), he tends to study cultural representations of law and of politics.

Kathryn Hendley is the William Voss-Bascom Professor of Law and Political Science at the University of Wisconsin–Madison. Her research focuses on the role of law in contemporary Russia, with a particular emphasis on how ordinary Russians experience the law in their daily lives. Her publications include *Everyday Law in Russia* (2017), as well as articles in such journals as the *American Journal of Comparative Law*, *Law & Social Inquiry*, *Law & Society Review*, *Post-Soviet Affairs*, and *Slavic Review*.

R. Daniel Kelemen is Professor of Political Science and Law and Jean Monnet Chair in European Union Politics at Rutgers University. His research focuses on the law and politics of the European Union and comparative law and politics. He has published six books and more than 60 articles and book chapters on these topics, including *Eurolegalism: The Transformation of Law and Regulation in the European Union* (2011) which won the Best Book Award from the European Union Studies Association.

Michael McCann is very honored to be the Gordon Hirabayashi Professor for the Advancement of Citizenship at the University of Washington and, currently, Director of the Harry Bridges Center for Labor Studies. He is author of *Rights at Work* (1994) and coauthor, with William Haltom, of *Distorting the Law* (2004). Michael was fortunate in graduate school, from 1977 to 1982, to benefit from the extraordinary mentoring of Bob Kagan.

R. Shep Melnick is the Thomas P. O'Neill Jr. Professor of American Politics at Boston College and cochair of the Harvard Program on Constitutional Government. He is the author of *Regulation and the Courts: The Case of the Clean Air Act* (1983), *Between the Lines: Interpreting Welfare Rights* (1994), and *The Transformation of Title IX: Regulating Gender Equality in Education* (2017), as well as many articles on courts, agencies, and public policy. He has also been a Research Associate at Brookings, President of the New England Political Science Association, and an elected member of the New Hampshire House of Representatives.

Van Swearingen is a lawyer in private practice at Rosen Bien Galvan & Grunfeld LLP, where he focuses on civil rights and other complex civil litigation. Mr. Swearingen received his J.D. from the University of California, Berkeley School of Law (Boalt Hall) in 2008, where he was Executive Editor of the *California Law Review*. He holds a master's degree in Public Policy from the Goldman School of Public Policy at the University of California, Berkeley, and a B.A. in Government from the University of Texas at Austin.

ACKNOWLEDGMENTS

This volume traces its origins all the way back to a 2007 conference celebrating Robert Kagan's body of research. The conference was held at the Center for the Study of Law and Society at UC-Berkeley, an institution that has nourished the scholarship of countless sociolegal researchers, among whom we are thankful to be part. We are grateful to the center, and especially to Rosann Greenspan, its Executive Director, whose efforts brought the conference to fruition. Thanks to all those who participated in that happy event.

We thank our editor, Natalja Mortenson, and her assistant at Routledge, Lillian Rand, for their kindness, persistence, and seemingly unlimited patience with this project as it took its many twists and turns.

We also would like to thank the authors of this volume, who went above and beyond. When we asked them to revise their chapters to make the book more conceptually unified, they were not just accommodating but creative in their responses. They pushed our thinking at every stage, and we are grateful to have learned from their contributions.

Last, and, of course, not least, we would like to thank Robert Kagan, our friend, colleague, and mentor. Bob has been a steady presence in our lives and careers. As we hope this volume demonstrates, his concepts and methods are at the forefront of efforts to understand—and, perhaps more importantly, how to ask questions about—the global burgeoning of law in its many forms. We dedicate this book to him.

1

INTRODUCTION

What We Talk About When We Talk About Law

Thomas F. Burke and Jeb Barnes

Politicians and pundits seem inclined to say two things about law: there is too much, and there is not enough. Too much, because law is "strangling" the economy (*Investor's Business Daily*, 2015), because "a flood" of lawsuits is sweeping through society (Brovard, 2015; Kilpatrick, 1984), because small business is "drowning" in regulation (Fox News, 2011). The metaphors are often aquatic, suggesting that like water, law is displacing the oxygen we need for our social institutions—profits for business, problem solving for governments, peaceful and orderly life for our communities. Law, this perspective suggests, is enveloping us, choking the life out of our workplaces, institutions and communities, and displacing traditional virtues of self-reliance with a culture of complaint (Hughes, 1993). Something must be done to restore "common sense" (Howard, 1994).

Yet sometimes the theme is reversed. When the drinking water of a community is fouled by pollution, when a minority group faces widespread discrimination, or when financial misdeeds create an economic meltdown, talk of overregulation and litigation is for the moment sidelined. We conclude that there is simply not enough law, that more must be fashioned, and urgently. As the saying goes, "There oughta be a law!"

In the battle between the "too much" and "need more" frames, the "need more" side is clearly winning on the ground. Across the globe, judicial power is on the rise, as whole sectors of public policy have become legalized, both within and among nations. We are told of "The Global Expansion of Judicial Power" (Tate & Vallinder, 1995), of the rise of a "Litigation State" (Farhang, 2010), and of the "Legalization" of world politics (Goldstein et al., 2001). We are warned of "Law's Allure" (Silverstein, 2009) and even "Juristocracy" (Hirschl, 2004). And while there has been a much-heralded move toward markets in place of government, "Freer Markets, More Rules" (Vogel, 1996) nicely summarizes the consequences—privatization and marketization, it turns out, typically require *more* law, not less.

The intensification of law is most obvious in the United States, where litigation and regulation reach into nearly every corner of society—schools and shopping malls, playgrounds and prisons, bedrooms and boardrooms—but it can be observed in many polities, some surprising. Recent books have heralded the judicialization of politics in Canada (Bogart, 2002), Australia (Sheehan, Gill, & Randazzo, 2012), among the nations of Europe (Kelemen, 2011; Sweet, 2000), across Latin America (Sieder, Schjolden, & Angell, 2005; Couso, Huneeus, & Sieder, 2010), in Southeast Asia (Dressel, 2012), and among authoritarian regimes around the world (Moustafa, 2014), including China (Stern, 2013). Sociolegal scholars are increasingly examining the "regulatory state" that is growing up in the developing world (Morgan, 2007; Bignami & Zaring, 2016). The growth of law is reflected in the constitutional courts that new democracies have created—and the legal systems that they have tried to build to attract foreign investment (Moustafa, 2014). The expansion of law can even be seen in Japan, the supposed poster child of the non-litigious society, where policymakers have reduced barriers to litigation in the past 20 years, stimulating rising litigation rates (Ginsburg & Hoetker, 2006). These scholarly accounts document the expansion of law both across countries and realms of social life.

The Need to Move Beyond Current Conversations

The profusion of law is a fundamental characteristic of politics and social life in the early 21st century, and it is understandable that there has been an accompanying profusion of academic commentary that attempts to make sense of it. We believe, however, that research on this topic has been hobbled by some serious limitations in both popular discourse and academic understandings of legal systems. A central premise of this volume is that scholars must find more productive ways to talk about the profusion of law.

The popular debate over law is hackneyed and even incoherent. When, for example, politicians, usually on the right, complain about regulation, they almost always portray it as a wound to business and a scourge on the economy. But of course this is a caricature. Regulation can in some instances foster business, or at least create certainty about standards and so generate economic investment and growth. For this reason businesses often crave regulation, and even fight for it. Moreover, much of the struggle over regulation—the part that goes on far from the glare of the media—is among firms in the same industry, each of which seeks to shape the rules to its advantage. But the popular discourse misses an even more fundamental point: Regulation often ratifies social concerns (safety, environmental protection, civil rights, privacy) that firms are already responding to, so that regulation is part of a broader politics of social norms in which myriad actors—communities, professions and social movements—play a role. The reduction of all this to "government versus business" misses much of what makes the politics of regulation so fascinating and complex.

The popular debate over litigation usually starts with an equally tired premise, that courts are taking over normal politics, encroaching on the prerogatives of elected representatives, and so damaging the democratic system. This bromide imagines a fixed boundary between law and politics that simply does not bear scrutiny, especially in the United States where courts, legislatures, and executive agencies are designed to share policymaking power, hopelessly blurring the line between law and politics. In practice, elected officials often prefer that the judiciary handle tricky political issues, passing laws designed to encourage litigation or crafting statutes that intentionally leave important matters unresolved (Graber, 1993; Lovell, 2003; Farhang, 2010). This sharing of power is reinforced from the bottom up, as groups both on the left and right actively combine lobbying and litigation in pursuing their policy agendas and thus ensure policy is considered in multiple forums (often simultaneously) (Melnick, 1994; Burke, 2002; Barnes & Miller, 2004; Keck, 2014).

Under these circumstances, the debate over litigation often is little more than a proxy for broader political struggles. Indeed, in the United States there is a long history of liberals and conservatives taking turns criticizing courts depending on how a particular line of judicial reasoning lines up with their own proclivities. During the New Deal, liberals decried the Supreme Court's political meddling when the Court ruled against their programs. Conservatives a few years later railed against the Warren Court for judicial policymaking, particularly in criminal justice and civil rights. Today, social conservatives lambast judicial activism on marriage equality while urging expansive readings of the First Amendment's protections of campaign finance. Liberals take the opposite stand, hailing the marriage equality decisions as vindications of basic rights while excoriating *Citizens United* and other campaign finance cases. A partisan hue colors cries of "judicial activism" from both left and right.

Academic researchers usually avoid the more silly aspects of popular debates about the legal system. Yet scholarship on the profusion of law is hampered by conceptual and methodological limitations. One symptom of these limitations is the welter of terms scholars use to describe the law's march: "legalization," "judicialization," "legalized accountability," "litigious policies," "juridification," the "litigation state," and various forms of "legalism" (Barnes & Burke, 2015). This proliferation of terms was probably inevitable as scholars in different countries and from different research traditions first addressed the spread of law to their corner of the world, but at this point the scholarly literature is starting to seem a Tower of Babel, with researchers in different disciplines and regions talking past one another and providing no easy way to aggregate their insights.

An underlying problem is that scholars differ in their understandings of law and so have strikingly different methodological approaches to studying its impact. Economists and some political scientists, on one side, tend to conceive of law as formal rules. They study rules as independent stimuli or "treatments" and try to isolate the effect of law on some outcome by comparing pre- to post-treatment periods, or by comparing polities that have the rules with those that do not. This approach has enormous practical and methodological appeal. It facilitates the collection of data across settings, and simplifies the research task by specifying a clear causal arrow from law to outcomes. Decades of law and society scholarship, however, have undermined the formal conception of law that underlies this approach as well as the use of simple causal models to think of its effects. Law and society scholars start from the premise that the law is not self-executing; it must be put into practice, and the process of implementing and enforcing the law substantially shapes its meaning. Much of the work that law does, after all, goes on before anyone reaches the courthouse, or even calls a lawyer. Law shapes the routines and conversations of people and organizations mostly without formal invocation. Moreover, the impact of law at the organizational level is highly variable. Organizations facing the same dictates respond in different ways. Some seek to circumvent the law through symbolic compliance, while others push far beyond what the law requires, and part of understanding the consequences of law is exploring the sources of this variation in response (Gunningham, Kagan, & Thornton, 2003; Barnes & Burke, 2012; Gray & Silbey, 2014). For these reasons, focusing on the rules—"law on the books" in the parlance of sociolegal scholars—is incomplete because it neglects the process by which law takes on life: "law on the streets."

Consider one simple example of how consequential the gap between "law on the books" and "law on the streets" can be. According to comparative legal scholars, American tort law and its counterparts abroad in the 1980s and 1990s were not all that different in terms of doctrine (Schwartz, 1991). Indeed, Dutch law might have been even more generous as a formal matter, because it allowed workers to bring tort suits directly against their employers where American law channeled employee claims into workers' compensation programs (Vinke & Wilthagen, 1992; Barnes, 2011). Yet the practice of tort law in the Netherlands and the United States during this period widely diverged. Although the incidence of asbestos-related diseases was five to ten times higher in Dutch workers in the 1970s and 1980s, only *ten* tort suits had reportedly been filed in the Netherlands as of 1991. In the United States, by contrast, asbestos litigation exploded into a "mass tort," so that, in 1990, one of every three civil cases filed in the Eastern District of Texas was an asbestos case (Judicial Conference Ad Hoc Committee, 1991, 8). The formal rules were more permissive in the Netherlands, but the degree of judicial involvement in the United States was far greater. To understand what's going on in this comparison, researchers have to dig more deeply into the political and policy settings of these countries and the lives of those plagued by asbestos to figure out why law was used in such disparate ways across the two countries.

When sociolegal scholars do this, they decenter the study of law, looking beyond the courthouse to examine how the law is shaped by the beliefs and actions of people far from the center of conventional legal authority. Human relations personnel, for example, interpret civil rights law in ways that reflect their managerial training, and so create practices that owe at least as much to managerialism as to the ideals of the civil rights movement (Edelman, Erlanger, & Lande, 1993). People with disabilities, Frank Munger and David Engel showed, interpret the commands of the Americans with Disabilities Act in line with their own social, political, and religious beliefs, and this in turn affects how they invoke (or, much more often, fail to invoke) the law (Engel & Munger, 2003). Operators of pulp mills and trucking companies interpret environmental regulations in light of the economic imperatives of their businesses, the social pressures they face at the local level and their organization's commitments to the law and its implementation (Gunningham et al., 2003; Thornton, Kagan, & Gunningham, 2008). You might assume that this proliferation of interpretations and practices is "corrected" by regulators and courts, but those formal institutions only rarely get involved. And even more radically, sociolegal scholars have shown that judges' and regulators' understanding of the law is itself shaped by the practices of the organizations and individuals the law affects (Edelman et al., 2011). So, in the social construction of the law, law and politics are mutually constitutive, which hopelessly confounds simple cause-and-effect models.

The fact is that both rules and practice matter. Ignoring one at the expense of the other distorts the way law works. Formal rules provide a framework for law-related practice and discourse, so understanding the rules is an important first step in studying the law. But looking only at formal rules obscures the mechanisms by which law is turned into social action. Understanding these mechanisms requires scholars to hit the streets and explore the myriad sites and contexts in which law does its work. The resulting focus on context and local practice makes it difficult to develop a common set of concepts about law, much less aggregate the insights from different stories. This challenge is further compounded by different legal traditions—common versus civil law versus post-communist—and cross-country variation within these traditions, as in the differences between Anglo and American common law practices (Atiyah & Summers, 1987). The blizzard of terms used to describe legalization/juridification/judicialization around the world in part reflects these different traditions, and the resulting accretion of many careful localized studies.

Thus we face a popular discourse about law that generates more heat than light, and an academic literature that raises difficult questions about how to proceed further.

The Goals of This Volume

This book seeks to move past the clichés of popular discourse about the legal system and advance the academic literature on the global intensification of law. To do so, we bring together scholars who study law in widely different settings—

a coal mine in Australia, prisons in California, regulatory bureaus in the European Union, the mean streets of Russia—but share a common starting point: they use approaches and concepts drawn from the work of Robert A. Kagan, a professor of political science and law at the University of California. Kagan, perhaps more than any other scholar, has tried to make sense of the profusion of law in all its forms that is characteristic of the late 20th and early 21st century governance. In a series of books and articles published over four decades, Kagan documented the growth of law around the globe. The bulk of his research has been on the politics and practice of regulation, but he has also written extensively about both the causes and consequences of the growing use of litigation.

Kagan's work has sometimes been cited by the "too much" school. But portraying him as a critic of litigation and regulation is far too simple, and ignores much of what is interesting in his work. Most importantly for this volume, it misses three useful tools Kagan has demonstrated for advancing how we talk about law, and how we should study its expansion.

First, Kagan's work gives us the conceptual tools to transcend popular debates on "too much" versus "too little" law, inspiring us to step back and examine the larger social and political context that gives debates about litigation and regulation their shape. Kagan shows (1991, 1994, 2001) that litigation, rather than an interruption of politics, is itself a form of governance, one that is often encouraged by elected officials and activists (see also Farhang, 2010; Burke, 2002; Barnes, 1997). Like any form of governance, it unfolds within particular political contexts and power relations, and has distinctive tilts and tendencies. Moreover, litigation competes with regulation as a mode of governance, and Kagan's research opens the way to understanding both their sources of political appeal and their consequences.

Second, Kagan's research, like that of the authors in this book, moves beyond the formal structures of litigation and regulation to show how law concretely shapes social action at the street level. This requires time to dig down into the intricacies of particular sites and organizations in which law is turned into practice. Good description—getting the story right—is foundational to any research agenda, and there is usually no convenient proxy measure for the complexities revealed at the ground level.

Third, Kagan's comparative framework, discussed below, gives us a shared conceptual language for talking about the profusion of law. The framework is general enough to be used in diverse contexts but specific enough to make meaningful distinctions across nations and fields of politics. This is crucial because it gives detail-oriented law scholars a set of tools for explaining how their work fits within the broader population of legalized policies. It also provides a measuring stick for identifying variation over time and across settings, which is essential to any empirical research agenda (Burke & Barnes, 2009).

Kagan's work gives researchers an example of how to deal with the most troubling obstacles in this field of study: 1) how to respond to popular debates about law without taking on their simplified framings, and 2) how to mediate between grand theories about law and the intensive fieldwork that is required to understand particular manifestations of law in action. We hope the body of this book will similarly provide examples for others to follow. The remainder of this introduction lays the foundation for the rest of the book, first through a quick review of Kagan's body of scholarship and then an analytic summary of the chapters that follow.

Kagan the Explorer

Like a botanist in the tropics confronting a profusion of flora, Kagan described a dense thicket of law spilling out of legislatures, bureaucratic agencies, and courts into contemporary societies. He attributed the profusion to the "relentless pressures of technological change, geographic mobility, global economic competition, and environmental pollution, which generate new inequalities, new injustices, new risks, and new cultural challenges to old norms" (Kagan, 2001, p. 6). This profusion takes widely varied forms—civil versus common law, "private" versus public law, constitutional versus statutory law, national versus state or provincial law, and state law versus local law. Much of this law is enforced by centralized bureaucracies, but some of it is promulgated by litigation, which can serve as a means not only to enforce rules but also to resolve disputes over the meaning of rules, challenge existing rules, and make new ones.

Kagan recognized that both the proliferation and diversity of forms of law posed a problem for sociolegal scholars. What should they do, Kagan asked, when "there is too much law to study"? (Kagan, 1995). Picking one particular stream of law seems arbitrary, trying to do it all impossible. Kagan's answer was twofold. First, reflecting the law and society research tradition in which he was trained, Kagan studied law not primarily in books or courtrooms but in the places where it mostly lives, in the everyday world of offices and factories, restaurants and schools. From his first book, a study of Richard Nixon's audacious attempt to regulate all prices and wages in the United States (Kagan, 1978), to his more recent research on water and air pollution (Gunningham et al., 2003; Thornton, Kagan, & Gunningham, 2008, 2009), Kagan investigated the law as it is experienced in everyday life.

But Kagan also recognized that studying individual sites of the law could be a road to nowhere, an endless series of studies about the details of particular instances of legalization without a framework for accumulation and generalization. To address this problem, Kagan, drawing on previous scholarship (Mashaw, 1983; Damaška, 1986), created ideal types of policy making and dispute resolution. Particularly important is his distinction between *adversarial legalism* and *bureaucratic legalism*, which is central to the chapters in this volume and so gives this book its title.[1]

To understand these terms, begin with a table that Kagan developed to distinguish all forms of dispute resolution and policymaking. Think of each cell as a

TABLE 1.1 Modes of Policymaking and Dispute Resolution

Organization of decision-making authority	*Decision-making style*		
	INFORMAL	⟷	FORMAL
HIERARCHICAL	Expert or political judgment		Bureaucratic legalism
↕			
PARTICIPATORY	Negotiation/ mediation		Adversarial legalism

Source: Kagan (2001).

way a polity can either settle a grievance among parties or make policy to address some social issue.

The horizontal axis is the level of *formality* in defining and determining the underlying issue, meaning the degree to which decision-makers use preexisting rules in resolving the matter. The use of rules involves all the paraphernalia of legal processes: precedents, records, documents, and written procedures. Informal processes, for example the use of expert administrative judgment by the Federal Reserve Board to adjust interest rates, are not closely constrained by preexisting substantive rules; the underlying policy decisions are made based on the professional judgment of its members and staff.

The vertical axis is the degree to which control over the decision-making process is *centralized*. In hierarchical processes, control is highly centralized, as in the example of the Federal Reserve Board, which controls monetary policy—the staff who serve under the board merely implement their commands. Participatory processes, at the other extreme, involve decision-making by bodies made up of roughly equal parties, for example legislators in Congress who each have one vote.

This volume focuses on the formal side of the table and the two cells there, adversarial legalism and bureaucratic legalism. In fact much of what is called the legalization or juridification of politics is the movement of power over decision-making from the informal to the formal side, from reliance on trusted experts, for example, or on legislative bodies, to institutions structured around adversarial or bureaucratic legalism.

Adversarial legalism involves formal and participatory structures, meaning that roughly equal parties—litigants are the paradigmatic example—drive the decision-making process. In adversarial legalism, parties dominate policy construction from the bottom up: They make policy by arguing over the meaning of substantive standards and procedural rules, the application of those rules to the decision at hand, and also the justice of the relevant rules and procedures used in the application. In the formulation and implementation of policy under adversarial legal regimes, then, everything is a matter of dispute, and all those affected by a decision are free to participate in the disputing process. There is an official decision-maker, but the decision-maker acts as a referee and so does not dominate the proceedings. Bureaucratic legalism, by contrast, is formal and hierarchical. It connotes a standard Weberian bureaucracy that centers on civil servants implementing formal rules from the top down, as is the case in many regulatory agencies.

The structural differences between adversarial and bureaucratic legalism correspond to different emphases in decision-making. In adversarial legalism, the decision-makers (for example, judges and juries in the American civil litigation system) are not tightly bound to a centralized higher authority and so a premium is placed on particularized justice, tailoring decisions to specific circumstances. In the bureaucratic model, civil servants are part of a centralized chain of command, so that emphasis is placed in the uniform application of rules across cases. For these reasons, adversarial legalism and bureaucratic legalism, though they both produce "law," are likely to be associated with different styles of law. Adversarial legalism will tend to produce a fluid, uncertain style that is unpredictable and inefficient but flexible; bureaucratic legalism is likely to be more predictable and hence more efficient, but also more rigid. Indeed, Kagan often defined adversarial legalism not as an authority structure but as a set of everyday practices—complex and punitive rules, and intense legal and political contestation over them (Kagan, 2007, pp. 166–167)—associated with adversarial legalism's decentralized, party-driven structure.

American law and legal institutions, Kagan argued, are suffused with adversarial legalism, with powerfully mixed consequences. Adversarial legalism's open-endedness makes it capable of great heroism, as when it is used to reform barbarous prisons, hold corporations accountable for reckless conduct, stop police from torturing suspects, or recognize the ways in which sexual harassment abuses women. Litigant activism can be a powerful force, prying out the secrets of institutions that inflict asbestos, tobacco, and pedophilic priests on society. Adversarial legalism made it possible for law to be, in the sociologists Philip Selznick and Philippe Nonet's terms, "responsive," that is, flexible and open to change in order to rectify social injustice (Nonet & Selznick, 1978). Further, Kagan argued that adversarial legalism is particularly attractive to American policymakers because, in a nation whose political institutions were designed to frustrate governmental activism, it gives them an alternative mechanism for addressing social problems. In an age of skepticism about government and tight fiscal constraints, adversarial legalism appears to be government on the cheap, a way of building state capacity to resolve social problems without seeming to add to existing governmental bureaucracies. But Kagan was more struck by the dark side of adversarial legalism: its costs, complexity, and unpredictability, features that result from its bottom-up structure and endless opportunities for rule contestation. These downsides often create a system that works poorly both for would-be plaintiffs, who often cannot afford to use it, and organizations, which struggle to manage uncertain legal threats.

Kagan was unusual among academics in that he worked at both the macro and micro levels, comfortable with making the big generalizations necessary for productive cross-national comparisons, but also with the more nuanced observations required for studies of particular sites, like ports, factories, and offices. As a result there is a tension in Kagan's work between structure and process, or between the apparent tilt of the structures of authority and the actual (and often highly variable) consequences that Kagan discovered when he studied law in action. American criminal law gives defendants, in theory, all kinds of ways in which to contest their prosecution, yet an overwhelming percentage of defendants forgo their rights and take a deal instead. Tort and civil rights law in theory promise all kinds of opportunities for injured plaintiffs, but most of those aggrieved "lump it." Adversarial legalism in theory offers too much law; in practice it often delivers too little. Where the main political criticism of adversarial legalism was "too much," the facts on the ground suggest a more complicated picture.

This was perhaps even more true of the larger part of Kagan's work, on bureaucratic legalism. Regulation, even in the United States, in structure looks quite close to the ideal type, with a hierarchical authority (OSHA, the EPA, the FDA) imposing rules and using the threat of punishment to elicit compliance. Kagan was part of a group of sociolegal scholars who showed just how complicated the politics of regulation really is, and how little it corresponds with this ideal type or to simple economic models of compliance and deterrence. Bureaucrats sometimes act like, well, stereotypical bureaucrats, "going by the book," as Kagan and Eugene Bardach (1982) found in their study of federal regulatory agencies, and the regulated sometimes respond as rational actors who worry only about the costs of punishment, but these are far from the only possibilities (Bardach & Kagan, [1982] 2002). Kagan was fond of comparing the regulatory politics of the United States to that of western Europe and Japan in which a less legalistic, more flexible, and cooperative relationship between regulated and regulators seemed to predominate (Kagan, 1987). Effective regulation, Kagan concluded, did not necessarily require detailed, highly punitive sanctions to deter purely rational business actors (Kagan & Axelrad, 2000).

The limits of the rational-actor model were apparent when, as Kagan often demonstrated in his research, organizations facing roughly the same threat of punishment reacted quite differently to a new law. A key variable in explaining regulatory response, Kagan and his coauthors argued, was the perceived cost of responding, as not all organizations enjoy the same "economic license" to follow new legal mandates. But the response to law is more than just a matter of weighing costs versus benefits. An organization's "management style" can also have a significant impact on its response to regulations, with some organizations acting as laggards who ignore the law, while others act as true believers who go well beyond compliance (Thornton, Kagan, & Gunningham, 2008). Kagan highlights the slew of actors and institutions that figure into response to law. It matters, for example, whether the officers within an organization who are charged with responding to regulations have internalized the norms of new laws, and this means that part of the politics of regulation is within the professions, where new norms are absorbed, translated, rejected and diffused. Communities surrounding organizations also play an important role. They can grant or deny what Kagan and his coauthors call the "social license" of the company: its legitimacy, based on community beliefs about regulations and their associated norms. A company unmoved by the threat of punishment may still worry about the damage to its reputation when it is seen to violate norms about safety, the environment, and civil rights (Thonton, Kagan, & Gunningham, 2003).

Political debates over too much or too little regulation, from this perspective, seem almost beside the point. For one thing, they center the problem in government regulations. Kagan and his colleagues showed that there is a much more complicated politics of norms in realms such as the environment, consumer protection, civil rights, and many others. Regulation is a field in which legal authority plays only a part. The corollary is that effective regulatory schemes have to go far beyond simply inducing compliance through fear of punishment. Policymakers must consider the wider, more complex politics of regulation that Kagan and his comrades have illustrated.

Bureaucratic legalism and adversarial legalism are both subjects of intense political controversy, and this is part of the reason Kagan's research became prominent. His writings on bureaucratic legalism speak to a highly polarized struggle over regulation; his work on adversarial legalism to a charged political debate over "litigiousness." There is, though, a significant downside to Kagan's ties to prominent political debates: They can obscure Kagan's core insights about how law works in society and how to study it. Both "adversarial legalism" and "bureaucratic legalism" can sound like put-downs, and Kagan's work frequently lists the pathologies associated with too much reliance on law. Kagan acknowledges, however, that adversarial legalism's negative attributes—its cost, unpredictability and inefficiency—are tendencies, not inevitabilities, and are at least partially offset by its virtues of innovativeness, flexibility, and responsiveness. Bureaucratic legalism, similarly, can be associated with the rigid "by the book" style that Kagan decried, but can also be handled in a flexible way that both corrals the "bad apples" who flout the law while empowering the vast majority who respond more positively, especially those who go beyond compliance. Thus framing Kagan's work in terms of the too much/too little debate drains much of what is interesting about it, and overlooks its potential to advance the field.

The critical move, we believe, is to analyze adversarial and bureaucratic legalism as forms of state authority, structures by which the state shapes society, and thus to investigate them as political phenomena. This shift takes us away from asking stale questions about the appropriate amounts of adversarial and bureaucratic legalism or whether they are always good or bad, and forces us to explore their characteristics and propensities, whom they empower and whom they weaken, what kinds of politics they create, what kinds of issues they highlight and obscure.

Only then can we begin to assess the conditions under which these structures of authority advance important policy goals and democratic values.

Volume Outline

The volume is divided into segments that illustrate different aspects of Kagan's approach to studying law. First, adversarial legalism is considered as a form of state authority, showing that adversarial legalism is a much more complex, contingent, and multisided phenomenon than the popular debate over litigiousness suggests. The second part comprises a trio of studies that explore adversarial and bureaucratic legalism from the ground up, through field research. The third part of the book examines Kagan's core concepts from a methodological perspective. Although commentators sometimes treat adversarial legalism as an American disease, scholars are increasingly finding it proliferating elsewhere and debating whether it can take a prominent role in nations quite different in tradition and political structure from the United States. With bureaucratic legalism, by contrast, the central questions are about regulatory style—what causes variations in style across nations, with what consequences? These questions seem particularly urgent with the threat of global climate change and the consequent need for effective regulation and coordination in developed and developing nations.

R. Shep Melnick's chapter begins the first part, illustrating the power of treating litigation as a form of governance. For those new to Kagan's ideas and law and society scholarship, this idea may be jarring. We are used to thinking of litigation as something separate from government, so that the doctrines by which judges rule, and the choices they make, are not considered as part of public policy. Government, according to this view, consists of the things done by legislatures and executive agencies—taxes, grants, subsidies, and regulations. In Kagan's terms, then, only bureaucratic legalism would be seen as the province of politics and public policy.

Melnick shows how Kagan's research challenges this view, and how our understanding of the American state changes once we think beyond the instruments of bureaucratic legalism. For years scholars considered American government weak or shrunken in comparison with other affluent democracies, but that was because they ignored the many ways that the United States has used nonbureaucratic means to achieve public ends. Melnick traces the creation of the "civil rights state," a befuddling array of instrumentalities designed to curb discrimination that went well beyond bureaucratic regulation, with judges, activists, legislators, and bureaucrats all playing a role. Analyzing the development of this civil rights state in the fields of employment discrimination, school desegregation, and bilingual education, Melnick uncovers the political roots of the surprising vitality of its operations. The civil rights state has grown up and managed to endure if not flourish during a period of rising concern about government. Melnick shows how adversarial legalism can provide a means of governance in tune with such difficult times for public ventures.

Kagan typically compared legal systems not by examining formal institutions but instead by probing how different nations handled similar policy problems. One such study compared how different nations responded to the carnage inflicted by tobacco smoking (Kagan & Nelson, 2001; Kagan & Vogel, 1993). The chapter by Michael McCann and William Haltom critically analyzes Kagan's research on tobacco policy. McCann and Haltom use the case of smoking to raise questions about Kagan's sometimes harshly critical view of adversarial legalism, and his explanations for why it seems so prominent in American public policy.

As usual, Kagan found in his study that the U.S. relied less than other nations on the typical mechanisms of bureaucratic legalism—taxes and regulation—and more on adversarial legalism, in which individuals bring lawsuits and defend their rights (including, of course, the right not to be around tobacco smoke). Here Kagan was critical; was this good public policy? Taxation seemed a far more straightforward and effective way to reduce smoking levels; the adversarial legal path seemed to result in suboptimal public policy.

McCann and Haltom take issue with Kagan's analysis on several fronts. Kagan, they say, sometimes treats adversarial legalism as a "tiger in the bush," a voracious animal that springs up and eats everything in sight. This is an approach all too easily aligned with popular culture's scapegoating of greedy lawyers and their rapacious clients. McCann and Haltom prefer Kagan's other frame, that of adversarial legalism as "ice cream or spice," a component of public policy that is fine in small bits but if eaten in too large a quantity can cause a stomachache. This framing, they argue, seems much more compatible with Kagan's understanding of adversarial legalism as a structure that people—often elected officials—choose to create, rather than something sprung on them. Moreover, McCann and Haltom argue that Kagan discounts the power of Big Tobacco to shape the politics of smoking, not simply by fighting regulations and taxes in the legislature, but by constructing the conflict over tobacco as a matter of individual responsibility. Adversarial legal policies regarding tobacco, they contend, are not the product of some fixed features of American culture, but instead of an array of powerful political forces in tobacco politics that have pushed activists toward courts and litigation. Moreover, McCann and Haltom remind us, adversarial legalism is just one aspect of a complex stew of tobacco policies jointly created by lawyers, judges, activists, legislators, and bureaucrats. Their chapter embeds the analysis of adversarial legalism within a broader political context, showing how adversarial legalism can serve as a vital, though flawed, lever for disadvantaged groups.

Moving beyond the United States, the chapter by Francesca Bignami and R. Daniel Kelemen, which takes the form of a colloquy, illustrates the usefulness of Kagan's concepts of adversarial and bureaucratic legalism in framing debates over the globalization of law. While scholars around the world report that "judicialization" is growing in the nations they study, it is less clear whether the growing power of courts and judges, and the growing use of litigation, suggest a global shift from bureaucratic legalism, centralized regulation, to adversarial legalism, the party-centered, decentralized mode of policymaking and dispute resolution that Kagan argues characterizes the United States. Bignami and Kelemen consider this issue in the context of Europe. Kelemen argues that "Eurolegalism" is becoming more adversarial-legal, but Bignami is skeptical. She notes that while the rules in Europe have become more complex and punitive, qualities associated by Kagan with adversarial legalism, the rules continue to be wielded by centralized authorities, as in bureaucratic legalism. Though Bignami and Kelemen disagree, their use of Kagan's concepts as a common lexicon sharpens their debate and raises questions about the political roots of legal style. Will the parliamentary democracies of Europe ever allow adversarial legalism to take root? And is the nexus between legal style and structure—centralized (bureaucratic) versus participatory (adversarial) legalism—as close as Kagan implies?

The chapters on civil rights, smoking policy, and the European Union are "top down"; the next three, comprising the second part of the book, are "bottom up." Kathryn Hendley's chapter tells a story about adversarial legalism through interviews with ordinary Russians involved in car crashes who must decide whether to sue for their injuries. Sociolegal research has long demonstrated one of the downsides of adversarial legalism: For it to work, everyday people who have their civil rights violated or feel they have been injured by a tobacco company must be willing to mobilize the law. Adversarial legalism decentralizes enforcement, putting government officials to the side, thus privatizing implementation—a structure that can have perverse consequences, with both underenforcement of serious wrongs and overenforcement of marginal or trivial law violations. Hendley's interviews show the many reasons why, even in the seemingly unfraught context of a dispute over a car crash, individuals might not choose to mobilize the law. But beyond this, the Russian setting of Hendley's research also raises questions about the prerequisites for an effective system of adversarial legalism. Adversarial legalism is sometimes seen as an end-run around corrupt, captured, or ineffective governments, and a way to create tolerably effective governance where social trust is low and dependence on bureaucrats unwise. In her Russian examples, though, Hendley shows that a lack of social trust and corruption in government also undermine the functioning of adversarial legalism.

The next chapter shifts to the consideration of bureaucratic legalism, with Neil Gunningham's analysis of the failures of workplace safety regulation at Australian mines. He examines the disjunction between the company's head office and the workers at the mines who must implement a company's response to regulation. The head office, Gunningham shows, was committed not simply to compliance but "beyond compliance" behavior, yet at the site level, manifest failures of implementation led to an appalling toll of injuries and death among mine workers. Gunningham uses the story to explain the challenges organizations face in implementing their responses to regulations, but like Hendley's chapter, his narrative can also be used to illustrate the ways in which legal authority often falls short. In theory the implementation of bureaucratic legalism is far more straightforward than adversarial legalism because it does not depend on private parties to bring lawsuits. A central authority, in this case the work safety agency, merely has to provide the right incentives to induce compliance among the regulated. But in this case, even when the company was induced to comply, in fact overcomply, the complexities of intra-organizational politics led to an implementation failure. The story suggests that to be effective, legal authority must penetrate all the way down to the level of the mine workers and their immediate bosses, a challenge not so different from the one involved in getting car accident victims to mobilize the law in Russia.

The chapter by Malcolm Feeley and Van Swearingen on the struggle to reform California prisons combines some of the themes of Hendley and Gunningham because it shows some of the challenges both of adversarial legalism and bureaucratic legalism. Litigation has become a common tool by which prisoners in the United States contest aspects of their incarceration, but in California, Feeley and Swearingen report, many prison lawsuits have been diverted to a less formal grievance procedure. This is a common response of organizations to adversarial legalism: Faced with the high costs of uncertain litigation, they attempt to create a more informal, low cost, and less threatening alternative system that can absorb (and neutralize) claims. The widespread use of alternative dispute resolution (ADR) provisions in employment contracts, which divert employees with discrimination claims from litigation into ADR systems, is an example, as are the ubiquitous provisions in consumer contracts (like the ones that pop up on your computer screen) that do the same. The problem, as Feeley and Swearingen, show, is that this can become a "cooling out" system that allows the organization to avoid any substantive change in its operations.

But Feeley and Swearingen also show how the remaining prison lawsuits have failed, and here their story is about both adversarial *and* bureaucratic legalism. Prison lawsuits, they say, are settled not by system-wide reforms, but by local, and seemingly ephemeral, changes in policy. This results in poor implementation of court orders. Here, as in the Gunningham chapter, we see that, in a world of complex organizations, implementing legal authority is as much a problem of internal politics as external governance. The chapter also demonstrates the close relationship between adversarial and bureaucratic legalism. Even where adversarial legalism is used to enforce norms (fairness, nondiscrimination, safety, environmental protection), the chapter suggests, complex organizations must be able to turn those norms into practices through a kind of intra-organizational bureaucratic legalism.

The third part of the book turns to methodological issues in sociolegal research. Because Kagan, unlike most sociolegal scholars, studies both litigation and regulation, in his terms both adversarial legalism and bureaucratic legalism as well as everything in between, he is able to compare the strengths and weaknesses of different types of legalism, to investigate their political roots, and to evaluate claims about their associated legal styles. Kagan asserts, for example, that adversarial legalism is associated with legal complexity, punitiveness, and high transaction costs generated by intense contentiousness; indeed, he sometimes even defines adversarial legalism in terms of those characteristics.

But is "legal style" a useful and valid variable? Cary Coglianese's chapter takes on this question. In his discussion of style, we see both the promise and pitfalls of Kagan's attempts to balance detailed observation and generalization or, in Coglianese's formulation, lumping versus splitting. On the plus side, the concept of style is flexible, reflecting insights from careful studies of legal systems, regulators, and regulated organizations. It can be deployed as an outcome to be explained ("dependent variable") or as an explanatory factor ("independent variable") to identify patterns of activity in legal systems, the use of regulatory powers by government officials and organizational cultures, and predispositions toward regulatory commands and litigation. Perhaps because this concept grows out of careful field observation, it has what Coglianese calls "verisimilitude," capturing something that those involved in the regulatory process immediately recognize as important, even if it is somewhat mercurial. The problem, and resulting challenge, is that the concept of style can take so many forms and have so many potential dimensions that it is hard to define rigorously, much less measure with any precision. The answer to these problems, Coglianese implies, is not to abandon style as a concept or replace it with some more general notion like culture or personality. Instead, scholars must strive to develop what was once called "middle-level theory" in which concepts are flexible enough to reflect the inherent diversity of street-level legal phenomena but precise enough to generate hypotheses and reliable measures. Kagan's work points the way towards useful mid-level theory about legal styles, but there is still much work to do in fully operationalizing this concept at the level of legal systems, regulatory behavior, and organizational responses to law.

In the final chapter, we look ahead and suggest some ways in which Kagan's core concepts might be deployed in future research, especially research aimed at comparing the growth of law over time and across nations. As law continues to expand its reach both in the United States and abroad, we believe that more scholars will be drawn to the questions Kagan has posed and the concepts he has developed. Kagan's distinctions between forms of legal authority give us a lens to view structural differences across nations and policy areas, organizing the unwieldy landscape of modern law. And his insistence that structures are just the beginning of the story, that the rule of law is much more flexible and circular than some would suggest, pushes us to look beyond the abstract and account for how law actually happens in the world. The result is a deeper understanding of the consequences, both heartening and disturbing, of the relentless march of law in contemporary society, what we need to do to study it, and what we might want to do about it.

Note

1 We do not use "legalism" here the way Kagan himself defines it in his first book, *Regulatory Justice*, as "the mechanical application of rules without regard to their purpose." (Kagan, 1978, p. 92) That meaning is akin to "going by the book" (Bardach & Kagan, 1982), as a later volume would refer to it.

References

Atiyah, P.S., & Summers, R.S. (1987). *Form and Substance in Anglo-American law: A Comparative Study of Legal Reasoning, Legal Theory, and Legal Institutions*. Oxford: Clarendon Press.

Bardach, E., & Kagan, R.A. (1982). *Going by the Book: The Problem of Regulatory Unreasonableness*. Philadelphia: Temple University Press.

Barnes, J. (1997). "Bankrupt Bargain?: Bankruptcy Reform and the Politics of Adversarial Legalism." *Journal of Law and Policy*, 13, 893.

Barnes, J. (2011). *Dust-Up: Asbestos Litigation and the Failure of Common Sense Policy Reform*. Washington, DC: Georgetown University Press.

Barnes, J., & Burke, T.F. (2012). "Making Way: Legal Mobilization, Organizational Response, and Wheelchair Access." *Law & Society Review*, 46(1), 167–98.

Barnes, J., & Burke, T.F. (2015). *How Policy Shapes Politics: Rights, Courts, Litigation, and the Struggle Over Injury Compensation*. New York: Oxford University Press.

Barnes, J., & Miller, M.C. (2004). *Making Policy, Making Law: An Interbranch Perspective*. Washington, DC: Georgetown University Press.

Bignami, F., & Zaring, D. (2016). *Comparative Law and Regulation: Understanding the Global Regulatory Process*. Northampton, MA: Edward Elgar Publishing.

Bogart, W.A. (2002). *Consequences: The Impact of Law and Its Complexity*. Toronto: University of Toronto Press.

Brovard, J. (2015). "How Disability Law Went Nuts." *USA Today*, July 29, 2015. Retrieved from www.usatoday.com/wlna/opinion/2015/07/27/ada-americans—disabilities-act-lawsuits/30702519/. Accessed 4/7/16.

Burke, T.F. (2002). *Lawyers, Lawsuits, and Legal Rights: The Battle Over Litigation in American Society*. Berkeley: University of California Press.

Burke, T.F., & Barnes, J. (2009). "Is There an Empirical Literature on Rights?" *Special Issue Revisiting Rights Studies in Law, Politics and Society*, 48, 69–91.

Couso, J., Huneeus, A., & Sieder, R. (2010). *Cultures of legality: Judicialization and Political Activism in Latin America*. Cambridge: Cambridge University Press.

Damaška, M.R. (1986). *The Faces of Justice and State Authority: A Comparative Approach to the Legal Process*. New Haven: Yale University Press.

Dressel, B. (2012). *The Judicialization of Politics in Asia*. Milton Park, Abingdon, Oxon: Routledge.

Edelman, L.B., Erlanger, H.S., & Lande, J. (1993). "Internal Dispute Resolution: The Transformation of Civil Rights in the Workplace." *Law & Society Review*, 27(3), 497.

Edelman, L.B., Krieger, L.H., Eliason, S.R., Albiston, C.R., & Mellema, V. (2011). "When Organizations Rule: Judicial Deference to Institutionalized Employment Structures." *American Journal of Sociology*, 117(3), 888–954.

Engel, D.M., & Munger, F. (2003). *Rights of Inclusion: Law and Identity in the Life Stories of Americans With Disabilities*. Chicago: University of Chicago Press.

Farhang, S. (2010). *The Litigation State: Public Regulation and Private Lawsuits in the U.S.* Princeton, NJ: Princeton University Press.

Fox News. (2011). "Regulation Nation: Drowning in Rules, Businesses Brace for Cost and Time for Compliance." September 12, 2011. Retrieved from www.foxnews.com/politics/2011/09/12/regulation-nation-drowning-in-rules-businesses-brace-for-cost-and-time-for.html. Accessed 4/17/16.

Ginsburg, T., & Hoetker, G. (2006). "The Unreluctant Litigant? An Empirical Analysis of Japan's Turn to Litigation." *The Journal of Legal Studies*, 35(1), 31–59.

Goldstein, J., Kahler, M., Keohane, Robert O., & Slaughter, A. (2001). *Legalization and World Politics*. Cambridge, MA: MIT Press.

Graber, M. (1993). "The Non-Majoritarian Difficulty: Legislative Deference to the Judiciary." *Studies in Political Development*, 7, 35–73.

Gray, G.C., & Silbey, S.S. (2014). "Governing Inside the Organization: Interpreting Regulation and Compliance." *American Journal of Sociology*, 120(1), 96–145.

Gunningham, N., Kagan, R.A., & Thornton, D. (2003). *Shades of Green: Business, Regulation, and Environment*. Stanford, CA: Stanford Law and Politics.

Hirschl, R. (2004). *Towards Juristocracy: The Origins and Consequences of the New Constitutionalism*. Cambridge, MA: Harvard University Press.

Howard, P.K. (1994). *The Death of Common Sense: How Law Is Suffocating America*. New York: Random House.

Hughes, R. (1993). *Culture of Complaint: The Fraying of America*. New York: Oxford University Press.

Investor's Business Daily. (2015). "Editorial: Is Obama Bashing Wall Street to Hide His Own Failures?" Retrieved from www.investors.com/wall-street-takes-a-beating-as-obama-covers-up-his-own-mistakes/#ixzz3TKxFPRBe. Accessed 4/7/16.

Judicial Conference Ad Hoc Committee. (1991). *Report of the Judicial Conference on Asbestos Litigation*. Washington, DC: U.S. Government Printing Office.

Kagan, R.A. (1978). *Regulatory Justice: Implementing a Wage-Price Freeze*. New York: Russell Sage Foundation.

Kagan, R.A. (1987). "What Makes Uncle Sammy Sue? Review of David Vogel, National Styles of Regulation: Environmental Policy in Great Britain and the United States." *Law & Society Review*, 21(5), 717–42.

Kagan, R.A. (1991). "Adversarial Legalism and American Government." *Journal of Policy Analysis and Management*, 10(3), 369.

Kagan, R.A. (1994). "Do Lawyers Cause Adversarial Legalism? A Preliminary Inquiry." *Law & Social Inquiry*, 19(1), 1.

Kagan, R.A. (1995). "What Socio-Legal Scholars Should Do When There Is Too Much Law to Study." *Journal of Law and Society*, 22(1), 140.

Kagan, R.A. (2001). *Adversarial Legalism: The American Way of Law*. Cambridge, MA: Harvard University Press.

Kagan, R.A. (2007). "Globalization and Legal Change: The 'Americanization' of European Law?" *Regulation & Governance*, 1(2), 99–120.

Kagan, R.A., & Axelrad, L. (2000). *Regulatory Encounters: Multinational Corporations and American Adversarial Legalism*. Berkeley: University of California Press.

Kagan, R.A., & Nelson, W.P. (2001). "The Politics of Tobacco Regulation in the United States." In R.L. Rabin & S.D. Sugarman (Eds.), *Regulating Tobacco*. New York: Oxford University Press, pp. 11–31.

Kagan, R.A., & Vogel, D. (1993). "The Politics of Smoking Regulation: Canada, France, the United States." In R.L. Rabin & S.D. Sugarman (Eds.), *Smoking Policy: Law, Politics and Culture*. New York: Oxford University Press, pp. 22–48.

Keck, T. (2014). *Judicial Politics in Polarized Times*. Chicago: University of Chicago Press.
Kelemen, R.D. (2011). *Eurolegalism: The Transformation of Law and Regulation in the European Union*. Cambridge, MA: Harvard University Press.
Kilpatrick, J.J. (1984). "U.S. Courts Drowning in a Flood of Lawsuits." *Spokane Chronicle*, January 12, 1984, 8.
Lovell, G. (2003). *Legislative Deferrals: Statutory Ambiguity, Judicial Powers, and American Democracy*. New York: Cambridge University Press.
Mashaw, J.L. (1983). *Bureaucratic Justice: Managing Social Security Disability Claims*. New Haven: Yale University Press.
Melnick, R.S. (1994). *Between the Lines: Interpreting Welfare Rights*. Washington, DC: The Brookings Institution.
Morgan, B. (2007). *The Intersection of Rights and Regulation: New Directions in Sociolegal Scholarship*. Aldershot, England: Ashgate.
Moustafa, T. (2014). "Law and Courts in Authoritarian Regimes." *Annual Review of Law and Social Science*, 10(1), 281–99.
Nonet, P., & Selznick, P. (1978). *Law and Society in Transition: Toward Responsive Law*. New York: Harper & Row.
Schwartz, G.T. (1991). "Product Liability and Medical Malpractice in Comparative Context." in P. Huber & R. Litan (Eds.), *The Liability Maze: The Impact of Law on Safety and Innovation*, pp. 28–80.
Sheehan, R.S., Gill, R.D., & Randazzo, K.A. (2012). *Judicialization of Politics: The Interplay of Institutional Structure, Legal Doctrine, and Politics on the High Court of Australia*. Durham, NC: Carolina Academic Press.
Sieder, R., Schjolden, L., & Angell, A. (2005). *The Judicialization of Politics in Latin America*. New York: Palgrave Macmillan.
Silverstein, G. (2009). *Law's Allure: How Law Shapes, Constrains, Saves, and Kills Politics*. New York: Cambridge University Press.
Stern, R.E. (2013). *Environmental Litigation in China: A Study in Political Ambivalence*. Cambridge: Cambridge University Press.
Sweet, A.S. (2000). *Governing With Judges: Constitutional Politics in Europe*. Oxford: Oxford University Press.
Tate, C.N., & Vallinder, T. (1995). *The Global Expansion of Judicial Power*. New York: New York University Press.
Thornton, D., Kagan, R.A., & Gunningham, N. (2003). "Sources of Corporate Environmental Performance." *California Management Review*, 46(1), 127–41.
Thornton, D., Kagan, R. A., & Gunningham, N. (2008). "Compliance Costs, Regulation and Environmental Performance: Controlling Truck Emissions in the U.S." *Regulation & Governance*, 2(3), 275–92.
Thornton, D., Kagan, R.A., & Gunningham, N. (2009). "When Social Norms and Pressures Are Not Enough: Environmental Performance in the Trucking Industry." *Law & Society Review*, 43(2), 405–36.
Vinke, H., & Wilthagen, T. (1992). *The Non-mobilization of Law by Asbestos Victims in the Netherlands: Social Insurance Versus Tort-Based Compensation*. Amsterdam: Hugo Sinzheimer Institute, University of Amsterdam.
Vogel, S.K. (1996). *Freer Markets, more Rules: Regulatory Reform in Advanced Industrial Countries*. Ithaca, NY: Cornell University Press.

2

ADVERSARIAL LEGALISM, CIVIL RIGHTS, AND THE EXCEPTIONAL AMERICAN STATE

R. Shep Melnick

According to the conventional wisdom, the American "state" is small, weak, and decentralized. The U.S. is the welfare state laggard that has never quite caught up with its older siblings in western Europe. Americans stubbornly remain more market-oriented and more tax-averse than citizens of other advanced industrial democracies. Some attribute this to American political culture, most importantly its devotion to individualism, its distrust of government authority, and its commitment to equality of opportunity rather than equality of results. Others emphasize our fragmented political institutions, especially our distinctive combination of federalism, separation of powers, and bicameralism. The extent to which American institutions and political culture reinforce each other makes it difficult to decide which of these two features is more important for explaining our predicament: our constitutional structure was designed to limit the authority of the central government, and our political culture provides no sustained impetus for major policy or constitutional change. Moreover, the conflict and inefficiencies created by our system of "separated institutions sharing power" no doubt increases distrust of government. As a result, those who favor a more assertive, European-style state usually call for both institutional reform—moving toward some form of parliamentary government and strengthening the authority of the national government over the states—and a new "public philosophy," one more suitable for our "collectivist age." Those who do not favor such changes, in contrast, celebrate "American exceptionalism" as a source of economic dynamism and a protector of our liberties.

But whether one likes or loathes American exceptionalism, is this picture of our political system still accurate? After all, the responsibilities of the federal government have grown by leaps and bounds since the 1960s. The continuing expansion of the American welfare state, especially with regard to health care, has significantly narrowed the gap between the U.S. and even the most generous European welfare states. Just as importantly, there are a variety of areas in which the "state" has been more aggressive on this side of the Atlantic. The most obvious is education: the U.S. took the lead in developing the common school, and still spends more on public education than almost any other nation. The U.S. has a military force that dwarfs that of European nations. The fact that Europeans live under a defense umbrella funded by American taxpayers makes it easier for them to pay for generous welfare-state benefits. The United States incarcerates far more people than any other advanced industrial democracy—as clear an example of the exercise of state authority as one can imagine. Not only has American regulation of pharmaceuticals been more rigorous than that of other nations, but the Food and Drug Administration created a regulatory model that has been copied around the world (Carpenter, 2010). Regulation and taxation of tobacco products is more extensive here than in Europe. The health, safety, and environmental regulation that first took shape in the 1970s not only dwarfs all previous regulatory efforts in American history, but has often been more stringent in the U.S. than abroad (Vogel, 1993). Deregulation of some sectors of the economy has been matched with both reregulation (especially of financial services) and new forms of regulation (especially state tort law). In his comparison of race policy in the U.S., Britain, and France, Robert Lieberman points out "the 'weak' American state" has "not only produced more active and extensive enforcement of antidiscrimination law; it also managed to challenge the color-blind presumptions of its own law and to forge an extensive network of race-conscious policies and practices that have proven strikingly resilient in the face of political and legal challenges" (2002, p. 139; also see Lieberman, 2005; Saguy, 2003; Bleich, 2003; Teles, 2001; Pedriana & Stryker, 2004; Dobbin & Sutton, 1998; Dobbin, 2009). Here it is Europe that has followed the American lead, not the other way around.

A number of important scholarly studies have shown that Americans consistently underestimate the reach and the strength of the American state because so many U.S. programs are consciously designed to reduce their visibility and to give the impression that they are not really government programs at all. We may mock Tea Party enthusiasts who rail against "big government" while warning politicians to "keep their hands off our Social Security and Medicare," but we should bear in mind that for decades Social Security and other middle-class entitlements have been sold as insurance programs in which worthy citizens get back what they have paid in earmarked taxes. For most of its existence, Social Security spending has not even been included in the budget of the United States. Christopher Howard's important book *The Welfare State Nobody Knows* (2007) demonstrates our heavy reliance on indirect forms of income support, most importantly tax deductions and exemptions (for health insurance, housing, pensions, child care, and much more) and loan guarantees (especially for housing and education). Such strategies are designed to avoid creation of new bureaucracies and to meet American voters' conflicting demands for more public benefits and less intrusive government. A particularly important consequence of this strategy, as Suzanne Mettler (2011) has shown, has been to obscure from voters the extent to which they rely upon and benefit from government programs.

For students of American politics, abstract talk about "the American state" has always had a strange ring to it. The U.S. is, after all, a nation of states—in fact 53 if one includes the national governments, the District of Columbia, and Puerto Rico; many more if one counts semisovereign Indian tribes and outlying territories. State and local governments raise about $2 trillion in taxes each year—a little more than the amount raised in taxes by the federal government—and, thanks to federal transfer payments, spend almost $2.5 trillion annually. The vast majority of public employees work for state and local governments. As a result, the federal government usually carries out its policies not by acting directly on citizens, but rather by regulating the activities of subnational governments. Through the use of grants-in-aid and federal mandates, the national government is able both to leverage its influence and to reduce its visibility. Looking only at federal spending or employment levels leads us to seriously underestimate the reach and the strength of the national government.

In recent years the American proclivity to employ unorthodox, indirect, and below-the-radar-screen policy instruments has become particularly striking. Consider the measures we have adopted to regulate tobacco, greenhouse gases, and asbestos. The 1998 multistate tobacco agreement imposed a $250 billion tax on tobacco products, placed numerous restrictions on tobacco advertising, marketing, and lobbying, and created substantial barriers to entry to protect established tobacco companies. This was the result a nationwide settlement of novel "unjust enrichment" suits brought by state attorneys general in state court. Since the payments made by tobacco companies to state governments were officially labeled "damages" rather than "taxes," they were never voted upon by either state legislatures or Congress (Derthick, 2004). The greenhouse gas regulations recently proposed by the U.S. Environmental Protection Agency were similarly the result of a court suit brought by state attorneys general. Ignoring the Clean Air Act's obvious focus on local ambient air quality, the Supreme Court ordered the EPA to regulate the emission of gases that are not dangerous at ground level, but which are likely to contribute to changes in the global environment. This meant that the EPA would regulate greenhouse gases unless Congress took action to *prevent* it from doing so—the reverse of the ordinary lawmaking process (Nolette, 2015; Melnick, 2014). In the long-running saga of asbestos tort litigation—which the Supreme Court once described as an "elephantine mass" that "defies customary judicial administration and calls for national legislation"—the courts again acted when Congress did not. Making novel use of bankruptcy laws, the federal courts created an elaborate administrative structure to compensate hundreds of thousands of asbestos victims. The cost of this program runs into the tens of billions of dollars, money that comes from trusts established by the scores of companies that declared bankruptcy in order to limit their tort liability (Barnes, 2011).

These developments expose two shortcomings of the conventional wisdom on "American exceptionalism." First, while Americans may be individualistic and distrustful of centralized government authority, this does not mean that they oppose the creation and expansion of many public programs. If programs can be framed in individualistic terms—or better still, in terms of individual rights—and if they can avoid creating a new bureaucracy, then they are more likely to garner widespread public support. A central reason for Social Security's continuing popularity is the common belief, long nurtured by its proponents, that it is a mechanism for individuals to fund their own retirement benefits. The redistributive features of Social Security are carefully hidden behind a confusing welter of rules and contingencies. Extensive and expensive benefits for individuals with disabilities have been successfully packaged and sold as rights to education, employment, and access to public facilities (Burke, 1997).

Second, American political institutions are far more malleable than the conventional wisdom appreciates. Most importantly, each "veto point" in the American system can at times become an "opportunity point" for promoting new programs or expanding old ones (Melnick, 2015). Over the long run, federalism probably does more to stimulate policy change than to inhibit it. Innovations originating in states such as California, New York, and Wisconsin quickly spread to other states, and then are endorsed (and imposed on other states) by the federal government. Although we often expect presidents to set the agenda for Congress, since 1970 a large number of important initiatives—ranging from health, safety, consumer, and environmental regulation to expansion of Medicaid, food stamps, the Earned Income Tax Credit, and education programs—have come from policy entrepreneurs in the House and Senate. Comparative studies have also shown that administrators in the U.S. are particularly entrepreneurial, actively building coalitions to support their policy proposals (Aberbach, Putnam, & Rockman, 1981). Focusing primarily on big initiatives produced by major legislation can lead commentators to miss some of the most important features of American public policy.

And then there are the courts. As both Paul Frymer (2008b) and John Skrentny (2006) have pointed out in important review articles, historians, political scientists, and sociologists frequently underestimate the American state because they "miss the important ways that courts contribute to the development of state power" (Frymer, 2008b, p. 789). Those who study state-building tend to equate "state" with "centralized bureaucracy." They see courts either as irrelevant or, more often, as obstacles to the creation of administrative capacity. Their images of courts comes from the *Lochner* era and the New Deal, when it was certainly reasonable to believe that strengthening the administrative capacity of both the federal government and the states required curbing the courts. Since the 1960s, though, the judiciary has "played a far more active and affirmative role in building the powers of the state and expanding its power to regulate civil society and the economy." In fact, according to Frymer, "judicial authority has been absolutely essential to the power and reach of the modern regulatory state." In area after area, litigation has been used to expand the scope of national programs. Examples range from entitlements such as disability insurance, Aid to Families with Dependent Children, food stamps, Medicaid, and Supplemental Security Income to environmental protection, tobacco and pharmaceutical regulation, housing and employment policy, and virtually every aspect of public education (Melnick, 1983, 1994, and 2007; Derthick, 1990; Erkulwater, 2006; Nolette, 2015; Dunn & West, 2009). The courts' role in the expansion of the American state has been obscured by scholars' obsession with federal constitutional law. Federal judges have been reluctant to read positive rights into the Constitution. (State court judges have not been so cautious in their interpretation of state constitutions, though.) Consequently, judicial expansion of such programs is usually effected through statutory interpretation, common law rulings (especially at the state level), and enforcement of often-ambiguous conditions on federal grants-in-aid. Such rulings may not be exciting enough for most political scientists and law professors to study, but they are ubiquitous enough to shape the American "state."

The New Deal Versus Adversarial Legalism

The most comprehensive and perceptive analysis of the crucial role played by law, courts, and litigation in the expansion of the American state is Robert A. Kagan's *Adversarial Legalism: The American Way of Law*. Far from a garden-variety critique of American litigiousness, *Adversarial Legalism* is above all a work of comparative politics, an examination of a new and quite different form of American "exceptionalism." The central theme of the book is not the weakness of the American state—the core assertion of almost all previous studies of American exceptionalism—but the way in which American adversarial legalism melds two ostensibly conflicting features of contemporary politics: the U.S.'s fragmented political institutions and the American commitment to activist government. Adversarial legalism is the unintended product of "something old and something new," namely, our 18th-century constitutional system that disburses political power in order to limit it; and our post-1932 demand for "total justice"—Kagan's shorthand for a political culture that "expects and demands comprehensive government protections from serious harm, injustice, and environmental damage—and hence a powerful, activist government" (Kagan, 2001, pp. 15 and 35). Adversarial legalism, he argues, must be understood as a distinctively American "mode of government," a fragmented, party-centered alternative to European-style bureaucratic centralization.

To understand this novel yet still peculiarly American "mode of government," it is useful to contrast it not only with that of western Europe—Kagan's central comparison—but also with its immediate predecessor in the U.S., the New Deal. The New Deal was in large part an effort to build a relatively centralized administrative state that is compatible with the U.S. Constitution (Milkis, 1993). This effort required reinterpretation of some of the Constitution's central features. Most obviously, the New Deal established the foundations of the modern regulatory and welfare state by significantly expanding the authority of the presidency and administrative agencies and by relaxing previous restrictions on the powers of the national government. According to the constitutional vision of the New Deal, Congress and the courts should defer to the president, who will give direction to executive agencies. National uniformity was prized even if it was not always attained. Where states retained significant control over joint programs, professionals in federal agencies would provide detailed guidance and advice, slowly weaning state and local administrators from their parochial habits (Derthick, 1970). These career administrators should be nonpartisan (which above all meant freed from the ties of patronage that had for so long weighed down federal programs), but at the same time should be "100% New Dealers"—that is, fully committed to an energetic public sector that would promote economic security, full employment, humane treatment of the disadvantaged, and conservation of natural resources. The epitomes of such New Deal agencies were the Social Security Agency, whose "program executives" guided the expansion of the welfare state for four decades (Derthick, 1979), and the National Labor Relations Board (NLRB), which oversaw the creation and maintenance of a new role for labor unions within the American economic system.

Given the long, intense battle between New Dealers and Progressives on the one hand and the federal judiciary on the other, it is little wonder that Roosevelt, his supporters, and his successors sought to insulate these agencies and programs from judicial review. Judicial restraint, a central norm of the New Deal and Progressive worldview, applied not just to constitutional interpretation but also to administrative law: both the statutes passed by legislatures and the rulings of administrative agencies are entitled to a strong presumption of legality. Both norms were emphasized by the Supreme Court justice with the closest ties to Roosevelt, Felix Frankfurter. Not only did New Dealers fear—for good reason—that federal judges would be hostile to aggressive action by the national government, but searching judicial review by hundreds of district court judges throughout the country threatened to destroy the national uniformity so highly valued by federal administrators.

It should be noted that while New Dealers were highly suspicious of courts, they were by no means opposed to framing issues in terms of individual rights. In 1944 FDR put forth an "Economic Bill of Rights" to supplement the "sacred Bill of Rights of our Constitution." This "Second Bill of Rights" includes "the right to earn enough to provide adequate food and clothing and recreation"; "the right of every family to a decent home"; "the right to adequate medical care"; "the right to adequate protection from the economic fears of old age, sickness, accident and unemployment"; and "the right to a good education." Each of these rights, Roosevelt argued, "must be applied to all our citizens, irrespective of race, creed, or color." "What all these rights spell," he explained, is "security." (It was no coincidence that the largest of all New Deal programs was not called "superannuation" or even "old-age pensions" as in Europe, but Social Security.) While 18th-century liberalism promised security from civil war and arbitrary government action by promoting limited government, this new form of liberalism promised security against the vagaries of the business cycle, the multiple hazards created by a dynamic capitalism, the pernicious prejudices of private citizens, and the insidious consequences of poverty and family decomposition—all of which required energetic government (Melnick, 1989).

New Dealers strongly believed that such rights could best be protected by expert agencies, not dilettantish judges. The Social Security Agency, for example, was firmly committed to the proposition that benefits should be considered earned rights. Longtime Social Security administrator Arthur Altmeyer reported that the agency worked hard to convince people "that because of contributions there were certain rights, statutory rights, that had to be recognized and achieved, and we had an obligation" (Derthick, 1979, pp. 21 and 31). Even in means-tested programs such as Aid to Families with Dependent Children and Old Age Assistance in which benefits were not tied to contributions, federal administrators sought to convince their counterparts in state government that benefits should be considered legal rights, and thus neither distributed nor withheld in a preemptory, arbitrary, or discriminatory manner (Tani, 2016). The NLRB was the chief protector of workers' right to organize and to engage in collective bargaining. The best way to protect this new form of rights was to insulate New Deal agencies from review by hostile courts. Recourse to litigation was a last resort, to be used only when other forms of government action proved unavailable.[1]

The effort to create something approaching a European-style state in a political system that imposed so many barriers to such an enterprise required New Dealers to negotiate a number of troubling compromises: with the barons on Capitol Hill, who retained authority to block New Deal laws and to control annual appropriations; with state governments, which continued to wield significant power within a system of "cooperative federalism"; with local Democratic machines devoted to patronage, corruption, and often parochial ethnic politics; with a federal judiciary still distrustful of administrative discretion and insistent that "it is emphatically the province and duty of the judicial department to say what the law is"; and with Dixiecrats who blocked any measure that threatened the racial caste system in the South.

By the late 1960s, all of these uneasy compromises had broken down. The first and most obvious casualty was the New Deal electoral coalition, which could no longer deliver the presidency to the Democratic Party on a regular basis. Just as important, but less frequently recognized, is the fact that New Deal institutional patterns withered as well, gradually replaced by the more fragmented and confrontational style of governance that Kagan calls adversarial legalism. Unlike the 1930s, this was not a case in which one well-developed constitutional vision replaced another. A variety of actors responded to new circumstances and new challenges, establishing on the fly new institutional patterns and ways of thinking about the role of government. Strategies that succeeded were copied; those that failed were quickly jettisoned. The new regime was built by many men and women who had no blueprint for—and often little awareness of—what they were constructing.

Civil Rights As Critical Juncture and Model for Emulation

The Civil Rights Movement provides a particularly useful window for understanding the character and the multiple causes of this seismic shift. The Kennedy and Johnson Administrations, civil rights organizations, and the northern and western Democrats who supported the Civil Rights Act of 1964 and the Voting Rights Act of 1965 were all staunch supporters of a New Deal–style solution to the problems of racial segregation, disenfranchisement, exclusion, and discrimination. Painfully familiar with the failure of constitutional litigation to end the disenfranchisement of black voters or the segregation of southern schools, they sought to replace time-consuming litigation with aggressive administrative action. They recognized that the Department of Justice and civil rights groups had won a number of important victories in the Supreme Court. But they could also see that southern district court judges—most of whom had been selected by segregationist senators—were capable of sabotaging even the clearest Supreme Court ruling.

We have become so accustomed to thinking of federal courts as protectors of the rights of racial minorities that we can easily lose sight of the compelling considerations that led civil rights advocates to seek administration alternatives to litigation. For decades after enactment of the 13th, 14th, and 15th Amendments, federal courts had read them extremely narrowly, at times undercutting congressional action to attack Jim Crow. *Brown v. Board* changed constitutional doctrine, but not educational practice: a decade after *Brown*, schools in the deep South remained as segregated as ever. This was a consequence of both lower court obstructionism and Supreme Court insouciance: between 1955 and 1968 the justices had virtually nothing to say about the explosive issue they had put on the national agenda. Nearly everyone agreed with Judge John Minor Wisdom's 1965 assessment of the progress of school desegregation: "The courts acting alone have failed" (*U.S. v. Jefferson County Board of Education I*, 372 F.2d 859 [1966]). By the early 1960s, it was equally clear that the Department of Justice's effort to use litigation to stop blatant discrimination against African-American voters had also failed (Landsberg, 2007). In 1949 the Supreme Court took the bold step of finding restrictive covenants unconstitutional, but that hardly made a dent in the extent of residential segregation. The greatest civil rights victory before 1964 was the desegregation of the military, the result of a presidential order.

Three key provisions of the legislation proposed by the Kennedy and Johnson Administrations in the period 1963–65 highlight the effort to move from litigation to "enlightened administration" in civil rights:

1. To combat discrimination by private employers, they proposed creating an Equal Employment Opportunity Commission (EEOC) with powers similar to those of the National Labor Relations Board. The EEOC would have authority to investigate complaints, promulgate legally binding rules, and issue enforcement orders on hiring practices, reinstatement, and back pay. It made no provision for private enforcement suits. Sean Farhang explains that the "administratively-centered enforcement framework" established by the House Judiciary Committee with the approval of the Johnson Administration "embodied the enforcement preferences" of Democratic civil rights advocates in Congress and leading civil rights groups (2010, p. 99).
2. What eventually became Title VI of the Civil Rights Act required all federal agencies to deny funding to recipients who engage in racial discrimination. This applied above all to state and local governments—including public schools. Since such discrimination was already unconstitutional, Title VI's significance lay in the fact that it added a swift administrative remedy for such unconstitutional action, and gave federal agencies authority to write rules defining what constitutes discriminatory behavior. In his explanation of the initial version of Title VI, President Kennedy stated that "indirect discrimination, through the use of Federal funds, is just as invidious" as direct discrimination "and it should not be necessary to resort to the court to prevent each individual violation" (H.R. Document #124, 88th Cong., 1st Sess. [1963], p. 12).
3. The "preclearance" provision of the 1965 Voting Rights Act took the unprecedented step of requiring "covered" states—that is, those states in the Deep South that Congress found had engaged in egregious discrimination against black voters—to receive prior approval before making any changes in their elections laws. States could seek approval either from the Department of Justice (DOJ) or from federal courts in the District of Columbia. Given the constitutional novelty of this provision—never before had a state been required to seek federal approval of legislation before it went into effect—the Johnson Administration did not dare vest preclearance authority solely in the Department of Justice. But in practice it was clear that DOJ would be the primary forum for resolving these issues. Here the delay associated with the judicial process worked against the states, which wanted either quick approval of their laws or specific guidance on what sort of changes would be needed to pass federal muster. This was particularly apparent when decennial redistricting plans became subject to preclearance review (Cunningham, 2001; Thernstrom, 2009).

Similarly, in 1967 the Johnson Administration endorsed fair housing legislation based on a bill backed by the Leadership Conference on Civil Rights that "would create a potentially powerful new watchdog agency called the Federal Fair Housing Board . . . patterned after the NLRB, and similarly armed with cease-and-desist authority" (Graham, 1990, p. 261).

Within a few years this effort to substitute administration for litigation had largely failed, both because Republicans opposed it and because state and local governments proved more resistant to administrative commands than supporters of this approach had assumed. The larger effort to enfranchise black voters, to desegregate southern schools, and to curb employment discrimination, however, most definitely did *not* fail. That is because civil rights groups and federal administrators discovered alternative regulatory strategies that relied as much on the judiciary as on the administrative action. Enforcement through private lawsuit lay at the heart of these strategies. Shifting to courts the responsibility for *enforcing* federal statutes also provides them with the opportunity to *interpret* these provisions. Federal judges were not inclined to stick close to the compromises embodied in civil rights statutes, leaving them with significant policymaking authority. This in turn made civil rights agencies more dependent on federal judges than on the White House—a consequence that proved much to the liking of civil rights organizations. The arrival of divided government in 1969—Republicans controlled the White House and Democrats at least one house of Congress for 20 of the next 24 years—reinforced civil rights advocates' commitment to these strategies by convincing them that they could no longer rely on support from the White House.

The symbiotic relationship that eventually developed between federal courts and federal civil rights agencies—usually with a critical assist from civil rights organizations and other private litigants—proved so successful that it was replicated in many other policy arenas. Most obviously, the Title VI model was used (virtually word for word) to attack gender discrimination in educational programs that receive federal funds. The same strategy was employed in §504 of the Rehabilitation Act of 1974, the Age Discrimination Act of 1976, and the Americans with Disabilities Act of 1990. Enforcement through private litigation also lay at the heart of the Education for All Handicapped Children Act of 1975 and the Age Discrimination in Employment Act of 1967. Starting in the early 1970s, environmental groups used private suits to promote more vigorous application of the Endangered Species Act and statutory provisions regarding management of federal lands. Federal courts began to recognize private rights of action to enforce conditions attached to a wide variety of federal grants-in-aid (Melnick, 2005b). As we will see, judges, members of Congress, administrators, and interest groups found their own reasons for embracing these new strategies.

This chapter explains why the New Deal model crumbled and how a viable alternative gradually appeared under both Title VII and Title VI of the 1964 Civil Rights Act. This is largely the story of the triumph and entrenchment of adversarial legalism. Although many similar stories can probably be told about other policy areas, few are as inherently important or as significant for blazing a new trail as these.

Title VII and the Rise of a Private Enforcement Regime

The 14th Amendment applies only to "state action," not to the behavior of private parties. Relying on Congress's authority to regulate interstate commerce, Title VII of the 1964 Civil Rights Act extended the prohibition on racial (and gender) discrimination to private employers. During the "longest debate" of 1964, no section of the proposed legislation was subject to more scrutiny and legislative bargaining than Title VII. Most of this debate centered on the extent of power delegated to the new Equal Employment Opportunity Commission. Could it promulgate binding rules and issue "cease and desist" orders, or would it be limited to filing suit in federal court? Could the EEOC initiate litigation itself, or would it be required to rely on private plaintiffs or attorneys in the Department of Justice? Given the vagueness of Title VII's substantive provisions, everyone understood how much hung on such questions of institutional design. The key participants drew on their recent experience to make educated guesses about the likely consequences of various enforcement options. Most of them guessed wrong.

A Law of Unintended Consequences

Passage of the 1964 act was not secured until the Johnson Administration and Senate Democratic leaders reached an agreement with Senate Minority Leader Everett Dirksen, who supplied enough Republican votes to end the southern Democrats' filibuster. The most important part of this compromise placed a number of limits on the power of the EEOC. It denied the EEOC power to issue cease-and-desist orders or even to file suit in federal court. It also explicitly denied the EEOC any authority to disrupt "bona fide" seniority systems, to prohibit the use of professionally developed aptitude tests, or to require an employer to achieve a racially balanced workforce.

The battle lines over Title VII reflected three decades of bitter partisan disagreement over labor relations. Republicans and Democrats alike viewed the issue of the EEOC's authority through the lens of their experience with the National Labor Relations Board. This was understandable since Title VII involved government regulation of business practices similar to that instituted by the NLRB. New Dealers in Congress and the administration favored creating an enforcement agency similar to the NLRB, with power to investigate complaints, promulgate legally binding rules, and above all issue enforcement orders on hiring practices, reinstatement, and back pay. They also sought to keep the federal courts at arms' length: their version of the legislation limited judicial review of the new agency to the Administrative Procedure Act's deferential "arbitrary and capricious" standard, and made no provision for private enforcement suits.

To business-friendly Republicans—including many of the senators whose support was needed to break the Dixiecrat filibuster—creating a new National Labor Relations Board was simply unacceptable. As the economist and Nixon advisor Arthur Burns once put it, "The words cease-and-desist and NLRB are inflammatory words to most businessmen. They find the NLRB in its activities among the worst in the federal government and in many instances, they are absolutely right in this evaluation" (quoted in Graham, 1990, p. 426). Republicans on the House Judiciary Committee warned that it would be "a major mistake to model legislation in the field on the National Labor Relations Board, which has one of the sorriest records of all the Federal agencies for political involvement" (quoted in Farhang, 2010, p. 101). House sponsors of the 1964 act eventually removed the cease-and-desist power from their bill in order to craft legislation that could pass the Senate. Hugh Davis Graham notes that this opposition "reflected the great battle over administrative reform of the 1940s, in which a coalition of Republicans and southern Democrats attacked the regulatory abuses they associated with the New Deal" (Graham, 1990, p. 130).

Even the weakened EEOC proposed by the House was too strong for Senate Republicans. According to Graham, the amendments Dirksen insisted upon were "devised primarily to limit the EEOC," which still "reminded Dirksen and his more conservative colleagues uncomfortably of its crusading earlier model: the NLRB" (1990, p. 146). They insisted upon removing the EEOC's authority to initiate court suits against employers. Although the Department of Justice was given power to pursue systematic "pattern and practice" suits, the vast majority of cases would be left to private litigation. The NAACP and other civil rights groups vigorously opposed this change, but were able to extract only minor concessions.

Sean Farhang provides this succinct summary of the changes made in the House and the Senate regarding enforcement of Title VII:

> While the key move of House Republicans on the fair employment provision had been to judicialize the enforcement forum, relying upon bureaucratic authority to execute the prosecutorial function, the key move of Republicans in the Senate, led by Dirksen, was to substantially *privatize* the prosecutorial function. They made private lawsuits the dominant mode of Title VII enforcement, creating an engine that would, in the years to come, produce levels of private enforcement litigation beyond their imagining.
>
> *(2010, p. 106, emphasis added)*

As Farhang suggests, the debate over the authority of the EEOC is instructive, not only because it illustrates the New Deal political divide on administrative power, but above all because the participants were so *wrong* about the consequences of these arrangements for civil rights. Hugh Davis Graham notes that both sides "had fallen into ossified, knee-jerk patterns of commitment and rhetoric" and ended up "betting on the wrong horse" (1990, p. 430–431).

One of the few people to recognize this at the time was law professor and influential EEOC consultant Arthur Blumrosen, who saw the potential for a private, litigation-based enforcement strategy. According to Blumrosen, "Based on a decade of experience, the civil rights movement should have welcomed the court enforcement, while those who wished to minimize the impact of the law should have preferred an administrative agency with seemingly broad powers which could be 'captured' by the interest it is set out to regulate" (1993, pp. 48–49). Farhang notes the irony that if Senate Republicans had accepted the House provisions on the powers of the EEOC, "the long run outcome would have been a far weakened enforcement regime" (2010, p. 147).

Reinterpretation Through Enforcement

What happened to so confound the predictions of all but the most astute participants in the 1964 debate? The most obvious answer is that federal judges proved more amenable to aggressive enforcement of Title VII than anyone had imagined. The federal judiciary that heard Title VII cases in the 1960s and 1970s was a far cry from the conservative institution the NLRB had faced in the 1930s.

In the late 1960s the NAACP Legal Defense and Education Fund (LDF) made Title VII cases a high priority. According to its chief litigator, Jack Greenberg,

> Between 1965 and 1970, LDF brought the cases that clear away the procedural obstacles to using . . . Title VII effectively and later, for some years, brought virtually all the cases that gave the law its bite. We enlisted scholars, economists, and labor experts every step of the way to target industries where lawsuits would do the most good.
>
> *(2004, p. 443)*

Greenberg was not exaggerating when he bragged that his organization handled more cases than the entire EEOC and that its Title VII litigation campaign "was a major triumph in making legal doctrine and achieving social gain—blacks, other minorities, and women won a dramatic increase in the number of jobs available to them and in the higher pay they received in those jobs." To be sure, LDF did have significant assistance, not just from other civil rights organizations but from the EEOC itself. The EEOC worked closely with civil rights organizations, often filing amicus briefs to support their position and issuing guidelines to provide them with legal ammunition.[2]

Saying that litigation by civil rights organizations with the assistance of the EEOC promoted enforcement of Title VII does not do justice to the enormous changes in public policy wrought by the employment discrimination litigation of the 1970s. It is more accurate to say that the federal courts *rewrote* Title VII, turning a weak law focusing primarily on *intentional* discrimination into a bold mandate to compensate for past discrimination, to prohibit employment practices that have a "disparate impact" on racial minorities (and, later, women), and above all to substantially increase the job opportunities available to African-Americans. Almost all laws combined broad aspirations with multiple constraints. In implementing these laws, some agency officials, interest groups, and members of Congress emphasize the broad purposes and try to minimize the constraints; others do the opposite. What is notable about Title VII is that supporters of an aggressive attack on employment practices were so despondent about the limitations imposed by the legislation passed by Congress in 1964. Emphasizing the section's "broad purposes" in effect required judges and administrators to ignore uncomfortably clear provisions of the law.

The version of Title VII enacted in 1964 not only granted few powers to the EEOC but also imposed a number of important substantive constraints on policymakers. One section of the law explicitly permits employers to use "professionally developed ability tests" as long as they are not "designed and intended or used to discriminate because of race, color, religion, sex, or national origin" (Graham, 1990, pp. 149–150). Another, added to appease labor unions, protected any "bona fide seniority or merit system." This meant that the significant advantages conferred upon white male employees by previous discriminatory actions could not be taken away, even if this "inevitably had the consequence of impeding the progress of minority employees and women into jobs from which they had previously been excluded" (Rutherglen, 2007, p. 152). Protecting seniority systems, one district court judge wrote in a frequently cited opinion, threatened "to freeze an entire generation of Negroes into discriminatory patterns that existed before the act" (*Quarles v. Philip Morris*, 279 F. Supp. 505 (E.D.Va., 1968), p. 516).

Even more important were Title VII's explicit endorsement of an "intent" standard and its concomitant rejection of any demands for racial balance in the workplace. The law provided that a court can impose sanctions on an employer only if it "finds that the respondent has *intentionally* engaged in or is *intentionally* engaging in an unlawful employment practice" (703(g), emphasis added). Anticipating the coming fight over affirmative action, §703(j) announced:

> *Preferential Treatment.* Nothing contained in this title shall be interpreted to require an employer . . . to grant preferential treatment to any individual or to any group because of the race, color, religion, sex, or national origin of such individuals or groups on account of an imbalance which may exist with respect to the total number or percentage of persons of any race, color, religion, sex, or national origin employed . . .

The bill's Senate floor leaders emphasized over and over again that Title VII prohibited only intentional discrimination, not failure to create a racially balanced workforce. According to Hubert Humphrey, Title VII "does not limit the employer's freedom to hire, fire, promote, or demote for any reason—or no reason—so long as his action is not based on race."[3] "Contrary to the allegations of some opponents of this title," Humphrey told the Senate, nothing in the act gave the EEOC or courts the power to create racial quotas:

> That bugaboo has been brought up a dozen times; but it is nonexistent. In fact, the very opposite is true. Title VII prohibits discrimination. In effect, it says that race, religion, and national origin are not to be used as the basis for hiring and firing. Title VII is designed to encourage hiring on the basis of ability and qualifications, not race or religion.
>
> *(110 Congressional Record 6549 [1964])*

The "Clark-Case memorandum"—a statement by Title VII's floor leaders designed to serve as a de facto committee report—similarly emphasized that the law does not require employers to "maintain a racial balance." To the contrary, "any deliberate attempt to maintain a racial balance . . . would involve a violation of title VII because maintaining such a balance would require an employer to hire or refuse to hire on the basis of race" (quoted in Graham, 1990, pp. 150–151). The eagerness of the act's chief sponsors to demonstrate that Title VII would not institute racial or gender quotas was not just a prudent legislative strategy. According to Hugh Davis Graham, "[T]he evidence suggests that the traditional liberalism shared by most of the civil rights establishment was philosophically offended by the notion of racial preference" (1990, p. 120). As President Kennedy put it a few months before his death, "I think it would be a mistake to begin to assign quotas on the basis of religion, or race, or color, or nationality. I think we'd get into a good deal of trouble" (quoted in Graham, 1990, p. 106).

Although EEOC staff members and civil rights advocates had initially shared this focus on intentional discrimination, they soon came to believe that a law limited to attacking overt discrimination and committed to protecting existing seniority and merit hiring systems would do little to change long-term employment patterns and practices. According to Alfred Blumrosen, "All of the EEOC's early interpretations of Title VII emerged from a unified idea—that the statute should be read so as to maximize its impact on employer practices" (1993, p. 67). As violence and unrest spread through the urban north, the EEOC became obsessed with "finding something that *works*, that gets *results*, even if that included race consciousness" (Skrentny, 1996, p. 115, emphasis in the original). Civil rights groups attacked the EEOC for shuffling paper while the cities burned. The EEOC, Skrentny has noted, "had a limited audience for its performance, and that audience was already booing loudly" (1996, p. 127).

Forced to choose between its ambitious definition of its mission and its allegiance to a statute it had no role in writing, the EEOC chose the former. According to Graham, the EEOC's staff and leadership were determined "to mount a 'wholesale' attack on institutionalized racism," even if this required them "to defy Title VII restrictions and attempt to build a body of case law that would justify its focus on effects and its disregard of intent" (1990, p. 250). Even the commission's official administrative history conceded that "eventually this will call for reconsideration of the amendment by Congress, or the reconsideration of its interpretation by the commission" (quoted in Graham, 1990, p. 250).

Blumrosen later argued that adhering to the restrictions embedded in Title VII "would have plunged Title VII investigations into an endless effort to identify an 'evil motive'" and prevented it from "changing industrial relations systems" (1993, p. 75). "Creative administration," he maintained, "converted a powerless agency operating under an apparently weak statute into a major force for the elimination of employment discrimination" (1971, p. 53). The Supreme Court openly embraced such "creativity" several years later when it issued its famous decision in *Steelworkers v. Weber*. Justice Brennan's majority opinion argued that while the explicit language of Title VII seemed to prohibit affirmative action programs developed by employers under pressure from the EEOC, judicial and administrative interpretation of Title VII should be guided by the "spirit" and overriding purpose of the law, which was to improve employment opportunities for racial minorities and thus to achieve "the integration of blacks into the mainstream of American society" (*United Steelworkers of America v. Weber* 443 U.S. 193 [1979]). This strategy of ignoring the constraints contained in the statute in order to change employment practices was not invented by the Supreme Court; it had been the mantra of the EEOC for more than a decade prior to Brennan's decision.

The big story in the first 15 years of litigation under Title VII was how willing the federal courts were to carry out the legislative revisions the EEOC expected would eventually need to come from Congress. Critics of these decisions have explained in detail how federal judges tortured the wording of the law.[4] Even the courts' defenders concede that judges played fast and loose with the statutory language. Frymer, for example, writes that "courts significantly rewrote aspects of the law . . . and, in the process, got rid of very carefully placed loopholes that unions and other civil rights opponents had demanded in order to pass the act, turning it from one that emphasized color-blindness to one that underscored affirmative action."[5] Some of this de facto revision of the statute was achieved in Supreme Court decisions such as *Griggs v. Duke Power*, *Albemarle Paper Co. v. Moody*, *Franks v. Bowman Transportation Co.*, *Steelworkers v. Weber*, and *Johnson v. Transportation Agency*. Nearly as important were such seminal lower court decisions as *Quarles v. Philip Morris*, *Contractors Association v. Secretary of Labor*, and a series of Fifth Circuit decisions on seniority systems (Blumrosen, 1993, pp. 95–96).

The Supreme Court's 1971 decision in *Griggs* was particularly important in establishing a "disparate impact" alternative to the act's explicit but inherently hard-to-prove "disparate treatment" test. Chief Justice Burger's opinion held that "[u]nder the Act, practices, procedures, or tests neutral on their face, *and even neutral in terms of intent*, cannot be maintained if they operate to 'freeze' the status quo of prior discriminatory employment practices" (410 U.S. 430). Under *Griggs*, once the plaintiff shows that a hiring, firing, or promotion practice will have a "disparate impact" on racial minorities (or women), the burden shifts to the employer to prove that the practice is "related to job performance" and justified by "business necessity." The Court later added a third stage: if the employer offers a convincing "business necessity" argument, the plaintiff then has an opportunity to show that this is merely a pretext for discrimination. None of these tests or requirements were mentioned in the original version of Title VII.

It is possible, of course, that if the EEOC had been given as much power as Democrats had originally hoped, it would have done much the same as the courts. After all, the courts often followed agency guidelines and advice. It is hard to believe, though, that such action by the EEOC would not have generated serious political opposition. Republicans would have said, "We told you so," and launched an attack on the "runaway bureaucracy." This almost certainly would have led Republican presidents Nixon and Ford to appoint commissioners less committed to amending the statute through administrative action. Labor unions, too, were highly dissatisfied with the new enforcement policies, adding significantly to the political pressure for greater restraint. The EEOC certainly was more susceptible to pressure from Congress and the president than were federal courts.

Not only were the federal courts more insulated from politics, but they also engaged in statutory revision in a slow, incremental, even stealthy fashion. It took years for the judicially revised Title VII to emerge. Meanwhile employers had time to adapt to the new regime. Even more importantly, the Congress that had passed the original Title VII no longer existed by the time the courts handed down their most important rulings. The power of southern Democrats plummeted in the 1970s, as did the number of Republicans in the House and Senate, especially after 1974. By 1975 liberal Democrats dominated the party leadership as well as key positions on the Judiciary Committees, the first stop for any legislative revision of judicial interpretations of the Civil Rights Act.

Skrentny points out that the judiciary was also skillful at *legitimating* this "new model of discrimination." A key part of the judicial art, he argues, is "asserting that what is new (the controversial case at hand) is *not* new" (1996, pp. 159–160). The novelty of the policy established in the pivotal case of *Griggs v. Duke Power* was disguised, not only by the Court's rhetorical effort to tie "disparate impact" analysis to the ultimate purposes of Title VII, but also by the fact that it was written by Chief Justice Burger for a unanimous Court. For all these reasons, the division of labor established by Title VII proved to be a particularly good mechanism for slowly redesigning the government's attack on employment discrimination without revising the underlying statute.

New Strategies, New Allies

By 1969 civil rights groups had come to appreciate the virtues of the institutional arrangement they had attacked only a few years before. Their faith in the courts was revived, and with the election of Richard Nixon their trust in the EEOC plummeted. The LDF's Jack Greenberg now told the Senate Judiciary Committee that "the entire history of the development of civil rights law is that private suits have led the way and government enforcement has followed." Liberal icon Joseph Rauh agreed "without reservation" (quoted in Farhang, 2010, p. 145). Congress continued to debate expansion of the power of the EEOC. But, as Farhang explains, the strategy of civil rights groups had changed significantly. While they continued to favor granting the EEOC cease-and-desist power, they were unwilling to give up private litigation to achieve it:

> [E]mpowered and partially financed (through attorney's fees) by the private enforcement provisions of the Dirksen compromise, civil rights groups found themselves at the leading edge of Title VII enforcement, wielding the weapon of private litigation to make what they judged to be new, meaningful, and gratifying inroads into labor markets previously foreclosed to African Americans .... Civil rights advocates could not, they had now decided, afford to rely solely upon the beneficence of bureaucrats, who themselves were dependent upon the beneficence of elected officials for resources and power, to enforce fair employment practices.
>
> *(2010, p. 146)*

As Greenberg put it, "[W]ith private enforcement we were the captains of our own ship. We took initiatives that more cautious government agencies wouldn't" (quoted in Farhang, 2010, p. 146). In 1972 Congress gave the EEOC power to file employment discrimination suits but not to issue cease-and-desist orders. The institutional issues that had loomed so large for New Dealers now seemed insignificant.

The role that private enforcement cases came to play in employment discrimination policy is indicated by the volume of suits filed in federal court. Private enforcement cases averaged less than 100 per year in the late 1960s. This grew to about 5,000 cases per year by the late 1970s, reached almost 10,000 annually in the 1980s, and then skyrocketed to over 22,000 per year in the late 1990s. In fact, employment discrimination cases now constitute almost one-fifth of all nonprisoner lawsuits brought under federal statutes (Farhang, 2010, pp. 2, 131–132, and 201). As these statistics indicate, strong incentives lead plaintiffs to file such cases and attorneys to help them do so.

The impressive growth of employment discrimination can be traced not just to the new interpretations of Title VII announced by the courts, but to congressional enactments that lower the costs and raise the benefits of litigation for plaintiffs and their lawyers. The best example of the former is the Civil Rights Attorney's Fees Award Act (CRAFAA) of 1976, which extended fee shifting to all civil rights laws (including Titles VI and IX, the subject of the next section of this chapter). The best example of the latter is the Civil Rights Act of 1991. Both provide significant support for Thomas Burke's argument that Congress has become a leading proponent of adversarial legalism (2002, chs. 2 and 5).

The congressional debate over CRAFAA offers a good illustration of how policymaking through litigation served the political needs of Democrats and liberal Republicans (not yet an endangered species) in the 1970s.[6] Although committed to improving the plight of racial minorities, women, the disabled, and other disadvantaged groups, they were growing increasingly wary of the emerging backlash against entitlement spending, social regulation, and the federal bureaucracy. They particularly feared being labeled supporters of "big government." Combining federal mandates on subnational governments and the private sector with enforcement through the courts provided a handy mechanism for squaring the political circle: this was an attractive way to provide more government protections without increasing government spending or expanding the federal bureaucracy (Melnick, 2005b). The Senate Report on CRAFAA emphasized that the bill would strengthen enforcement of civil rights law "while at the same time limiting the growth of the enforcement bureaucracy." Senate Minority Leader Hugh Scott claimed that this legislation "would cost the government nothing" and "would make the civil rights laws almost self-enforcing" (quoted in Farhang, 2010, p. 155). What politician could object to that?

Ironically, while Congress has repeatedly demonstrated its support for the court-centered private enforcement regime, the Supreme Court has become a major *critic* of this form of adversarial legalism, frequently making it more difficult for plaintiffs to get into court, to win their cases once there, to receive attorneys' fees, or to collect large damage awards. By the late 1980s, a slim conservative majority on the Court had begun to whittle away at the Title VII precedents established over the preceding two decades. Decisions of the Rehnquist Court increased the burden of proof for plaintiffs, provided additional defenses to employers, and generally made it harder for plaintiffs to prevail in "disparate impact" cases. A series of rulings announced by the Court in June 1989 produced a firestorm of criticism from civil rights organizations, Democrats in Congress, and the now substantial employment discrimination bar. In 1990 Congress passed legislation overturning a number of Title VII decisions of the Rehnquist Court. President Bush vetoed the legislation, denouncing it as a "quota bill." Congress responded by passing the Civil Rights Act of 1991, which overturned even more Court decisions and significantly expanded the damages available to plaintiffs in employment discrimination cases. This time President Bush signed the legislation, which contained enough ambiguities to allow both sides to declare victory (Govan, 1993). The 1991 act made it easier than ever for plaintiffs to prevail in employment discrimination cases and—even more importantly—significantly increased the value of winning. As a result, the number of Title VII cases filed in federal court quickly shot up once again.

No one would ever suggest that the resulting process is either pretty or efficient. George Rutherglen, a leading legal expert on Title VII, has noted that the law's enforcement scheme is "inherently more complicated than any simple mechanism for purely administrative or judicial enforcement." Consequently, "the legal doctrine governing these issues has become ever more complex, making litigation of employment discrimination cases highly technical and specialized. . . . [C]onsidered together, these policies yield a complex system of enforcement that threatens to sidetrack employment discrimination cases into a multitude of collateral procedural issues" (2007, pp. 157–159). Uncertainty, procedural complexity, redundancy, lack of finality, high transaction costs—these are the central features of adversarial legalism described by Robert Kagan.

The result, though, is *not* weak government regulation. Facing the prospect of paying very large damage awards if they lose in court, employers inevitably look for ways to avoid the financial risks (and bad publicity) of litigation. And the EEOC has been eager to offer them a "safe harbor" from the uncertainties of adversarial legalism. Since 1979 the EEOC has maintained that employers can protect themselves from disparate-impact suits by adopting "voluntary" affirmative action plans (Blumrosen, 1993, ch. 15). The major effect of the 1991 Civil Rights Act was to increase employers' incentives to sail into this "safe harbor." With employers facing greater potential losses and a heavier burden of proof, Rutherglen notes, "affirmative action becomes less and less a voluntary option and more and more a mandatory requirement. It becomes the only realistic way to avoid liability under the theory of disparate impact" (2007, p. 90). This is why many business leaders oppose "reverse discrimination" attacks on affirmative action: victory in these cases would have left them perched precariously between the Scylla of disparate-impact lawsuits and the Charybdis of "reverse discrimination" challenges, depriving them (to milk this metaphor even further) of any "safe harbor" in a sea of legal uncertainty. Whatever the flaws of adversarial legalism, it does not produce a less powerful central government.

The Transformation of Title VI

Title VI of the 1964 Civil Rights Act established the principle that "no person in the United States shall be excluded from participation in, be denied the benefits of, or be subject to discrimination under any program or activity receiving Federal financial assistance." It directed federal agencies to issue "rules, regulations, or orders of general applicability" to carry out this provision, and to terminate funding for any "particular program" that failed to comply. Although Titles VI and VII both target racial discrimination, in several ways they are mirror images of each other. The original version of Title VII applied only to private employers, not public officials. Title VI, in contrast, applies primarily to state and local governments. Title VII was extremely controversial in 1963 and 1964, the focus of the most important bargaining over the legislation. Little attention was paid to Title VI, which Hugh Davis Graham describes as "the sleeper that would become by far the most powerful weapon of them all" (1990, p. 83).

Most importantly, while Title VII was designed to be enforced by the courts, Title VI was consistently presented as a mechanism for replacing costly, time-consuming constitutional litigation with decisive administrative action. The Congress that had focused so intently on the judicial enforcement role of Title VII said nothing about the role of the courts in implementing Title VI. There is no mention of private enforcement suits either in the statute itself or in its legislative history. This was not an oversight. Since it was already unconstitutional either for state and local governments to discriminate on the basis of race or for the federal government to support such activity, suits by aggrieved private individuals were already available—just too cumbersome to be effective. While Title VII made illegal private activities that had previously been legal under federal law, Title VI applied new administrative sanctions against those who violated preexisting *constitutional* norms.

Congressional debate on Title VI focused exclusively on the extent of the powers granted to federal agencies. The House and the Senate imposed several constraints on their authority: rules issued under Title VI must be approved by the president himself; federal agencies must give Congress 30 days' advance warning of funding terminations; state and local governments are entitled to public hearings prior to termination of funds and judicial review after the fact; and such terminations apply only to the particular program found guilty of discrimination, not to the entire institution receiving funding. Congress later prohibited agencies from using "deferrals" to avoid these restrictions. Having delegated substantial power to federal administrators, members of Congress wanted to make sure they did not wield it precipitously, arbitrarily, or without giving Congress a heads-up.

From Carrot to Stick

We know from detailed accounts of school desegregation that administrative action under Title VI initially proved a potent weapon for change (Halpern, 1995; Orfield, 1969; Graham, 1999; Skrentny, 1996) Desegregation guidelines issued by the Department of Health, Education, and Welfare (HEW) in 1965 and 1966 were a crucial component of the "reconstruction of southern education" accomplished at long last in the late 1960s and early 1970s. The threat of fiscal sanctions was made particularly compelling by the new pot of money Congress made available to southern school systems when it passed the landmark Elementary and Secondary Education Act of 1965. But it still took a subtle combination of judicial and administrative action to desegregate southern schools. According to Gary Orfield, who has provided one of the best descriptions of OCR's early years, "The policy shift announced by the Office of Civil Rights was possible only because of a series of helpful court decisions" (1969, p. 340).

The breakthrough on school desegregation came in the period 1966–67, when judges on the Fifth Circuit incorporated key elements of HEW's guidelines into their opinions and remedies in 14th Amendment cases. In its most important ruling, *U.S. v. Jefferson County Board of Education*, Judge John Minor Wisdom explained that since "the courts acting alone have failed," administrative action under Title VI "was necessary to rescue school desegregation from the bog on which it had been trapped for years." HEW's guidelines "offer, for the first time, the prospect that the transition from a *de jure* segregated dual system to a unitary integrated system may be carried out effectively, promptly, and in an orderly manner" (*U.S. v. Jefferson County Board of Education I*, 372 F. 2d 859 [1966]). If administrative guidelines provided courts with the "judicially manageable standards" essential for desegregating schools, the courts offered HEW's Office for Civil Rights crucial political support and credible sanctions. As Stephen Halpern explains in his detailed analysis of this court-agency partnership,

> HEW officials realized that federal courts were a good ally, and the agency had few allies in beginning the politically touchy task of enforcing Title VI . . . Time after time, the Fifth Circuit intervened . . . to give HEW's school desegregation efforts "a boost." Moreover, in meetings with angry southern educators HEW officials could claim that their hands were tied—that court decisions and hence, indirectly, the Constitution itself, required HEW to be as insistent as it was.
>
> *(1995, p. 73)*

According to Halpern, in the southern desegregation effort "the synergistic power of the bench and bureaucracy working together was apparent." Federal judges "lauded HEW's 'expertise' in writing the Guidelines, and HEW officials, in turn, extolled and relied on the 'objective' policies of the courts." He also notes the irony of this arrangement: "The enforcement of a law intended as a substitute for litigation became heavily dependent on and linked to the standards advanced in litigation" (1995, pp. 73, 67, and 76).

It did not take long for administrators throughout the federal government to discover that termination of funding for state and local governments is too blunt and extreme a sanction to be politically palatable or administratively attractive in ordinary times. In a report highly critical of federal agencies' lax enforcement of Title VI, the United States Commission on Civil Rights identified a central dilemma facing these funding agencies: "Although funding termination may serve as an effective deterrent to recipients, it may leave the victim of discrimination without a remedy. Funding termination may eliminate the benefits sought by the victim" (U.S. Commission on Civil Rights, 1996, p. 40). Just as importantly, funding cut-offs threatened to damage relations between the federal agency and those state and local officials with whom they worked on a regular basis—not to mention antagonizing members of Congress upon whom administrators relied for appropriations. Statistics provided by Beryl Radin vividly demonstrate the weakness of this sanction. Between 1964 and 1970, the period in which OCR was most aggressive and most successful in attacking southern school segregation, it initiated administrative proceedings against 600 of the more than 4,000 school districts in the South. Federal funding was "terminated in 200; in all but four of these 200 districts, federal aid was subsequently restored, often without a change in local procedures" (Radin, 1977, p. 14). Not only was the termination process procedurally cumbersome and politically hazardous, but some of the most recalcitrant rural districts were willing to forgo federal funds rather than desegregate (Halpern, 1995, pp. 51–52; Orfield, 1969, pp. 241–243). At that point, litigation was the only option. As Congress replaced small categorical grants with much larger block grants in the 1970s, termination of funding became all the more awkward.

Federal courts offered a more imposing enforcement tool, the structural injunction. During the 1960s, judges in school desegregation cases created detailed, demanding regulatory regimes tailored to the specific circumstances of each school district. These injunctions were modified on a regular basis. Many remained in effect for decades. Public officials who violated these injunctions could be found in contempt of court, a powerful weapon for compelling compliance. In the five years after *Jefferson County,* the Fifth Circuit also adopted novel procedural rules that sharply limited the authority of obstructionist district court judges, significantly reduced the cost to civil rights organizations and the Department of Justice of mounting desegregation litigation, and in effect turned appellate review into a form of administrative oversight. Frank Read, who has provided us with a detailed account of these innovations by the Fifth Circuit, notes that the appellate procedures produced a "quantum leap in school desegregation activities." Between December 1969 and September 1970, the newly created standing panels of the Fifth Circuit issued 166 "opinion orders" on desegregation (Read, 1975, p. 32; see also Read & McGough, 1978). With school districts throughout the South facing the near certainty of specific judicial desegregation orders, funding sanctions faded into irrelevancy.

What courts—especially those in the Fifth Circuit—needed from administrators were guidelines to make their newly acquired tasks manageable. If these agency rules had merely tracked previous court rulings defining racial discrimination under the 14th Amendment, then they would have been of little help or little policy significance. But agency rules under Title VI went far beyond what the courts had deemed constitutionally required. In order to provide specific guidance to recipients of federal funding, agency rules often created a presumption in favor of racial proportionality. OCR's 1966 desegregation guidelines, the most important set of rules ever issued by that organization, set specific targets for the percentage of black students enrolled in formerly white schools. The Fifth Circuit's embrace of these guidelines not only broke the logjam on school desegregation, but constituted a major step in the redefinition of "desegregation." Although the 1964 act specifically stated that "desegregation" did not mean assigning children to particular schools in order to achieve racial balance, OCR took the first step in that direction and the courts, claiming to defer to agency expertise, took many more. Together they established the expectation that all school districts that had previously engaged in segregation must reconstitute their schools so that none of them were "racially identifiable"—which in effect meant that the racial composition of each school must reflect the racial composition of the district as a whole.

This redefinition of desegregation coupled with the enhanced enforcement capacity of the federal courts produced what Gary Orfield has called the "reconstruction of southern education" in the late 1960s and early 1970. It also raised the enormously controversial issue of busing, first in the South, then in northern and western cities. Both Congress and the White House prohibited OCR from participating in busing cases. This did not mean that OCR merely walked away with its tail between its legs. Instead it looked for new ways to promote equal educational opportunity using the institutional arrangements now at its disposal. With the blessing of the Nixon White House, it undertook a major investigation of racial discrimination in New York City schools and promoted bilingual education for Latino students (Rebell & Block, 1985; Davies, 2007, ch. 7).

New Groups, New Rights, New Incentives

Bilingual education provides a good example of the division of labor between federal courts and federal agencies that eventually emerged under Title VI. In 1970 the Office for Civil Rights in HEW issued new rules on "school districts with more than 5% national origin minority group children." The regulations announced that

> when the inability to speak and understand the English language excludes national origin minority group children from effective participation in the educational program offered by the school district, the district must take affirmative steps to rectify the language deficiency in order to open its instructional program to those students.
>
> *(Quoted in Davies, 2007, p. 151)*

The original rules were not very specific about the content of those "affirmative steps." But within a few months it had issued detailed guidelines for bilingual education. HEW Secretary Elliot Richardson told a Senate committee that OCR would require schools with a significant number of non-English-speaking students to engage in

> total institutional reposturing (including culturally sensitive teachers, instructional materials and educational approaches) in order to incorporate, affirmatively recognize, and value the cultural environment of ethnic minority children so that the development of positive self-concept can be accelerated.
> *(Quoted in Davies, 2007, p. 153)*

Failure to follow these guidelines would constitute discrimination on the basis of "national origin" and thus call for termination of federal funding to the school district.

The impetus for these regulations came not from Latino groups but from idealistic young lawyers in the Office of Civil Rights. They received unexpected political support from the White House, which was courting Hispanic voters in anticipation of the 1972 election. But OCR had neither the capacity nor the political will to translate these demanding guidelines into enforcement action. By 1974 it had reviewed only 4 percent of the covered school districts. It found over half of the review districts out of compliance. Some of these districts agreed to a remedial plan. Others refused to negotiate at all. On only one occasion did the Office of Civil Rights take even the first step towards termination of federal funds (Davies, 2007, pp. 147–157).

Once again it was the federal judiciary that came to the rescue of the OCR. In 1974 the Supreme Court heard a Title VI bilingual education class action suit filed by legal assistance lawyers representing Chinese-American parents in San Francisco. In its brief opinion in *Lau v. Nichols* (414 U.S. 563 [1974]), the Court avoided the question of whether the 14th Amendment required school districts to provide education in students' native language by finding that the school was bound by HEW's Title VI regulations. Those regulations, the Court held, were well within the power granted to HEW by Title VI. The court implied—but did not specifically state—that the regulations could be enforced by the federal courts. The next year HEW issued more specific bilingual education guidelines, known appropriately as the "*Lau* remedies." Federal district courts in New York and New Mexico ordered school districts with large numbers of Hispanic students to comply with them (Davies, 2007, pp. 160–161).

In school desegregation cases federal judge had required school districts to comply with HEW's guidelines in order to remedy *constitutional* violations. But no one claimed that failure to provide bilingual education constituted a violation of the Constitution. *Lau v. Nichols* thus marked a subtle yet important shift that few appreciated at the time: the federal courts were now willing to entertain private suits to enforce administrative regulations issued under Title VI, even those without any clear connection to the 14th Amendment. This transformed a mechanism designed to create an *administrative alternative to constitutional litigation* into one that *combines broad rulemaking authority for federal agencies with judicial enforcement through private suits.*

One can argue that Title VI was intended to give agencies authority to issue "prophylactic" regulations that extend beyond the basic requirements of the Constitution. At the same time, though, Congress placed many restrictions on the agency's power to enforce these rules. Everyone knew that cutting off funding was a highly visible action that most agencies would take only in unusual circumstances. Termination of funding is not cheap: it requires the expenditure of a significant amount of political capital.

The addition of judicial enforcement for private rights of action significantly altered this political equation. Now agencies could write broad Title VI regulations and allow others to take the political heat for enforcing them, something civil rights organizations and federal judges were happy to do. Even more importantly, federal judges could enforce these rules not by ordering the termination of funding—by far the most obvious remedy for the violation of Title VI—but by issuing injunctions requiring recipients to alter their practices in specific ways to comply with agency rules. After all, private parties did not go to court asking for termination of funding for the programs in which they participated; they wanted state and local officials to use federal money in different ways.

For years the Supreme Court heard many cases under Title VI and its various "clones" (especially Title IX of the 1972 Education Amendments and §504 of the 1974 Rehabilitation Act) without directly addressing the underlying questions of who could file suit and what kind of relief courts could order. The lower courts understandably took the Supreme Court's silence as a green light to entertain private rights of action and to issue injunctions requiring compliance with agency rules.

In the 1970s, private rights of action under Title VI and Title IX were usually brought by civil rights organizations. Not only were these cases too expensive for most private individuals to pursue, but prospective injunctive relief promised few benefits for those initially aggrieved. Eventually, though, the Supreme Court authorized federal judges to award *monetary damages* to plaintiffs in some Title VI and Title IX cases. The Court first permitted the award of back pay in a splintered, garbled decision on racial discrimination in the employment practices of the New York City Police Department (*Guardians Association of NYC Police Dept. v. Civil Service Commission* 463 U.S. 582 [1983]). A decade later, the Court announced that federal courts can require public schools to pay damages to students who have been subjected to sexual harassment by teachers (*Franklin v. Gwinnett County Public Schools* 503 U.S. 60 [1992]). Later it ruled that a student could sue a school district for monetary damages when it fails to take adequate steps to prevent sexual harassment by a fellow student (*Davis v. Monroe County Board of Education* 526 U.S. 629 [1999]).

The combination of congressionally authorized attorney's fees and judicially authorized monetary damages significantly increased incentives for private parties to file suits under Titles VI and IX. Eventually a private bar developed to litigate these cases. This had the effect not just of increasing the number of cases filed, but of augmenting the political support for this enforcement mechanism. A better example of path dependency in action would be hard to find.

A Remedial Scheme on Trial

In 2001 Justice Stevens composed the following ode to the "integrated remedial scheme" that the courts, Congress, and agencies had developed under Title VI:

> This legislative design reflects a reasonable—indeed inspired—model for attacking the often-intractable problem of racial and ethnic discrimination. On its own terms the statute supports an action challenging policies of federal grantees that explicitly or unambiguously violate antidiscrimination norms (such as policies that on their face limit benefits or services to certain races). With regard to more subtle forms of discrimination (such as schemes that limit benefits or services on ostensibly race-neutral grounds but have the predictable and perhaps intended consequence of materially benefiting some races at the expense of others), the statute does not establish a static approach but instead empowers the relevant agencies to evaluate social circumstances to determine whether there is a need for stronger measures. Such an approach builds into the law flexibility, an ability to make nuanced assessments of complex social realities, and an admirable willingness to credit the possibility of progress.
>
> *(Alexander v. Sandoval 532 U.S. 275 [2001])*

In the case then before the Court, the state of Alabama had refused to comply with Department of Justice rules requiring drivers' tests to be conducted in Spanish as well as English. The department claimed that Alabama's English-only rule would have a disproportionate impact on those born outside the U.S., and therefore violated Title VI. For Justice Stevens this rule reflected

> the considered judgment of the relevant agencies that discrimination on the basis of race, ethnicity, and national origin by federal contractees are significant social problems that might be remedied, or least ameliorated, by the application of a broad prophylactic rule.

Since the issue in this case, *Alexander v. Sandoval*, was virtually identical to the one decided by the Court a quarter-century before in *Lau v. Nichols*, Stevens considered it an easy one to resolve.

Surprisingly, Stevens lost. As he bitterly and accurately complained, "in a decision unfounded in our precedent and hostile to decades of settled expectations, a majority of this Court carves out an important exception to the right of private action long recognized under Title VI." The Court's majority held that while private parties could sue to enforce the explicit statutory mandate contained in the first section of Title VI, they could not sue to enforce agency *regulations* issued under its second section. Since the Court had repeatedly deferred to federal agencies' interpretation of Title VI in previous cases, this was an odd ruling, to say the least.

Alexander v. Sandoval was in part a reflection of the Rehnquist Court's hostility to affirmative action and to "effects" tests in discrimination cases. The Court's five-member majority in essence said, "Since we interpret Title VI to outlaw only *intentional* discrimination, we will not allow agencies to impose a broader definition through the rulemaking process." But *Sandoval* also indicated that some members of the Court—perhaps a majority, but a fleeting one at best—entertained serious doubts about the entire array of institutional arrangements that have grown up around Titles VI and IX. Under *Sandoval*, it would seem, when agencies seek to go beyond the Court's interpretation of Title VI and the 14th Amendment, they are on their own in the enforcement process. They must invoke the awkward funding termination process rather than rely on court-based enforcement by private parties.

It is too early to write the obituary for Steven's "inspired model" for attacking discrimination. In a 2005 "retaliation" case brought under Title IX, a closely divided Court seemed to retreat from *Sandoval*'s narrow interpretation of judicially enforceable rights contained in cross-cutting federal mandates (*Jackson v. Birmingham Board of Education* 544 U.S. 167 [2005]). In the past it has not been unusual for Congress (at least when Democrats are in the majority) to respond to restrictive court rulings by passing legislation that explicitly authorizes private damage suits to enforce agency rules.

It is more useful to examine the reasons behind the growth of this enforcement regime than to speculate about the likelihood of its demise. The institutional arrangements that gradually evolved under Titles VI and IX were the product of two convictions. The first is that for every federal right there should be an effective federal remedy, created, if necessary, by the courts. As the Supreme Court stated in an earlier "implied private right of action" case, *J.I. Case v. Borak*, "[I]t is the duty of the courts to be alert to provide such remedies as are necessary to make effective the congressional purpose" (377 U.S. 426 [1964], 433). The second is that neither the tools wielded by civil rights agencies under these statutes nor those employed by the courts were themselves adequate for uprooting subtle yet invidious forms of discrimination. Implicit in the Court's marrying of private damage suits with administrative regulation is the recognition that neither federal agencies nor federal courts can go it alone in creating an effective regulatory regime.

Conclusion: Friends With Benefits

No one set out to build the "inspired model" of civil rights regulation lauded by Justice Stevens. It was the product of serendipity, strategic miscalculation, experimentation, opportunistic lawyering, and, most importantly, successful adaptation by a variety of key actors. The policymaking model described above has frequently been emulated, but rarely explicitly championed or even described. In the long run, these arrangements survived and prospered despite their obvious drawbacks because they fit so well with key features of the new political environment. Years of divided government eroded Democrats' and civil rights leaders' faith in the executive branch and in New Deal institutional norms. Growing public suspicion of "big government"—and especially centralized bureaucracy—led advocates to search for ways to attack various forms of discrimination without seeming to expand the power of federal bureaucrats. Adversarial legalism offered something to a number of key players—including judges, administrators, members of Congress, and advocacy groups.

The stories of Titles VI and VII show that adversarial legalism can promote aggressive federal regulation of the private sector and subnational governments through a new division of labor between judges and administrators, one that inverts our usual assumptions about the executive and judicial branches. Administrators focus on writing rules and guidelines, leaving to politically insulated judges the job of enforcing them through private rights of action. Freed from the politically onerous job of taking enforcement actions against well-connected businesses and state and local officials, civil rights agencies have been emboldened to promulgate aggressive regulations they could never hope to carry out on their own. These administrative rules supplied judges with the "judicially manageable standards" they so often have difficulty devising on their own. Each branch built on the initiatives of the other, and avoided responsibility by claiming to defer to the judgment of the other. Judges deferred to "expertise" of civil rights agencies; those agencies deferred to the courts' interpretation of statutes and the Constitution. Courts' ability to issue injunctions, to award monetary damages, and to provide attorney's fees not only put real teeth into the enforcement process but provided strong incentives for private litigants to monitor the behavior of employers and recipients of federal funding. The growth of the civil rights bar, in turn, provided crucial political support for these institutional arrangements when they were threatened by adverse Supreme Court decisions.

In the early 1970s, just as these new patterns were emerging under civil rights statutes, innovative judges on the D.C. Circuit were marking the arrival of what Judge David Bazelon famously called "a new era in the long and fruitful collaboration of administrative agencies and reviewing courts" (*EDF v. Ruckelshaus*, 439 F.2d 589 [D.C. Cir., 1971], 597). According to his colleague Harold Leventhal, courts and agencies "are in a kind of partnership for the purpose of effectuating the legislative mandate" (*Portland Cement Assoc. v. Ruckelshaus*, 486

F.2d 375 [D.C. Cir., 1973], 394). "Our duty," Judge Skelly Wright, a third member of that court, announced, "is to see that the legislative purposes heralded in the halls of Congress, are not lost in the vast halls of the federal bureaucracy" (*Calvert Cliffs Coordinating Committee v AEC*, 449 F.2d 1109 [D.C. Cir., 1971], 1111). These quotations capture the sense that judges had come to view their job not as *constraining* administrators, but as *collaborating* with them to produce more effective—and often more ambitious—government programs (Melnick, 1985). In Justice Stevens' words, these judges demonstrated an "admirable willingness to credit the possibility of progress."

As the history of Title VII so vividly illustrates, sometimes vindicating broad "legislative purposes" means ensuring that inconvenient statutory provisions *are* in fact "lost in the vast halls" of the bureaucracy and reviewing courts. One might have thought that this would spark a hostile response from Congress. But, as Thomas Burke has shown, Congress is one of the most reliable supporters of adversarial legalism (2002, chs. 2 and 5). When the Supreme Court rewrote Title VII in the 1970s, Congress took no action. But when the Supreme Court curtailed attorneys fees, limited opportunities for private suits, and made it more difficult for plaintiffs to win disparate impact suits, Congress repeatedly enacted laws to reverse these decisions. Moreover, Congress created a variety of Title VI and Title VII "clones" designed to limit discrimination on the basis of gender, disability, age, veteran status—and even membership in the Boy Scouts.

One great advantage of this form of policymaking for members of Congress is that it allows them to pass vague legislation without delegating authority to the executive branch, which since 1968 has usually been in the hands of the other party. Not surprisingly, adversarial legalism began to take shape in this country in the 1970s, a period characterized by divided government, extreme hostility between Congress and the president, a shift in power in Congress from the conservative old guard to the much more liberal and entrepreneurial "Watergate babies," and an outpouring of important legislation, much of it enacted without presidential support. The Congress that did so much to encourage adversarial legalism after 1970 was a far different body than the one that wrote the Civil Rights Act of 1964—which helps explain why subsequent Congresses showed so little concern with respecting the compromises included in that legislation. When Republicans suddenly seized control of Congress in 1995, they made a number of efforts to reduce the role of the federal courts, especially their authority to impose "unfunded mandates" on state and local governments. But this effort was sporadic and usually unsuccessful. Ever ready to demonize government bureaucracy, Republicans were often even more eager than Democrats to depart from New Deal–style delegation of authority to the executive branch.

In a famous study first published in 1967, Lloyd Free and Hadley Cantril noted that the American public is "ideologically" conservative but "operationally" liberal (Free & Cantril, 1967). While Americans are distrustful of government in general, they support virtually all the particular activities the government undertakes—and want more of almost everything. After 1968 this contradiction grew more intense: public expectations grew while trust in government declined precipitously. The public expected the federal government to fight racial and gender discrimination, improve education, expand the economic opportunities of the disadvantaged, protect the environment, reduce crime, wage one "war" on drugs and another on cancer, promote energy self-sufficiency, guarantee health care for all, create a full-employment economy, and provide a "safety net" for those unable to find work (Cantril & Cantril, 1999, ch. 2; Mayer, 1993, pp. 451–462 and 486–90; Cook &. Barrett, 1992; Weaver, 2000, ch. 7). When asked what they want from government, citizens typically offer a Gomperesque reply: "more." After the Great Society, it became nearly impossible to argue that any of these tasks were outside the constitutional realm of the federal government.

Yet, as innumerable public opinion polls have demonstrated, confidence in government fell precipitously after 1965. In the mid-1960s three-quarters of Americans thought the federal government could be trusted to do the right thing most of the time. By the mid-1970s, only about one-third of Americans shared that view. Conversely, in the mid-1960s slightly less than one-third of the public believed the "government is run by a few big interests looking out for themselves." Ten years later, over two-thirds agreed with this statement. Despite a few ups and downs, public trust in government remained low for the next 20 years (Orren, 1997; Lipset & Schneider, 1987).

Surprisingly, between 1965 and 1975 trust in government fell furthest and most precipitously among those who described themselves as liberals and Democrats (Lipset & Schneider, 1987, p. 333). According to Nie, Verba, and Petrocik, by 1972 "liberals were more opposed to big government than were conservatives" (1976, p. 127). There were, of course, many reasons for this. Liberals came to identify "big government" with Richard Nixon, the war in Vietnam, the military-industrial complex, captured regulatory agencies, and ineffective, insensitive, unresponsive bureaucracy. Such doubts about the beneficence of government were most pronounced among those affiliated with civil rights organizations. After all, they had spent years challenging the discriminatory practices of public school systems, state agencies, and local police departments. They had also witnessed firsthand the tepid response of federal agencies. Many came to view public schools—the unit of government that has the greatest direct effect on ordinary people's lives—as instruments of oppression rather than as avenues for advancement.

This put liberals in the awkward position of arguing that more authority should be given to a national government that they—and the American public generally—did not trust. For many activists of the 1960s, Hugh Heclo has noted, "the federal government was part of the 'establishment' that had to be attacked. And yet it was also the resource that lay most readily at hand to pursue the social reformations [they] urged." In marked contrast to the reform tradition stretching from the Progressives to the New Deal and the Great Society, this new cadre of reformers proved "in a certain sense to be antigovernment":

> Government responsibilities were to be vastly expanded, while government autonomy had to be restricted at every turn. Distrust required opening up policy-making to public view and assuring access for formerly marginalized groups. Confidence in administrative discretion, expertise, and professional independence had to be replaced by continuous public scrutiny, hard-nosed advocacy, strict timetables, and stringent standards for prosecuting the policy cause in question.
>
> *(Heclo, 1996, pp. 52)*

Fortunately for these liberal activists, the "paradox of policy expectations and institutional suspicion" could be resolved: "Federal policy powers could be vigorously increased so long as they were sufficiently distrusted and controlled by activists." The "energetic use of national policy" can be harnessed "for transforming American society" only if it is "accompanied by an equally vigorous suspicion of that power and whoever might exercise it"(Heclo, 1996, pp. 51–52).

Building public programs by exposing government's failures—this was the formula that not only resolved liberal activists' ambivalence about government authority but allowed them to make full use of their allies in the media, on congressional subcommittees, and on the federal bench. After all, journalists, oversight committees, and judges do not run government programs. Their responsibility is to show that something is wrong and to demand (usually indignantly) that the situation be corrected. Blame-casting is their job, and if blame could be cast at a Republican administration, so much the better.[7]

The language of individual rights was particularly well suited to the purposes of these ambivalent activists, for the rights most vigorously promoted in the 1970s were at one and the same time (1) claims for government assistance, and (2) protections against bureaucratic discretion. The right to a free and appropriate education, the right to a nutritionally adequate diet, the right to equal access to public transportation, the right to breathe clean air, the right to adequate health care, the right to a workplace free from racial discrimination or sexual harassment—all this required substantial governmental effort. But the fact that these were rights rather than mere programs meant that government officials would be subject to elaborate procedures, multiple rules, and constant oversight. This understanding of rights produced not the limited government we associate with Locke and *Lochner*, but the peculiar combination of governmental activism and political fragmentation that characterizes adversarial legalism.

In recent years the most persistent critic of adversarial legalism has been the Supreme Court. The Court's decisions in *Sandoval*, in the Title VII cases overturned by the Civil Rights Act of 1991, and in a large number of cases limiting the jurisdiction of the federal courts indicate that since the late 1980s the Supreme Court has had second thoughts about the wisdom of the policies and institutional arrangements described above. Indeed, one could say that over the past two decades opposition to adversarial legalism has become a guiding theme of Supreme Court jurisprudence (Siegel, 2006; Melnick, 2005a). One cannot hope to understand the divisions in the Rehnquist and Roberts Courts without appreciating the extent to which the justices disagree profoundly on whether the civil rights state created through adversarial legalism constitutes an "inspired model" for attacking discrimination or a judicially abetted perversion of federalism and separation of powers.

Once created, institutions are hard to displace. Despite repeated warnings about imminent retrenchment, the civil rights policies and institutions established in the 1960s and 1970s have proved remarkably resilient. Legal protections first provided to African-Americans on the basis of the extraordinary and unique injury done to them have now been extended to a variety of additional groups, some of them defined in rather ambiguous and arbitrary terms. Much of this regulatory regime remains, to use Suzanne Mettler's term, submerged. But it is not weak or ineffective, and it will not soon fade away.

Notes

1 The obvious example is civil rights, where the Roosevelt Administration created a new administrative unit, the Civil Rights Division, within the Department of Justice in order to do through the courts what it could not do through Congress or unilaterally. See McMahon, 2004, chs. 5–6. The division achieved some notable victories, but for reasons discussed below, such courtroom triumphs were seldom converted into substantial change on the ground.
2 Blumrosen describes the many ways the EEOC attacked discrimination, encouraged litigants, and promoted affirmative action in chs. 5, 6, 10, 12, and 14–16. Also see Graham, 1990, pp. 190–254; Skrentney, 1996.
3 Quoted in Rutherglen, 2007, p. 17. Justice Rehnquist's dissent in *Weber* provides many more examples of such statements by the leading of supporters of the Civil Rights Act.
4 See, for example, Justice Rehnquist's dissent in *Weber*; Justice Scalia's dissent in *Johnson v. Transportation Agency*; Meltzer, 1980; Graham, 1990, chs. 9 and 15; Belz, 1991; Lund, 1997.
5 2008a, 87. The most extensive and sophisticated effort to justify the courts' deviation from conventional statutory interpretation is Eskridge 1994. I highlight the connection between *Weber* and Eskridge's theory of statutory interpretation in Melnick, 1995.
6 The following paragraph draws on Farhang, 2010, pp. 147–155.
7 For a graphic example, see Derthick, 1990, especially chapters 7 and 8. Samuel Huntington has described the 1970s as "the great age of exposure," noting that "exposure could not occur until the authority of the executive branch—that is, the plausible targets of exposure—had been weakened, and it could not occur until the power of the press and Congress—that is, the necessary agents of exposure—had been enhanced." 1981,190.

References

Aberbach, J., Putnam, R., & Rockman, B. (1981). *Bureaucrats and Politicians in Western Democracies*. Cambridge, MA: Harvard University Press.
Barnes, J. (2011). *Dust-Up: Asbestos Litigation and the Failure of Commonsense Policy Reform*. Washington, DC: Georgetown University Press.

Belz, H. (1991). *Equality Transformed: A Quarter-Century of Affirmative Action*. Piscataway, NJ: Transaction Press.

Bleich, E. (2003). *Race Politics in Britain and France: Ideas and Policymaking Since the 1960s*. Cambridge: Cambridge University Press.

Blumrosen, A. (1971). *Black Employment and the Law*. New Brunswick, NJ: Rutgers University Press.

Blumrosen, A. (1993). *Modern Law: The Law Transmission System and Equal Employment Opportunity*. Madison: University of Wisconsin Press.

Burke, T. (1997). "On the Rights Track." In P. Nivola (Ed.), *Comparative Disadvantage? Social Regulation and the Global Economy*. Washington, DC: Brookings Institution Press, 242–318.

Burke, T. (2002). *Lawyers, Lawsuits, and Legal Rights: The Battle Over Litigation in American Society*. Berkeley: University of California Press.

Cantril, A.H., & Cantril, S.D. (1999). *Reading Mixed Signals: Ambivalence in American Public Opinion about Government*. Washington, DC: Woodrow Wilson Center Press and Johns Hopkins University Press.

Carpenter, D. (2010). *Reputation and Power: Organizational Image and Pharmaceutical Regulation at the FDA*. Princeton, NJ: Princeton University Press.

Cook, F.L., & Barrett, E.J. (1992). *Support for the Welfare State: The Views of Congress and the Public*. New York: Columbia University Press.

Cunningham, M. (2001). *Maximization, Whatever the Cost: Race, Redistricting, and the Department of Justice*. Westport, CT: Praeger.

Davies, Gareth. (2007). *See Government Grow: Education Politics from Johnson to Reagan*. Lawrence: University of Kansas Press.

Derthick, M. (1970). *The Influence of Federal Grants: Public Assistance in Massachusetts*. Cambridge, MA: Harvard University Press.

Derthick, M. (1979). *Policymaking for Social Security*. Washington, DC: Brookings Institution Press.

Derthick, M. (1990). *Agency Under Stress: The Social Security Administration in American Politics*. Washington, DC: Brookings Institution Press.

Derthick, M. (2004). *Up in Smoke* (2nd ed). Washington, DC: CQ Press.

Dobbin, F. (2009). *Inventing Equal Opportunity*. Princeton, NJ: Princeton University Press.

Dobbin, F., & Sutton, J.R. (1998). "The Strength of a Weak State: The Rights Revolution and the Rise of Human Resources Management Divisions." *American Journal of Sociology*, 104, 441–76.

Dunn, J., & West, M. (Eds.) (2009). *From Schoolhouse to Courthouse: The Judiciary's Role in American Education*. Washington, DC: Brookings Institution Press.

Erkulwater, J. (2006). *Disability Rights and the American Safety Net*. Ithaca, NY: Cornell University Press.

Farhang, S. (2010). *The Litigation State: Public Regulation and Private Lawsuits in the U.S.* Princeton, NJ: Princeton University Press,

Free, L., & Cantril, H. (1967). *The Political Beliefs of Americans*. New Brunswick, NJ: Rutgers University Press.

Frymer, P. (2008a). *Black and Blue: African Americans, the Labor Movement, and the Decline of the Democratic Party*. Princeton, NJ: Princeton University Press.

Frymer, P. (2008b). "Law and American Political Development." *Law and Social Inquiry*, 33, 779–803.

Govan, R.C. (1993). "Honorable Compromises and the Moral High Ground: The Conflict between the Rhetoric and the Content of the Civil Rights Act of 1991." *Rutgers Law Review*, 46(1), 1–242.

Graham, H.D. (1990). *The Civil Rights Era: Origins and Development of National Policy*. New York: Oxford University Press.

Graham, H.D. (1999). "Since 1964: The Paradox of American Civil Rights Regulation." In Melnick and Keller (Eds.), *Taking Stock: American Government in the Twentieth Century*. Cambridge: Woodrow Wilson Center Press and Cambridge University Press, 187–218.

Greenberg, J. (2004). *Crusaders in the Courts: Legal Battles of the Civil Rights Movement*. Anniversary Edition. Northport, NY: Twelve Tables Press.

Halpern, S. (1995). *On the Limits of the Law: The Ironic Legacy of Title VI of the Civil Rights Act*. Baltimore: Johns Hopkins University Press.

Heclo, H. (1996). "The Sixties' False Dawn: Awakenings, Movements, and Postmodern Policy-Making." *Journal of Policy History*, 8(1), 34–63.

Howard, C. (2007). *The Welfare State Nobody Knows: Debunking Myths about U.S. Social Policy*. Princeton, NJ: Princeton University Press.

Huntington, S. (1981). *American Politics: The Promise of Disharmony*. Cambridge, MA: Harvard University Press.

Kagan, R. (2001). *Adversarial Legalism: The American Way of Law*. Cambridge, MA: Harvard University Press.

Landsberg, B.K. (2007). *Free at Last to Vote: The Alabama Origins of the 1965 Voting Rights Act*. Lawrence: University of Kansas Press.

Lieberman, R. (2002). "Weak State, Strong Policy: Paradoxes of Race Policy in the United States, Great Britain, and France." *Studies in American Political Development*, 16: 138–61.

Lieberman, R. (2005). *Shaping Race Policy: The United States in Comparative Perspective*. Princeton, NJ: Princeton University Press.

Lipset, S.M., & Schneider, W. (1987). *The Confidence Gap*. Baltimore: Johns Hopkins University Press.

Lund, N. (1997). "The Law of Affirmative Action in and After the Civil Rights Act of 1991: Congress Invites Judicial Reform." *George Mason Law Review*, 6, 87.

Mayer, W.G. (1993). *The Changing American Mind: How and Why American Public Opinion Changed Between 1960 and 1988*. Ann Arbor: University of Michigan Press.

McMahon, K. (2004). *Reconsidering Roosevelt on Race: How the Presidency Paved the Road to* Brown. Chicago: University of Chicago Press.

Melnick, R.S. (1983). *Regulation and the Courts: The Case of the Clean Air Act*. Washington, DC: Brookings Institution Press.

Melnick, R.S. (1985). "The Politics of Partnership." *Public Administration Review*, 45, 653.

Melnick, R.S. (1989). "The Courts, Congress, and Programmatic Rights." In S. Milkis & R. Harris (Eds.), *Remaking American Politics*. Boulder, CO: Westview Press, 188–212.

Melnick, R.S. (1994). *Between the Lines: Interpreting Welfare Rights*. Washington, DC: Brookings Institution Press.

Melnick, R.S. (1995). "Statutory Reconstruction: The Politics of Eskridge's Interpretation." *Georgetown Law Journal*, 84, 91–121.

Melnick, R.S. (2005a). "Deregulating the States: The Political Jurisprudence of the Rehnquist Court." In T. Ginsburg & R. Kagan (Eds.), *Institutions and Public Law: Comparative Approaches*. New York: Peter Lang, 69–95.

Melnick, R.S. (2005b). "From Tax and Spend to Mandate and Sue: Liberalism after the Great Society." In S. Milkis & J. Mileur (Eds.), *The Great Society and the High Tide of Liberalism*. Amherst, MA: University of Massachusetts Press, 387–410.

Melnick, R.S. (2007). "Entrepreneurial Litigation: Advocacy Coalitions and Strategies in the Fragmented American Welfare State." In J. Soss, J. Hacker, & Susanne Mettler (Eds.), *Remaking America: Democracy and Public Policy in an Age of Inequality*. New York: Russell Sage Foundation Press, 51–73.

Melnick, R.S. (2011). "The Crucible of Desegregation: 'Unitary' Schools in a Divided Court." Paper prepared for delivery at the Annual Meeting of the American Political Science Association, Seattle, Washington, Sept. 1–4.
Melnick, R.S. (2014). "The Conventional Misdiagnosis: Why 'Gridlock' Is Not Our Central Problem and Constitutional Revision Is Not the Solution." *Boston University Law Review*, 94, 767.
Melnick, R.S. (2015). "Gridlock and the Madisonian Constitution." In B. Wittes & P. Nivola (Eds.), *What Would Madison Do? The Father of the Constitution Meets Modern American Politics*. Washington, DC: Brookings Institution Press, 68–94.
Meltzer, B.D. (1980). "The Weber Case: The Judicial Abrogation of the Antidiscrimination Standard in Employment." *University of Chicago Law Review*, 47, 423–66.
Mettler, S. (2011). *The Submerged State: How Invisible Government Policies Undermine American Democracy*. Chicago: University of Chicago Press.
Milkis, S. (1993). *The President and the Parties: The Transformation of the American Party System Since the New Deal*. New York: Oxford University Press.
Nie, N., Verba, S., & Petrocik, J. (1976). *The New American Voter*. Cambridge, MA: Harvard University Press.
Nolette, P. (2015). *Federalism on Trial: State Attorneys General and National Policymaking in Contemporary America*. Lawrence: University of Kansas Press.
Orfield, G. (1969). *The Reconstruction of Southern Education: The Schools and the 1964 Civil Rights Act*. New York: Wiley-Interscience.
Orren, G. (1997). "Fall from Grace: The Public's Loss of Faith in Government." In J. Nye, P. Zelikow, & D. King (Eds.), *Why People Don't Trust Government*. Cambridge, MA: Harvard University Press, 77–108.
Pedriana, N., & Stryker, R. (2004). "The Strength of a Weak Agency: Enforcement of Title VII of the 1964 Civil Rights Act and the Expansion of State Capacity, 1965–71." *American Journal of Sociology*, 110, 709–60.
Radin, B. (1977). *Implementation, Change and the Federal Bureaucracy: School desegregation Policy in H.E.W., 1964–1968*. New York: Teachers College Press.
Read, F. (1975). "Judicial Evolution of the Law of School Integration since Brown v. Board." *Law and Contemporary Problems*, 39, 7.
Read, F., & McGough, L. (1978). *Let Them Be Judged: The Judicial Integration of the Deep South*. Lanham, MD: Scarecrow Press.
Rebell, M., & Block, A. (1985). *Equality and Education: Federal Civil Rights Enforcement in the New York City School System*. Princeton, NJ: Princeton University Press.
Rutherglen, G. (2007). *Employment Discrimination Law: Visions of Equality in Theory and Doctrine* (2nd ed). New York: Foundation Press.
Saguy, A. (2003). *What Is Sexual Harassment?" From Capitol Hill to the Sorbonne*. Berkeley: University of California Press.
Siegel, A. (2006). "The Court Against the Courts: Hostility to Litigation as an Organizing Theme in the Rehnquist Court's Jurisprudence." *Texas Law Review*, 84, 1097.
Skrentny, J. (1996). *The Ironies of Affirmative Action*. Chicago: University of Chicago Press.
Skrentny, J. (2006). "Law and the American State." *Annual Review of Sociology*, 32, 213–44.
Teles, S. (2001). "Positive Action or Affirmative Action? The Persistence of Britain's Antidiscrimination Regime." In J. Skrentny (Ed.), *Color Lines: Affirmative Action, Immigration, and Civil Rights Options for America*. Chicago: University of Chicago Press, 241–69.
Tani, K.M. (2016). *States of Dependency: Welfare, Rights, and American Governance 1935–1972*. New York: Cambridge University Press.
Thernstrom, A. (2009). *Voting Rights and Wrongs: The Elusive Quest for Racially Fair Elections*. Washington, DC: American Enterprise Institute Press.

U.S. Commission on Civil Rights. (1996). *Federal Title VI Enforcement to Ensure Nondiscrimination in Federally Assisted Programs*, June.

Vogel, D. (1993). "Representing Diffuse Interests in Environmental Policymaking." In K. Weaver, & B. Rockman (Eds.), *Do Institutions Matter? Government Capabilities in the United States and Abroad*. Washington, DC: Brookings Institution Press.

Weaver, R.K. (2000). *Ending Welfare as We Know It*. Washington, DC: Brookings Institution Press.

Supreme Court Decisions

J.I. Case v. Borak 377 U.S. 426 (1964), at 433.
Griggs v. Duke Power 401 U.S. 424 (1971).
Lau v. Nichols 414 U.S. 563 (1974).
Albemarle Paper Co. v. Moody, 422 U.S. 405 (1975).
Franks v. Bowman Transportation Co. 424 U.S. 747 (1976).
United Steelworkers of America v. Weber 443 U.S. 193 (1979).
Guardians Association of NYC Police Dept. v. Civil Service Commission 463 U.S. 582 (1983).
Johnson v. Transportation Agency, 480 U.S. 616 (1987).
Franklin v. Gwinnett County Public Schools 503 U.S. 60 (1992).
Gebster *v. Lago Vista Independent School District* 524 U.S. 274 (1998).
Davis v. Monroe County Board of Education 526 U.S. 629 (1999).
Alexander v. Sandoval 532 U.S. 275 (2001).
Jackson v. Birmingham Board of Education 544 U.S.167 (2005).

Lower Court Opinions

U.S. v. Jefferson County Board of Education I, 372 F.2d 859 (1966).
Quarles v. Philip Morris, 279 F. Supp. 505 (E.D.Va., 1968).
EDF v. Ruckelshaus, 439 F.2d 589 (D.C. Circuit, 1971).
Calvert Cliffs Coordinating Committee v. AEC, 449 F.2d 1109 (D.C. Circuit, 1971).
Contractors Association v. Secretary of Labor Association 442 F.2d 159 (3rd Circuit, 1971).
Portland Cement Assoc. v. Ruckelshaus, 486 F.2d 375 (D.C. Circuit, 1973).

3

SEEING THROUGH THE SMOKE

Adversarial Legalism and U.S. Tobacco Politics

Michael McCann and William Haltom

Introduction

Robert Kagan's model of adversarial legalism (AL) is one of the most important and provocative contributions to comparative sociolegal analysis developed over recent decades. Kagan's framework not only powerfully captures the distinctive legalistic politics that mark contemporary U.S. political culture, but it helps to explain how this type of politics developed, the forces that sustain it, and the implications of its continued pull on American life and around the world. No contemporary scholar of law and politics can ignore the compelling logic of this fundamental analytical framework.

We attempt in this essay to explore the promises and limits of the adversarial legalism framework by applying it to one important policy area—tobacco policy in the U.S. over the past 50 years. This is a particularly useful policy window for such a project, as Bob Kagan has written three separate essays on tobacco policy (Kagan & Skolnick, 1993; Kagan & Vogel, 1993; Kagan & Nelson, 2001)[1] and addressed the topic again in a chapter on tort law for his classic book *Adversarial Legalism* (Kagan, 2001). We argue that Kagan's approach offers a quite clear-sighted comparative understanding of tobacco policy, and of law generally, but we also suggest that development or reframing of some themes would deepen its value as a macro-level analytical framework.

This chapter begins with a brief historical overview of tobacco policy and politics in the United States, followed by a summary of Kagan's own analysis and its relationship to the AL model. We then draw on our own research (Haltom & McCann, 2004; McCann, Haltom, and Fisher, 2013) to show how Kagan's approach at once clears the air through penetrating analysis and yet invites further clarification or refinement of its own premises.

A Quick Overview of Tobacco Policy and Politics in the U.S

The history of tobacco politics after World War II in the U.S. is well known among sociolegal scholars, and there is probably no better general overview than that provided in Kagan and Nelson's essay "The Politics of Tobacco Regulation in the United States" (2001). This essay includes a very handy chronology of events in the history of tobacco policy in post–World War II America. Although it is useful, the chronology does not capture well the changing discursive frameworks and institutional dynamics that drive the policy contests. Other scholars thus have tended to construct the history of tobacco policymaking in terms of distinct periods or waves (Rabin 2001; Mather, 1998; Haltom & McCann, 2004), each with its own distinctive framing exchanges and venues of the policy contest. We thus begin with a very quick summary of those waves, which will be invoked often in our later discussion.

The first wave of political activity, from the late 1960s through the early 1980s, is longest but least central to the discussion here. The primary disputes were over the certainty of scientific evidence about the health hazards of tobacco as well as about corporate liability for consumer choices, which was largely overshadowed by consensus on consumer responsibility for risks. The surgeon general reported in January 1964 that consumption of tobacco was related to various diseases; the next year congressional legislation was passed that required warnings on cigarette packs. On the one hand, Big Tobacco defended itself by contesting the reliability and conclusions from disparate scientific studies, aided by the skewed studies that the industry sponsored. On the other hand, the industry welcomed the mandate of package labeling as further justification for pinning the blame for injury on those who chose to consume tobacco products despite acknowledged risks. The industry tolerated taxes by state and national authorities as a necessary concession to ward off further regulation. Individual lawsuits challenging harms escalated in number, but all failed due to successful corporate defense as a matter of disputable science and individual responsibility for assumed risk. State policies varied widely in specifics, with first moves toward restrictions on smoking in various indoor venues in the latter part of this period. This was a classic era of litigation-based, lawyer-driven adversarial politics.

The second wave is usually marked from 1983 to 1992. In this period, the surgeon general's warning of the effects from secondhand smoke was instrumental to the banning of smoking on airplanes and selective banning of smoking in some private spaces in a few states. Growing scientific evidence of the harmful effects caused by smoking put the tobacco industry on the defensive, leading to what often has been labeled a "Scorched Earth, Wall of Flesh" strategy of well-funded attrition against increasing numbers of lawsuits. This proved very successful until Mark Edell, a veteran of litigation against asbestos companies, managed in *Cipollone v. Liggett* to generate serious discovery revealing gross duplicity and knowing manipulation of scientific data by tobacco companies, leading to a verdict and damages for plaintiffs from a jury, despite the more than $50 million expended by the tobacco industry for its legal defense (Kluger, 1996, pp. 663–677). The jury award was eventually reversed on appeal, but the symbolic victory spurred more litigation during the late 1980s in which plaintiffs accused tobacco companies of irresponsibility and duplicity, aided by whistleblowers' disclosures and adversaries' discovery (Zegart, 2000, p. 47).

Other lawyers enriched or empowered by asbestos fees or enraged by tobacco power organized a third wave of litigation in the 1990s, a period during which litigation surged to the fore in the policymaking process (Haltom & McCann, 2004, pp. 232–236). From about 1992 until mid-1998, lawyers aimed not merely to compensate those injured directly or indirectly by tobacco products but also to raise the prices of tobacco products and boost the legal fees of tobacco companies. In addition, liability suits delivered on the promise of discovering new information that could be publicized against the tobacco companies (Mather, 1998, pp. 907–908). More importantly, anti-tobacco litigation arrayed class actions, private suits, and actions by attorneys general of multiple states against "Big Tobacco," an entity defined largely, strategically, and symbolically by its adversaries. The third wave culminated in the Master Settlement Agreement negotiated among tobacco companies, private attorneys, states, and Congress. The largest civil settlement in U.S. history involved, ultimately, hundreds of billions of dollars.

After the 1998 Master Settlement Agreement, the Supreme Court of the United States rejected FDA jurisdiction over nicotine products under existing law, the Department of Justice initiated a RICO lawsuit, and Big Tobacco suffered huge jury verdicts in Florida and California. The most important development was the intensification of allegations that "criminalized" the tobacco industry for duplicity and disinformation about its harmful products. The wave of litigation that crested in the MSA subsided in the later era, but mass media, legislators, and executive branch officials arguably became more important to the criminalizing project (McCann et al., 2013). This fourth period is largely or completely subsequent to the publication of Professor Kagan's primary accounts, so we assess the degree to which developments in this period do or do not conform to the adversarial legalist framework.

Adversarial Legalism in the Tobacco Wars

Bob Kagan's writings provide as powerful and insightful an analysis of the tobacco legacy through the 1990s as any we have encountered. Not the least of the virtues is his framing of the key analytical questions and concepts by thinking comparatively. He begins his most important essay[2] on the topic by recognizing that "tobacco, once unchallenged, is on the defensive" (Kagan & Nelson, 2001, p. 11). The most important reason for this change is "the diffusion of scientifically based knowledge about tobacco's carcinogenic properties" that began in the 1950s and grew over subsequent decades. "But," he notes, "the response, both by governments and by popular cultures, has not been uniform" (Kagan &Nelson, 2001, p. 12). Japan has done little to discourage smoking; many western European countries have taxed more, more aggressively restricted advertising, and emphasized more warnings to discourage smoking; and the U.S. has been more aggressive in banning smoking from workplaces and restaurants as well as adopting a "punitive," stigmatizing approach to the "evil" tobacco industry.[3]

Kagan draws on his larger analytical framework regarding adversarial legalism to explain the curious approach adopted in the United States. Above all, his analysis underlines at length that tobacco policy in the U.S. has been a "fragmented, freewheeling process" that has involved many organized interest groups and entrepreneurial activists seeking to "capitalize on the structural fragmentation of power in the American constitutional system" and routinely pursuing "forum-to-forum reversals of fortune" (Kagan & Nelson, 2001, p. 15). This dynamic process of lobbying legislatures, administrative agencies, courts, and the general public at both national and local levels produced, not surprisingly, a complex, volatile, often inconsistent mix of policies. Kagan is especially persuasive in demonstrating the triumph of pluralist politics in the U.S. that is highly responsive to the maneuverings of particularistic issue entrepreneurs but short on capacities for centralized state action responsive to majority preferences and collective interests in effective government.[4]

Second, Kagan underlines as well that this politics expressed "enduring characteristics of American political culture" (Kagan & Nelson, 2001, p. 33). He emphasizes in most writings the powerful pull of *individualism*, which seems to assure attention to rights of both smokers and nonsmokers as well as express a marked distrust of centralized government regulation and a distaste for high taxes of any kind. At the same time, a moralistic, populist propensity of citizens to demand "total justice"[5] has fed select paternalistic policies protecting youth and limiting spaces where smoking is allowed as well as vengeful demands for action against corporate producers. Again, these conflicting pressures have supported the complex patchwork of policies that make distinctive the U.S. approach to tobacco policy. Public opinion was unstable and variable on specific policies and policy mechanisms, Kagan documents. However, he suggests that the overall policy mix seems to have resisted the excessive pull of interest groups on either side of the issue and tends to be consistent with what Americans overall seem to endorse (Kagan & Nelson, 2001, pp. 15, 32).[6]

Finally, " . . . only in the United States has litigation against tobacco companies become a prominent (and sometimes dominant) aspect of national tobacco control efforts" (Kagan & Nelson, 2001, p. 12). This is hardly surprising, Kagan explains in familiar terms, because the "unusual openness and malleability of the American legal system has opened the road to another mode of entrepreneurial action" (Kagan & Nelson, 2001, p. 14). Kagan highlights this theme of entrepreneurialism among lawyers, who are motivated by a mix of idealism and substantial material return from huge contingency fees, as the most distinctive feature of U.S. tobacco policy. To his credit, Kagan distinguishes attorneys from health advocates in the tobacco policy arena, a theme that underlies our own approach. Moreover, he recognizes that, while lawyers have not entirely dominated the process, they have "helped transform the public dialogue about tobacco companies" (Kagan & Nelson, 2001, p. 32), contributing greatly to the moralistic, punitive attacks on the tobacco industry (Kagan & Nelson, 2001, pp. 33–35). Kagan does not defend the behavior of the tobacco industry, but he finds important the distinctive way that the tobacco companies have been "criminalized" in the adversarial, legalistic context of our political culture.

All in all, Kagan makes a good case that tobacco policy reflects the characteristic tension between growing desires of citizens for strong welfare and regulatory state action, on the one hand, and longstanding preferences for a fragmented, limited state structure, on the other, that feeds reliance on lawyers, litigation, and legal processes (see Kagan & Nelson, 2001, p. 15). Kagan for the most part separates his incisive analytical explanation regarding the unique features of U.S. tobacco policy from his moderately critical normative assessment, but the two perspectives are undeniably linked. His most important and familiar critique is that U.S. policy on tobacco is characteristically "unpredictable and erratic," and hence inefficient (Kagan & Nelson, 2001, p. 35). As is often the case in the U.S., the prominent role of litigation has lined private attorneys' pockets but produced only limited benefit for those who have suffered the most and, arguably, for the consuming public in general. Indeed, Kagan uses the data on public opinion to show that the work of lawyers has been the least supported or respected dimension of the overall tobacco policy process (Kagan & Nelson, 2001, pp. 29–30). This tactic fits his overall position that adversarial legalism inhibits informed, rational, realistic, incrementally coordinated policy in which government leaders and professional policy experts play a more prominent, consistent role.

Clearing (or Blowing?) Yet More Smoke

The remainder of this chapter takes a closer look at the issues raised by Kagan, based to a large extent on our own long-developing research agenda and specific empirical findings about U.S. tobacco policy. Much of what we have found supports Kagan's analysis, empirically and conceptually. But we also have reason to urge greater conceptual development and refinement in, plus some friendly amendments to, his analysis. In the process, we seek at once to celebrate and to challenge the adversarial legalism framework itself. We organize our discussion into four general lines of inquiry, which generally move from largely theoretical or interpretive to more empirically grounded investigative matters.

Adversarial Legalism: An Elusively Elastic Concept

Kagan's model of adversarial legalism aims to provide a flexible approach to identifying specific types of processes and propensities in policymaking and implementation. Its flexibility as a concept is, we think, its greatest strength, especially as it facilitates comparative analysis. But this elasticity also is sustained in part by a fundamental epistemological tension in analytical modes, tensions that are neatly captured in Kagan's own metaphors.[7] Early in his majestic 2001 book, Kagan tends to treat legalism, in his words, like ice cream or spicy food. As such, adversarial legalism can be gratifying and even healthy in small doses, but it can be unpleasant and even unhealthy in excessive doses. It thus is a potentiality that is not self-actuating or autonomous, but rather depends on the actions of agents in historically contingent contexts; its presence and effects vary with the quantity as well as timing and duration of indulgence in combination with other factors.[8] This mode fits the more complex, process-based, and normatively measured version of Kagan's approach. When applied to the empirical world, this version of the AL approach tends to be lighter and more fluid, highly attentive to change over time and complexity; it recognizes that lawyers, litigation, and legal mobilization efforts can vary in motive, style, and impact as they mix with other modes of interaction and institutionally embedded agents in public life. In this mode, Kagan's analysis parallels the more behavioral (and less interpretive) versions of legal mobilization, cause lawyering, and legal disputing analysis by other sociolegal scholars who emphasize the variability of legal action in different contexts. It also is especially useful for comparative analysis that distinguishes unique American institutional arrangements and cautions about selective "transfer" of select institutional elements to other legal systems.

By the end of the book, however, AL assumes a form like "tigers in bushes . . . lying in ambush and which need to be tamed" (see Nelken, 2003, p. 822). In this mode, adversarial legalism is a discrete, actively embodied force that overtakes human agents and causes harm; its persistent dangers must be actively disciplined or caged for society to function reasonably. In this version, the lines between AL as general analytical framework and actual, discrete, reified force "in" the world are blurred; the analysis becomes more positivist and expresses more normative bite as well, underlining the scholar's impassioned effort to locate the dangerous forces and encourage caution, if not reform. This version of the framework is, in our view, less attentive to the dynamic interactions among institutional, instrumental, and ideological factors, more inclined to view litigation and lawyers as insular than as interdependent and contingent forces, and less open to viewing legal action as a desirable, much less noble, form of political participation. It veers closer to the type of highly critical, positivist account of judicial impact studies offered by Gerald Rosenberg (1991; see also McCann, 1992, 1996).

In our reading, the first, more supple, process-based, and contingent version of adversarial legalism is the most common mode of analysis featured in Bob Kagan's repertoire. The institutional focus is most compelling and most adaptable to comparative analytical and empirical study. The essay with Robert Nelson about tobacco policy on which we focus here mostly is cast in this mode, although, as in the larger book, it oscillates between the two and gravitates toward the second, more positivist and critical mode as the essay progresses. Sometimes, it seems, the tiger has eaten the ice cream as an appetizer for larger prey. We can see the tendency in the early chronology offered by Kagan and Nelson that distinguishes among "federal politics," "state and local politics," and "litigation" in U.S. tobacco policy (2001, pp. 17–18). This may make sense in a chronology, but the demarcations of discrete actions obscure the complex interactions among all three modes of activity in discussing the events, including especially around the complex Master Settlement, thus underlining their relative autonomy and distinctions in arguably misleading ways. As one of us has written elsewhere about that essay, "This division may be useful for some purposes but will impair readers' appreciation of lawsuits as civic participation by adjudicative means" (Haltom, 2002, p. 187). We see this tendency ascend in the later, long section on public opinion, which uses variable opinion data both analytically and normatively to show that litigation is the least approved or preferred mode of regulation in the mix of U.S. tobacco policies. Again, the earlier complexity of the process-based historical narrative yields to the enterprise of isolating lawyers and litigation as discrete, uniform, largely predatory, arguably undemocratic forces. In this mode, Kagan's analysis diverges from efforts of other law and society scholars[9] to highlight how litigation, rights claiming, and lawyer actions are highly contingent interventions that vary widely in motive, intent, and impact in different social contexts.[10]

Kagan's tacking back and forth between different epistemological modes is common to much social scientific analysis, including our own efforts. Indeed, these are arguably classic tensions characteristic of rigorous thought itself (Pitkin, 1972). Most of us scholars want to have it "both ways" to some extent, and arguably the challenge is usually one of getting the balance right, avoiding either too much descriptive detail without analytical focus or too much narrow separation of discretely defined factors that obscure their complex interdependencies (see McCann, 1996; McCann & Haltom, 2006). But choices about the balances among these modes matter much. For example, David Nelken has identified how these two approaches produce quite different challenges for comparative analysis (2003, 2009), an important topic that is lamentably beyond the scope of this chapter. The problem is especially acute when one considers how other scholars appropriate Kagan's approach. We think here, for example, of Martha Derthick's *Up in Smoke* (2001), which draws a clear distinction between "adversarial legalism" and "ordinary politics" of policy development in the U.S., and then advances a reductionist broadside against the "anti-majoritarian" role of litigation and unaccountable lawyers in the tobacco policy case. In our view, her analysis is lacking precisely the subtlety, complexity, and big-picture sensibility displayed by Kagan's generally more balanced critical approach. Derthick's normative assessment seems to drive or at least heavily bias her analysis far more than does Kagan's, which sustains the tension. But we also wonder whether Kagan's focus on adversarial legalism as a discrete and problematic mode of politics is not all too easily exploited for the normative lawyer thumping and litigation bashing by Derthick and many others in the contemporary scene.[11] At the same time, the emphasis on a wide variety of generally defined institutional and cultural factors that are designated to encourage adversarial legalism permits a characteristic elusiveness to his case studies.[12] Our discussion in the next few sections raises a variety of questions associated with each dimension of the tension.

Fragmented Government and Its Problems

Kagan's argument about the possibilities and propensities that lead to adversarial legalism turns to a large extent on the "fragmented" nature of political institutions in the United States. At a very general level, it is fairly easy to understand what Kagan means by this characterization of institutional structure and how it increases the demand or trend toward reliance on lawyer-driven legalistic processes. His most focused discussion of the topic is a 15-page section of his major tome (Kagan, 2001, pp. 40–54). Building on a typology developed by Mirjan Damaška, Kagan locates the U.S. state as "leaning" strongly toward the "coordinate" mode of administrative structure and "reactive" mode of state role performance, although he recognizes how New Deal–era reforms added elements of stronger national statism. But the list of characteristics for U.S. government, which has "in comparative terms, remained structurally and politically fragmented," is long and diffuse: coordinate organization, wide openings for civilian influence, skepticism about state-enforced norm, reliance on adversarial argument, federalistic decentralization, administrative decentralization, splintered authority among separate powers at state and federal levels, deadlocked legislatures, hyper-pluralistic party structures, and, of course, judicialized and adversarial legalistic politics in many senses, among other features.

This list is familiar and we do not contest that most of these specific terms are somewhat applicable to aspects of U.S. governance. The U.S., for example, surely does have a patchwork of policies at different local, state, and national levels; we cannot argue there. But does this long list of features capture what is most unique or problematic about U.S. tobacco policy? Conversely, does the critical focus on adversarial legalism really do justice to the problematic aspects of U.S. policymaking? What is lost by the focus on adversarial legalism and emphasis on "fragmentation" as a secondary, contributing set of factors? In short, our work suggests that what gets buried in the mix is the conspicuously problematic interdependent roles of U.S. legislatures. Kagan himself at points gives some attention to this, usually by invoking the term congressional "deadlock."[13] By this he seems to indicate that Congress has not, and perhaps cannot, formulate strong, effective policy to reduce harms to citizens, provide adequate health care to those in need, and render accountable private corporate power. To this, we reply, "Bravo!"

But this emphasis on deadlock can be misleading. After all, Congress *has* acted on tobacco policy at various times. It succeeded in passing legislation to require warning labels, to prohibit sales of tobacco products to minors, and to regulate advertising in various ways and venues. Does adversarial legalism help explain why these and not other actions—such as authorizing more active regulation by the FDA[14]—were taken? Moreover, Congress did step up to act in the mid-1990s after the litigation campaign by the state attorneys general. In short, by dramatically increasing the cost to the tobacco companies and the windfall tax revenue that government would receive, legislators scuttled the national settlement, sending it back to the states and their lawyers to work out. Similarly, at the state level the elected politicians jumped on the bandwagon to grab all the revenues they could to buoy strained budgets, with only limited regard for compensating those victims most harmed by tobacco, for increasing health services for those afflicted by smoking, or for reducing consumption by the young. The problem was equally one of narrowly interested action and publicly responsible inaction, of opportunistic revenue-grabbing as much as stalemate or deadlock by legislators. Were legislators any less punitive, unpredictable, or self-interested than the teams of lawyers and attorneys general?

Our point is that the focus on multiple dimensions of fragmentation that lead to the central problem of adversarial legalism, however relevant, can easily obscure or minimize the specific features of the institutional framework in which elected officials work.[15] These problems in legislative capacity and performance are related to the U.S. scheme of winner-take-all elections, localized representation, the rise of mass-mediated political communication, and other factors that weaken parties in government.[16] Institutional incentives encourage legislative policy inaction until a "crisis" or "disaster" can be identified, or statutes that are so vague and general that they muster majority support only because of their symbolically appealing but substantively thin content. Meanwhile, Congress routinely expands the authority of the federal judiciary and specifically invites, defers to, even begs for courts to address electorally divisive conflicts over major issues and to interpret and enforce the typically vague terms of routine statutes (Graber, 1993; Lovell, 2003; Burke, 2002; McCann & Lovell, 2005).

It simply is not clear that lawyers, litigation, and legalistic maneuvering should get the bulk of blame for acting when legislators do not act at all, for acting in ways authorized and invited by legislators, or for acting in ways similar to legislators. After all, lawyers, attorneys general, and litigation coalesced loosely to break decades of logjam and forced a systemic response, however imperfect. Many lawyers deserve condemnation for their greedy, self-interested manipulations, to be sure, but were they more of the problem than elected officials? And what of the many private and public attorneys who deserve praise for their nobler actions in pushing for some degree of desirable policy, even though perhaps they gave in too willingly to the politicians and corporate adversaries? Moreover, the core features of the policy proposals that they advanced through the settlement were structured very much like the types of increased tax that European legislators imposed and Kagan seems to celebrate as rational (see Haltom & McCann, 2004, p. 239, fn 20).

In short, we are unconvinced that the focus on adversarial legalism of institutional sources clearly or correctly targets the biggest obstacles to sound government in the contemporary United States. It is troubling enough that contemporary mass media routinely scapegoat efforts of lawyers and legal groups to use litigation to balance the scales of political power (we leave "justice" to others), often relegating to the background congressional dysfunctionality and inaction that prompted the resort to litigation in the first place. Kagan is far more illuminating in his account and subtle in his critique than other scholars, such as Derthick (2001), who draw on the adversarial legalism framework. We enthusiastically applaud his acuity in this regard. He is also on the mark, we think, in recognizing the failure of national government to develop a sound national health insurance program and to regulate industry effectively and consistently. But we wonder how the legacy of tobacco politics might look if the primary, or at least coequal, analytical focus were on the failures of elected politicians rather than just relegating it to one of many background features that help explain the problematic reliance on lawyer-driven adversarial legalism.

Social Questions

A corollary to the preceding discussion of state structure is worth noting, at least briefly. Kagan demonstrates his skills as a political scientist by focusing on state institutions and behavioral expressions of national culture, but he is typically less focused on the deeply embedded inequalities of social power.[17] For example, in his major tome he explains that "the coordinate structure of American government . . . encouraged civil rights leaders to circumvent the legislative deadlock by turning to the courts" in the 1950s and 1960s (2001, p. 45). This is uncontestable. But what it overlooks is that legislative deadlock was a result, not just of porous, fragmented structure, but of the widespread support for exclusionary racist policies that exploited congressional structures, even amid the enormous pressures for action created by the cold war and clearly understood by executive officials and other leaders. Moreover, the very system of fragmented, decentralized federalist structure as well as institutionalized checks and balances itself owed a great deal to historical compromises between North and South over the status of slavery at the formative constitutional moment, through antebellum struggles, Reconstruction, and subsequent institutional developments of the post–World War II civil rights era. Racist dominance has not been merely facilitated by our inherited structures of government; it has been a major historical force shaping our institutional development of government into the present. Kagan does not hesitate in acknowledging that racial discrimination and inequality continue, nor is he in any way reluctant to condemn it.[18] But in his analysis he accords little attention to the relationship between fragmented state structure, deadlocked institutional capacity, and deeply entrenched social hierarchies.[19]

A parallel argument could be made regarding private corporate power in the tobacco legacy. Kagan does not overlook the power of Big Tobacco. He devotes a substantial paragraph to outlining the multiple dimensions of power wielded by the tobacco industry in recent decades (Kagan & Nelson, 2001, p. 13), and he recognizes at various points that the tobacco industry has formidable resources and position to advance its agenda within the porous American institutional structure of government. But most of this analysis, in the essay (Kagan & Nelson, 2001, p. 13) and the book, addresses corporate power as an *instrumental* force expending resources to advance its interests, mostly by blocking regulation and defending itself in the courts. Big Tobacco is primarily treated as just a big interest group in Kagan's analysis. This is all fine, even sophisticated.[20] But even in contemporary terms of corporate power, the tobacco industry is in a league by itself, with its formidable role in the Business Roundtable, its huge investment in the mass media, and its diversification in many corporate sectors. Indeed, one cannot even imagine the modern tort reform movement without understanding the formative, extensive role of organized tobacco interests in its many complex manifestations (Haltom & McCann, 2004). Some analysts (Deal & Doroshow, 2002) have estimated that the tobacco industry provided as much as half of the entire financial support for the American Tort Reform Association, at once bankrolling and leading the massive effort to saturate American public life with powerful images and compelling rhetoric vilifying lawyers and litigation. Moreover, tobacco's indirect structural power grounded in the taxes it provides government, the jobs and products it supplies, and especially its long influence in knowledge production and ideological generation (see Haltom & McCann, 2004, ch. 7) gets little more than occasional or indirect nods.[21] It makes some sense to compare Big Tobacco and entrepreneurial legal advocates at the instrumental level, but we think the mismatch in social power is often too minimized, as are the factors that can alter the mismatch for short periods. Big Tobacco is rather bigger than a focus on lobbying efforts captures. Entrepreneurial issue groups like plaintiffs' lawyers—no matter how much money and savvy and connections they generate—simply do not have the structural power in economic relations to match huge producer groups like tobacco; the interest group game does not pit like players against one another over the long haul.[22]

More generally, the role of private hierarchical power—including tobacco interests—in constructing and constituting the fragmented American system receives virtually no mention in the conventional account of adversarial legalism. From the overwhelming commitment to protecting the "different and unequal faculties for acquiring property" that Madison deemed the "first object of government" through the long history of U.S economic development, the American legal system has played a fundamental role in privileging large, dynamic, corporate forms of nongovernmental power subject to only limited piecemeal governmental control (Nedelsky, 1990; Horwitz, 1979; Miller, 1976). Hierarchical wealth and concentrated capital not only have benefited from a fragmented, decentralized government in which common law courts and judicial review play a major role; the former—however internally diverse, complex, and contested—have been formative, driving forces constructing and sustaining the latter state structure and legalistic politics. Kagan is right to emphasize the U.S. institutional forms as somewhat "exceptional" among western polities, but the most striking aspect of this exceptional system is the ways that official law (courts, judges, lawyers) has been used to structure and support a unique mode of capitalist development. It is worth recognizing that the most litigious, adversarial, legalistic "sue and settle" sector of U.S. society in recent decades has been in corporate contract, securities, antitrust, and patent disputes led by "mega-lawyers" (Galanter, 1996; Galanter & Palay, 1991). Tobacco has been a major part of business and corporate complexes since early America, and that is hardly unrelated to its long, deep roots in shaping American social relations and practices (Kluger, 1996). Indeed, the tobacco industry arguably has exhibited the most ruthlessly adversarial, strong-arm political uses of litigation in the contemporary era. Perhaps our point is no more than a footnote that adds more historical dimensions to Kagan's already complex account of the U.S system. But in our view, recognition of this historical legacy of corporate social power changes the story of contemporary tobacco politics into more than just a contest of contemporary interest (or entrepreneurial) groups.[23]

On Political Culture and Public Opinion

Much of Kagan's analysis of tobacco policy, and of the tendencies toward adversarial legalism in the U.S. and beyond, turns on claims about political culture and specific studies of public opinion. We welcome this focus, because it parallels our own studies of tobacco policy and of law and politics generally. Much of our approach parallels that of Kagan to some degree (see McCann & Haltom, 2006), as do our empirical findings, but both conceptually and empirically we again are inclined to refine and rethink his contributions.

We begin first with trying to sort out conceptual matters. Kagan relies heavily on various features of U.S. "culture" to supplement his argument about how fragmenting structures encouraged adversarial legalism. He often makes claims about "the public" and public opinion. What does he mean by these terms? Kagan often joins the term "culture" to adjectives such as "enduring" and "deeply rooted," thus suggesting norms or values that run deep and are fairly stable.[24] He sometimes speaks of culture in very general terms, with many referents, but he tends to give greatest attention to the propensities for "individualism" that date back to early America as well as to late 20th-century propensities of Americans to seek "total justice."[25] The former value feeds into the suspicion of strong, centralized government, the hostility toward paternalistic policies, and the fondness for decentralized, dispersed institutional power; the latter places high demand for egalitarian legal rights to social insurance and "other ways of compensating victims of unfair treatment, personal injury, and unexpected health costs" (2001, p. 9). Together, these cultural demands for justice and dispersed state power nurture the forces of adversarial legalism generally (2001, p. 44), forces that are quite apparent in the tobacco policy legacy. Kagan's terminology becomes less clear when he refers specifically to "political culture" and "legal culture," although the former is often linked to the individualistic, fragmenting propensities and the latter to the legalistic commitment to total justice fed by the legal profession. The relationship between culture and public opinion, which Kagan emphasizes in his study of tobacco, is also at times unclear. Our most plausible interpretation is that opinion measures public attitudes or "sentiments," which are citizen judgments about particular phenomena as they judge facts in light of their contradictory cultural values. Opinion is often deemed both "notoriously unstable" on some issues and "remarkably stable" in other regards (Kagan & Nelson, 2001, pp. 34–35).[26]

Our own research follows these conceptual lines to some degree and supports much of Kagan's analysis, evidence, and argument. It is easy to identify how the contradictory mix of support for legal remedies and skepticism toward centralized government policy have contributed to, or at least tolerated, the pastiche of tobacco policies as well as to the emergence of litigation as an important force by the 1990s. Kagan's judgment that "on balance, contemporary U.S. tobacco policy seems to reflect American public opinion much more than it does the preference set of either the tobacco industry, public health activists, or anti-tobacco lawyers" (p. 32) likewise seems sensible. However, these claims are also unsurprising. After all, even casual observers would expect public opinion and public policy to be at greater distance from political poles than from each other. At the same time, Kagan argues that litigation has played a "dominant" role in U.S. tobacco policy, but that "anti-tobacco litigation by private litigants and state actors alike has been based on asserted norms that do *not* seem to be in accord with American public opinion" (33). How can the dominant mode of policy action be unsupported and yet the net overall result of policy be quite acceptable to the majority or mainstream? More broadly, such claims raise questions about the problematic relationship of public opinion to "enduring" cultural forces.

Our own approach thus has added several other elements for consideration. First, we examine not only the distribution of public opinion toward discrete policies and modes of action, but also the noteworthy shifts in opinion over time in response to changing dynamics of the policy contest. Our reliance on organizing concepts of distinct periods or waves in the tobacco legacy is very useful in this regard. Second, we are even more interested in changing terms of public knowledge and knowledge production that are generated about tobacco disputes over time. We thus systematically study, along with the actions of contending disputants, the levels and content of media coverage about tobacco politics, including but not limited to litigation, during these periods (McCann et al., 2013). Building on our earlier work presented in *Distorting the Law*, we coded a carefully selected sample of nearly 600 newspaper articles in *The New York Times* from the last three periods of policy action. In each period, we coded both for general thematic frames[27] for making sense of the legal contests, focusing on themes related to attributions of "responsibility" for harm, and for characterizations of participants, which might reinforce or undercut the authors of such frames. Moreover, we distinguished between two categories of articles—those that were largely about litigation ("litigation heavy") and those that were "litigation light," focusing instead on health experts, science, or non-litigation-oriented politics. This empirical approach enabled us to develop a more coherent, detailed, and nuanced picture about what attentive citizens probably know about law and politics and how they know it. After all, most of what citizens (and elites) know about policy processes comes from the corporate-generated news and mass infotainment, the major source of legal knowledge in modern mass society.[28] Our focus on the media enables us to examine how common but indeterminate cultural conventions and strategies are mobilized by political contestants and then reconstructed for mass audiences. We then review public opinion in these various periods in light of news coverage; while the former is quite vague and rarely asks the range of questions we do, some notable parallels and connections are evident.

So what did we find? We can only summarize our findings in this chapter, but we will give some select bits of evidence that illustrate our logic. The broader outlines support Kagan to a large extent. For one thing, tobacco politics, including litigation episodes, was covered extensively by the mass media. To give one indicator, Lexis-Nexis Academic found 7,830 items (reports, features, op-eds, letters to editor) published in *The New York Times* alone between January 1984 and December 2005, which averages to around 356 items per year, or roughly an item every day during that period. Moreover, the amount of coverage that was litigation-heavy or litigation-light varied each year, but generally was distributed across the periods as expected. The bulk of coverage looked past litigation during Wave Two, 1984–1992, except in 1988 when the *Cipollone* case was won at the trial level. Litigation became the dominant focus of attention in Wave Three, especially once trial lawyers teamed up with state attorneys general in 1994 through the Master Settlement in 1998. Wave Four saw a return to patterns closer to Wave Two, although there was more litigation-heavy coverage overall and especially in several specific years (2001, 2003, 2005).

We think it significant that our study of thematic frames in the news underlines the cultural power of "individualistic" values in the U.S. that Kagan emphasizes. However, we show that individualism cuts in disparate ways. As we demonstrated in *Distorting the Law*, individualistic understandings of justice do tend to support rights-oriented legal actions against large corporations. But this individualism is almost entirely implicit, rather than explicit, in media coverage, and we think also in ordinary discourse. By contrast, the ethos of "individual responsibility" has been mobilized by corporations and conservative legal reformers to stigmatize rights claiming, litigation, plaintiffs, and lawyers as greedy and irresponsible (see Engel, 1984; Haltom & McCann, 2004). This frame dominated news coverage until 1989, and then dropped to a less significant but steady presence in the disputes over the next 15 years. See Graph 3.1 (McCann et al., 2013, p. 305).

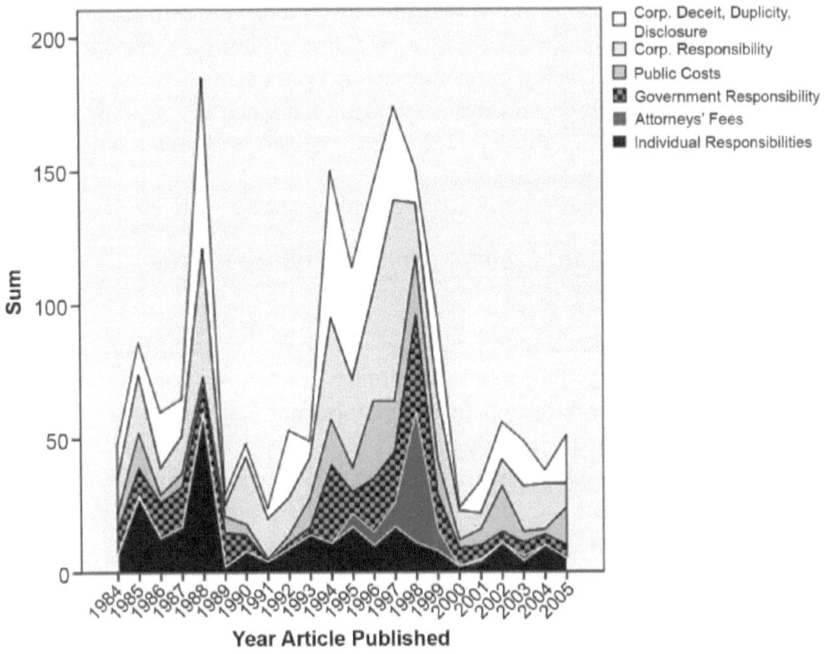

GRAPH 3.1 Distribution of Six Thematic Frames, 1984–2005

The individual responsibility frame declined in salience with important changes in the dynamics and issue-framing by participants in tobacco politics. Prior to 1990, polls suggested that public values privileging individual responsibility discouraged heavy regulation of and litigation against tobacco companies. But this changed during the 1990s, when frames that disadvantaged tobacco interests—corporate responsibility, corporate duplicity/disclosure, public costs of tobacco-related harms, and governmental responsibility—all increased significantly; indeed, each theme alone received more attention than did individual responsibility. The first two outpaced the latter by a 3–1 margin, and collectively the pro-plaintiffs' frames trounced those that favor Big Tobacco.

Our constructivist approach thus aims to contribute a more subtle, revealing, and important story about how disputes over tobacco played out in cultural knowledge production and opinion-shaping processes. Focusing on cultural frames in mass knowledge production reinforces the importance of understanding cultural norms and values as more intrinsically indeterminate, multivalent, and complex in their implications than Kagan's behavioral approach suggests. A legal or political mobilization approach captures the processes by which cultural norms are mobilized, constructed, reconstructed, and reproduced through both routine practices and active contests among social groups in multiple institutional settings. Norms and values become powerful not as discrete, autonomous forces or propensities, but as they are embedded and enforced in institutional conventions as well as reproduced and reenacted variably through human interactions.[29] We are careful not to speculate confidently about how citizens, overall or as subgroups, understood and processed these frames, even when we can show striking parallels in public opinion. But it is clear that key players on all sides of the dispute were vying to shape the media and responding in turn to changing story lines.

Beyond Tort Litigation: Criminalizing Big Tobacco in the Fourth Wave

Most of the developments addressed so far can be read as consistent, or at least not at odds, with Kagan's general interpretation, and especially his argument that lawyers and their litigation became "dominant" aspects of U.S. tobacco policymaking and that their campaigns "helped transform the public dialogue about tobacco companies" (Kagan & Nelson, 2001, p. 32). However, our findings regarding developments in the period after the Master Settlement through 2010 significantly revise or even refute Kagan's analysis. It is at these later stages that our interpretive focus on changing cultural framings of legal norms and claims yields the most important results, which go well beyond Kagan's AL framework. Our study shows that litigation and legal mobilization activities differed markedly in character and produced quite different results in different eras; tort litigation was unsuccessful in court and barely noticed in public life prior to 1988, came to dominate only in the mid-1990s, and then quickly gave way to increased legislative and executive action, from the Master Settlement Agreement to the authorization of FDA regulation that the industry had long resisted. Why? Kagan's relatively undifferentiated approach to adversarial legalism and to the role of "values" like individualism provides relatively vague, static responses to the question. The dramatic changes in substantive constructions and institutional players in the early 1990s and continuing for the following decades are not well explained by the adversarial legalist framework. We offer several dimensions for this claim, all supported by data in Graph 3.1, but grounded primarily in the actual political history.[30]

First, the significant jury verdict for the plaintiff in *Cipollone* generated considerable attention and, arguably, legitimate stature to legal challenges by nonsmoking victims against Big Tobacco. Even more important, Judge Lee Sarokin, alleging that the "tobacco industry may be the king of concealment and disinformation," applied the "crime/fraud exception" to the case, producing a discovery process for that trial that unleashed abundant evidence demonstrating that corporations knew that cigarettes were extremely harmful, took actions to increase the addictiveness of tobacco products, and blatantly lied about what they knew (*Frontline* Online, 1998a). As a result, Big Tobacco could be reasonably considered to be duplicitous, legally liable for harm, even a fraudulent lawbreaker. The dominant frame of reform action shifted from one of demonstrating indirect tortious liability to one of "criminalizing" Big Tobacco (McCann et al., 2013). This frame was augmented by revelations of prominent insider whistleblowers Merrell Williams and Jeffrey Wigand, who provided additional evidence of willful corporate deception and disinformation. This shift is clearly evidenced as the thematic frames of corporate duplicity and corporate responsibility for harm skyrocketed in 1988, and ascended once again dramatically in the mid-1990s.

At the same time, private attorneys, who routinely were stigmatized as greedy and self-interested, receded into the background as state attorneys general took the lead, further conferring the legitimacy of publicly appointed prosecutors—a legitimacy generally lacking among contemporary elected politicians—to the legal campaign (Mather, 1998). Mississippi State Attorney General Michael Moore told *Frontline* that the evidence provided by whistle blowers Wigand and Williams sealed his commitment to take on Big Tobacco on new terms:

> I saw with my own two eyes, seven tobacco executives raise their right hand and swear, before Congress, that nicotine was not an addictive drug. . . . And then, the very next couple of weeks, I had in my hand, a memo that proved that they were lying. *This is evidence of a crime.* And when an Attorney General of this country has evidence of a crime, he has a duty to put it in the hands of those people who can do something about it . . . We sent them to the Justice Department. We sent them to the Food and Drug Administration. And we saved a copy to use in our case.
>
> *(Frontline, 1998a; italics added)*

At this point, congressional officials and the executive branch took leading roles in further advancing the criminalizing frame. FDA chief David Kessler began to campaign against the criminal "conspiracy" of the "deadly" tobacco industry, making the key charge now a "question of intent" (2001). While recognizing that he did not have authority to prosecute a case, he explained in 1998 the shift several years earlier to new modes of legal claiming and charging: " . . . the criminal case, as I understand it, is you lied. You lied to federal authorities. You lied to the FDA. You lied to the Congress. You committed conspiracy . . . to defraud the United States Government" (*Frontline* Online, 1998b). After the dissembling congressional testimony by tobacco executives in 1994, Congressman Marty Meehan (Democrat of Massachusetts), a former prosecutor, delivered a "prosecution memo" to U.S. Attorney General Janet Reno. And it was in this context of increased allegations of conspiratorial criminal fraud that the Master Settlement Agreement was brokered in Congress. The almost unparalleled scale of punitive damages (nearly $250 billion) was represented and justified largely in public regulatory, deterrent, and punitive, which is to say quasi-criminal, terms. And "punishment" was the term that the tobacco industry used repeatedly in the wake of the settlement, largely to fend off further lawsuits. As Florida judge Robert Kaye noted in the *Engle* case, "The industry is trying to say 'We have been punished enough because we agreed to pay so much money to the states'" (McQuillen, cited in McCann et al., 2013, p. 299).

The Master Settlement did not quiet the storm for Big Tobacco. Attorney General Reno in 1997 established a full-time task force in the Fraud Section of the Criminal Division of DOJ to investigate the allegations of conspiracy under the RICO Act, drawing heavily on evidence made available by whistleblowers and civil discovery processes. A DOJ civil lawsuit under RICO developed over the next year. The criminalization frame became common media fodder in subsequent years. A *Denver Post* headline summarized the frame in covering District Court judge Gladys Kessler's 2006 ruling against the industry in the RICO lawsuit: "TOBACCO'S CRIMINAL PLOT." Our study demonstrates not just the increased media indulgence in this framing, but also the parallel dramatic drops in public opinion polls regarding "trust" in the industry and increases in support for FDA regulation (McCann et al., 2013). We also show that it was this "plummeting" corporate image that led Philip Morris, the largest tobacco corporation, to change its name to Altria in 2001 and to break with other manufacturers in expressing open support for FDA regulation in an effort to regain legitimacy, redefine itself as "socially responsible," and insulate itself from further litigation. Under official and public scrutiny as a criminal enterprise, the tobacco industry was subjected to centralized, national bureaucratic regulatory authority by 2009.

Conclusion

We take away a number of important lessons from this complicated story. Most generally, the history of tobacco disputing was far more complex, variable, and dynamic than Kagan's adversarial legalism model accommodates. The relative success of lawyers and litigation in framing issues, and in challenging long-prevailing frames proffered by industry, was historically contingent and highly variable; it depended on changing discursive strategies, knowledge generation, instrumental tactics, and institutional alliances. As many law and society scholars have demonstrated, litigation campaigns and the work of "cause lawyers" are hardly unitary, but differ in strategy, organizational form, style, and outcome in different contexts. The tobacco legacy became a model for much other mass tort litigation, but subsequent campaigns differed markedly even as they mimicked various maneuvers, and each has differed greatly from other legacies of social policymaking involving lawyers, legal forums, and litigation.

One could still argue that the shift from legalistic tort litigation to the punitive criminalizing discourse precisely illustrates the characteristic form of U.S. adversarial legalism. Kagan himself points to the process of criminalizing Big Tobacco. But he does not explain in any depth or detail the many dimensions of that shift in institutional and discursive frames. Moreover, to identify criminalization with adversarial legalism is arguably misleading. For one thing, lawyer-driven litigation was only one of several institutional processes at work. We have just hinted at the degree to which mass media, insider whistleblowers, congressional leaders, and executive branch officials played fundamental roles in escalating challenges to Big Tobacco and leading toward expansion of bureaucratic regulatory authority over the industry. The lawyers were not the lone, or even the primary, inventors or advocates of criminalizing frames. There was a great deal of adversarialism along the way, but adversarial battles were waged increasingly beyond the courts. Moreover, granting attention to the substantive terms of the changing debate, especially as it played out in the national media, suggests that simply identifying "adversarialism" is of limited value to understanding dynamic political relationships. Finally, escalating claims framed in criminalizing terms eventually led to a series of more cooperative bargains and relationships among government and industry. None of this refutes Kagan's "adversarial legal" model, but we wonder whether the model helps us to understand, much less to expect or predict, the dramatic turns—from tort to criminal (or crim-tort) framings of the conflict, from private litigation to public government action—in the tobacco legacy.

We venture further to draw from the tobacco legacy a speculative hypothesis. Our research has shown that, while tort litigation produced mostly stalemates and little positive change or constructive governance for many decades, the litigation eventually triggered the emergence of the criminalizing frame and expanded institutional engagement, eventually expanding the authority of centralized, national bureaucratic apparatus to regulate domestic tobacco production, sales, and taxation. In short, an era of sustained adversarial legalism arguably was critical to creating the possibilities for statist regulatory politics that more resemble the quasi-corporatist European model or even New Deal-era governance that Professor Kagan seems to appreciate. Given the extraordinary economic, political, and legal power of the tobacco industry, we wonder whether rational, coordinated governance could have been produced by any other means.[31] This question is amplified by recognition that the tobacco legacy recalls other historical examples where sustained periods of decentralized, fragmented, individualized disputing primarily led by lawyers in courtrooms have paved the way to industry willingness to submit to more routinized, bureaucratic regulatory and administrative governance. One might point to the history of personal injury litigation at work that produced standardized worker's compensation insurance schemes and eventually the Occupational Safety and Health Administration (OSHA), labor clashes in and beyond courts that led to routinized NLRB governance, the legacy of civil rights litigation that gave way to legislation authorizing the private-litigation-based enforcement of the EEOC and eventually a more bureaucratic, routinized, and centralized EEOC, among others. In each case, bureaucratic governance did not replace adversarial legalism but was added to earlier forms of fragmented legalistic disputing to produce a more complex, multilayered institutional mix of governance forms. Understanding American government as a volatile and varied hybrid mix of adversarial legalism and more statist governance is hardly a position that Professor Kagan would reject, although such complex multiplicity of institutional forms can be obscured by the sole emphasis on adversarial legalism.

Of course, there is reason to think that forms of national governance around the world generally are moving in the opposite direction today, from older modes of centralized state corporatist rule toward more decentralized, fragmented, legalistic relations in the neoliberal era. The key mover and beneficiary of these trends is expanding multinational capital. And that returns us to our previous point: that adversarial legalism is the form of governance that seems to be most preferred by and supportive of highly concentrated business power and limited popular democratic control. That is the lesson that we derive from American history. But we should also be careful not to assume that the ascendance of neoliberalism around the world is drifting toward a unitary form of American-style adversarial legalism. We surely can see evidence of expanded legalization, litigation, and roles of courts, court-like procedures, and legal professionals in many contexts. But whether this is undercutting or merely adding new dimensions to alternative or older forms of statist governance, and whether adversarialism in any meaningful, deep sense is diminishing or increasing as legalism advances, are open questions beyond the scope of this chapter but surely ripe for further study (see Kagan, 2007; *EPS Forum,* 2006). Bob Kagan's rich legacy of scholarship long will be, and should be, an invaluable guide for such inquiries.

Notes

1 To reduce verbiage, in the remainder of this chapter we cite the Kagan and Nelson chapter as Kagan & Nelson, 2001; the larger book by Kagan is cited as Kagan, 2001.

2 We will refer only to Kagan here, even though the 2001 and 1993 essays are coauthored, because Kagan is the common author of the three cited sources and, of course, the focus of the essay collection in which our analysis appears. We focus on the paper coauthored with Nelson (2001) because it is the most direct and recent engagement that addresses the dramatic events of the 1990s, although it is consistent with his other essays.

3 Compare, for example, Mather's similar claim about tobacco policy in the United Kingdom: "Public health experts and government officials defined the tobacco control policies through education, regulation, and taxation. Tort lawyers were nearly invisible. Smokers generally accepted their illnesses as their own responsibility. Anti-tobacco interests lobbied for stronger regulation but the government's 1992 White Paper stopped short of banning tobacco advertisements. The idea of suing manufacturers was virtually unknown" (Mather, 2009: 10).

4 The reader may find this sentence a bit vague. But we try to stay close to the terms of Kagan's own framework.

5 The reference is to Friedman, 1985. Kagan does not explicitly discuss the pull of "total justice" in his 2001 essay, but he makes a similar argument in the essay and makes much of it in his 2002 book as well as in other related writings on adversarial legalism in the U.S.

6 "There may be limits to how far American public opinion can be molded by either side in the tobacco wars" (15). "On balance, contemporary U.S. tobacco policy seems to reflect American public opinion more than it does the preference set of either the tobacco industry, public health activists, or anti-tobacco lawyers" (32).

7 We first were drawn to the significance of these metaphors by the thoughtful review essay of David Nelken (2003). We draw some broader epistemological implications than does Nelken, but our angles of analysis share much in common.

8 This "potentiality" is variously discussed as a passive opportunity that aggressive political actors might exploit or an alluring temptation to which citizens of weaker constitution might succumb too easily. In either case, the potential danger or harms variably depend on the actions of people.

9 We refer especially to scholars working in the traditions of legal mobilization (Scheingold, 1974; McCann, 1994), cause lawyering (Scheingold & Sarat, 2004), and ordinary legal disputing and consciousness study (for review, see McCann & Haltom, 2006). Not surprisingly, most studies in these traditions are heavily case-study oriented, qualitative in methods, and grounded in process-based or interpretive epistemologies.

10 For example, Kagan does not distinguish in either his assessment or that of public opinion variously among early private lawsuits, the *Cipollone* case, the Castano group cases, the attorneys' general actions leading to the Master Settlement, or the large, private class actions by Stanley Rosenblatt and others—all of which we would contend are quite different in style, venue, and impact. See below.

11 Consider Kagan's concluding claims in the 2001 article: "The unique role of litigation in the United States, however, has produced outcomes that arguably conflict with or frustrate public sentiment . . ." (32).

12 After advancing the "majoritarian" critique in the previous footnote (fn 7), Kagan then recognizes that judicial action looks different in the classic pluralist point of view, thus enabling him to register his stinging critique while appearing analytically complex and nimble. This is what we mean by claiming that Kagan at once tends to be analytically positivist and critical even while overall remaining somewhat elusive. We do not suggest anything untoward in these maneuvers; it is the sign of a smart, effective analyst.

13 "In this political structure it is especially difficult for hopeful reformers to assemble legislative majorities to enact potentially new policies into law and easier for opponents to find a veto point at which to block the enactment of policies they oppose." Kagan & Nelson, 2001, p. 13.

14 The FDA found itself in regular conflict with Congress over the terms of its regulatory authority in the 1990s. The Supreme Court weighed in by ruling that the FDA under David Kessler's leadership exceeded the statutory authority granted by Congress, foiling efforts of the Clinton Administration, health experts, and various social advocacy groups to support the FDA campaign to rein in the tobacco industry. See Kessler (2001).

15 Our critique about lack of differentiation and analytical focus in this section expresses a plea for greater isolation of discrete variables in the complex mix of factors.

16 To his credit, Kagan identifies these problems in his contextualization of how adversarial legalism develops. But they receive little attention beyond background contextualization, and are barely mentioned in the analysis of tobacco policy.

17 Professor Kagan's Ph.D. is in sociology (Yale, 1974), but he fits in well with the conventions of political science, in which field he long has held his primary faculty position.

18 The literature on this topic is far too abundant to document here. But a good example of how examining the role of racism in structuring state development redefines efforts to analyze later civil rights struggles and impacts is Paul Frymer's wise book, *Black and Blue* (2008).

19 We tend to think that Kagan's emphasis on "culture" as relatively autonomous or discrete social norms and values that influence social action is part of the conceptual problem at stake. Our own view of culture focuses on norms, discourses, and frameworks of meaning construction that are routinely produced and reproduced by dominant institutions, social groups, and conventions. In short, culture is the product and producer of unequal social power; we cannot adequately understand "enduring cultural values"

without making study of the "social question" front and center. Specifically, in the context of this part of our chapter, one cannot understand either inherited institutions or cultural values independent of capitalist development and racism or racialized social relations. See our response to his review of our book (McCann & Haltom, 2006).

20 One conspicuous feature receiving little attention from Kagan is the extraordinary mismatch between the corporate legal defense teams of Big Tobacco and private plaintiffs' attorneys. See Zegart, 2000.

21 Kagan does link the particular trajectory of American capitalism to the fragmented state and overall dispersal of power in his book (2001, pp. 51–54). Much of this seems right, but somewhat curiously the driving force seems to be preexisting cultural tendencies or state structures encouraging dispersal of power and fragmentation, rather than dominant business groups and commitments as forces in this history. Moreover, the rise of massive hierarchical corporate forms in the late 19th and 20th centuries are just treated as "business," as if they are but larger, more complex forms of small businesses. The scale, forms, and influence of U.S. business power are not ignored but also are not much recognized or treated as important in our reading of Kagan's work. The very premise of "fragmentation" almost determines the incomplete story that is told about American power, a story that is quite contestable from other frameworks attentive to continuities in hierarchy.

22 That lawyers did eventually produce some modestly successful challenges to the tobacco industry reflects the former's savvy strategic skills, their ability to generate and combine financial resources, and the ways in which the legal system sometimes does level a bit highly unequal social power in the interest of fairness.

23 Neither traditional pluralist nor majoritarian frameworks capture issues of unequal social power very well, in our view. We develop a similar approach to our study of guns and gun litigation—another area of mass tort litigation.

24 Kagan claims on p. 33 of the 2001 book that "those distinctive features" of U.S. tobacco policy "reflect enduring characteristics of American political culture."

25 See note 5 for discussion of Kagan's argument about "total justice," drawing on Friedman (1985).

26 We find Kagan's claims about the relative stability, instability, and overall implications of public opinion regarding tobacco policy inconsistent and selective at times. See below.

27 The key frames were: corporate responsibility for harm; corporate duplicity; good science; individual responsibility for harm; governmental responsibility; public costs; junk science; attorneys' fees or motives; shared responsibility; parental responsibility. The first four frames tend to support critics and/or plaintiffs challenging the tobacco industry, while the other frames tend to favor claims or actions of the tobacco industry, although in longer presentations of our findings we show that matters are rather more complex than such binary separation suggests.

28 Our book (2004) underlines the complex interaction between Big Tobacco, corporate news production, and other corporate forms of knowledge production in society. Again, we place issues of organized power at the center of our understanding of cultural norms, values, and meaning-making activity.

29 One implication of viewing cultural conventions as indeterminate, contested, and multivalent is to relax the assumed causal force of ideas, norms, values, and frameworks of meaning. Cultural conventions are internalized and significantly shape and restrict how members "know," but they vary widely in meaning and force as reconstructed and enacted by differently situated subjects. As such, we often stress that cultural norms are at once constitutive and instrumental (Haltom & McCann 2004).

30 This entire section draws directly and extensively on our article, "Criminalizing Big Tobacco" (McCann et al., 2013).

31 We surely do not want to suggest that FDA regulatory authority will not be constrained by the power of the industry that it is charged with regulating. Rather we are simply pointing to the change in the institutional *forms* of governance, which seems

to be Kagan's own focus. Our own inclination is to assume that effective governance that protects public health will require continuation in multiple forms of institutional action by multiple institutional players.

References

Burke, T.F. (2002). *Lawyers, Lawsuits, and Legal Rights: The Battle Over Litigation in America*. Berkeley: University of California Press.

Deal, C., & Doroshow, J. (2002). *The CALA Files: The Secret Campaign by Big Tobacco and Other Major Industries to Take Away Your Rights*. New York: Center for Democracy and Justice.

Derthick, M. (2001). *Up in Smoke: From Legislation to Litigation in Tobacco Politics*. Washington, DC: CQ Press.

Engel, D. (1984). "The Oven Bird's Song: Insiders, Outsiders and Personal Injuries in an American Community." *Law & Society Review*, 18, 551–82.

"EPS Forum: The Americanization of European Law?" Symposium Featuring R. Daniel Kelemen, R. Kagan, & Lisa Conant. *European Politics & Society*, Newsletter of the European Politics & Society Section of APSA (Fall Winter 2006) 6(1), 1–12.

Friedman, L.M. (1985). *Total Justice*. New York: Sage Foundation.

Frontline Online. (1998a). "Inside the Tobacco Deal: Interview With Michael Moore." Retrieved from www.pbs.org/wgbh/pages/frontline/shows/settlement/interviews/moore.html. Accessed 2/21/09.

Frontline Online. (1998b). "Inside the Tobacco Deal: Interviews With David Kessler." Retrieved from www.pbs.org/wgbh/pages/frontline/shows/settlement/interviews/kessler.html. Accessed 2/21/09.

Frymer, P. (2008). *Black and Blue: African Americans, the Labor Movement, and the Decline of the Democratic Party*. Princeton, NJ: Princeton University Press.

Galanter, M. (1996). "Real World Torts: An Antidote to Anecdote." *Maryland Law Review*, 55, 1093.

Galanter, M., & Thomas Palay, M. (1991). *Tournament of Lawyers: The Transformation of the Big Law Firm*. Chicago: University of Chicago Press.

Graber, M.A. (1993). "The Nonmajoritarian Difficulty: Legislative Deference to the Judiciary." *Studies in American Political Development*, 7, 35–73.

Haltom, W. (2002). Review of *Regulating Tobacco*, by R.L. Rabin & Stephen D.S (Editors). *Law and Politics Book Review*, 12, 185–8.

Haltom, W., & McCann, M. (2004). *Distorting the Law: Politics, Media, and the Litigation Crisis*. Chicago: University of Chicago Press.

Horwitz, M. (1979). *The Transformation of American Law, 1780–1860*. Cambridge, MA: Harvard University Press.

Kagan, R.A. (2001). *Adversarial Legalism: The American Way of Law*. Cambridge, MA: Harvard University Press.

Kagan, R.A. (2007). "Globalization and Legal Change: The "Americanization" of European Law?" *Regulation & Governance*, 1(2), 99–120.

Kagan, R.A., & Nelson, W.P. (2001). "The Politics of Tobacco Regulation in the United States." In R. L. Rabin, & S.D. Sugarman (Eds.), *Regulating Tobacco*. New York: Oxford University Press, pp. 11–38. (referenced as K&N 2001 in text).

Kagan, R.A., & Skolnick, J.H. (1993). "Banning Smoking: Compliance Without Enforcement." In R.L. Rabin & S.D. Sugarman (Eds.), *Smoking Policy: Law, Politics, and Culture*. New York: Oxford University Press, pp. 22–41.

Kagan, R.A., & Vogel, D. (1993). "The Politics of Smoking Regulation: Canada, France, the United States." In R.L. Rabin & S.D. Sugarman (Eds.), *Smoking Policy: Law, Politics, and Culture*. New York: Oxford University Press, pp. 22–48.

Kessler, D. (2001). *A Question of Intent: A Great American Battle with a Deadly Industry*. New York: Public Affairs.

Kluger, R. (1996). *Ashes to Ashes: America's Hundred-Year Cigarette War, the Public Health, and the Unabashed Triumph of Philip Morris*. New York: Knopf.

Lovell, G. (2003). *Legislative Deferrals: Statutory Ambiguity, Judicial Power, and American Democracy*. New York: Cambridge University Press.

Mather, L. (1998). "Theorizing About Trial Courts: Lawyers, Policymaking, and Tobacco Litigation." *Law and Social Inquiry*, 23 (Fall), 897–937.

Mather, L. (2009). "Lawyers as Conduits for Culture: Litigation Against Tobacco in Britain and the United States." In D.M. Engel, & M. McCann (Eds.), *Fault Lines: Tort Law as Cultural Practice*. Stanford, CA: Stanford University Press, pp. 192–210.

McCann, M. (1992). "Reform Litigation on Trial." *Law and Social Inquiry*, 17(4) (Fall), 715–43.

McCann, M. (1994). *Rights at Work: Pay Equity Reform and the Politics of Legal Mobilization*. Chicago: University of Chicago Press.

McCann, M. (1996). "On Being More Positive . . . Causal versus Constitutive Explanations: Or On the Difficulty of Being So Positive . . . " *Law and Social Inquiry*, 21(2), 457–82.

McCann, M. (2006). "Legal Rights Consciousness: A Challenging Analytical Tradition." In B. Fleury-Steiner & L.B. Nielsen (Eds.), *The New Civil Rights Research*. Farnham: Ashgate, pp. ix–xxx.

McCann, M, & Haltom, W. (2006). "On Analyzing Legal Culture." *Law & Social Inquiry*, 31, 739–56.

McCann, M., Haltom, W., & Fisher, S. (2013). "Criminalizing Big Tobacco: Legal Mobilization and the Politics of Responsibility for Health Risks in the United States." *Law & Social Inquiry*, 38 (2) 288–321.

McCann, M., & Lovell, G. (2005). "A Tangled Legacy: Federal Courts and the Politics of 'Democratic Inclusion.'" Chapter 12. In C. Wolbrecht & R. Hero, with P.E. Arnold & A.B. Tillery (Eds.), *The Politics of Democratic Inclusion*. Philadelphia: Temple University Press, pp. 257–80.

Miller, A.S. (1976). *The Corporate State*. Westport, CT: Greenwood Press.

Nedelsky, J. (1990). *Private Property and the Limits of American Constitutionalism*. Chicago: University Chicago of Press.

Nelken, D. (2003). "Beyond Compare? Criticizing "The American Way of Law." *Law & Social Inquiry*, 28(3),799–831.

Nelken, D. (2009). "Law, Liability, and Culture." In D.M. Engel & M. McCann (Eds.), *Fault Lines: Tort Law as Cultural Practice*. Stanford, CA: Stanford University Press, pp. 21–38.

Pitkin, H. (1972). *Wittgenstein and Justice*. Berkeley: University of California Press.

Rabin, R.L. (2001). "The Third Wave of Tobacco Tort Litigation." In R.L. Rabin & S.D. Sugarman (Eds.), *Regulating Tobacco*. New York: Oxford University Press, pp. 176–206.

Rosenberg, G.L. 1991. *The Hollow Hope: Can Courts Bring about Social Change*? Chicago, IL: University of Chicago Press.

Scheingold, S.A. (1974). *The Politics of Rights: Lawyers, Public Policy, and Political Change*. New Haven: Yale University Press.

Scheingold, S.A., & Sarat, A. (2004). *Something to Believe In: Politics, Professionalism, and Cause Lawyering*. Palo Alto: Stanford University Press.

Zegart, D. (2000). *Civil Warriors: The Legal Siege on the Tobacco Industry*. New York: Bantam/Delta.

4

KAGAN'S ATLANTIC CROSSING

Adversarial Legalism, Eurolegalism, and Cooperative Legalism in European Regulatory Style

Francesca Bignami and R. Daniel Kelemen

Robert Kagan is known primarily as a scholar of American public law, but Kagan's studies of America have always been informed by a comparative perspective. Though many scholars and pundits speak of "American exceptionalism," Kagan is one of the rare few who understands that the truly exceptional features of American politics and law can only be recognized on the basis of detailed study of other polities. Early on, Kagan saw that to succeed as an Americanist, he must also become a comparativist. He has done so with such success that his work on comparative law and regulation not only has contributed to his insights on the U.S., it also has made landmark contributions to the study of law and regulation across Europe and Asia.[1]

In this chapter we focus on one particular contribution Kagan has made to the study of law and politics in the European Union, namely in stimulating a debate over the potential spread of "adversarial legalism" to Europe. In the mid- to late 1990s, Kagan was in the midst of producing a series of papers that would culminate in his path-breaking 2001 book, *Adversarial Legalism: The American Way of Law*. In this work, he developed a concept, "adversarial legalism," that captured the distinctive features of American legal and regulatory style and he explained the origins and persistence of that style. As part of his research, he engaged in comparative studies of regulation in European countries, highlighting the advantages many enjoyed as compared to the U.S. in terms of being more cooperative and informal, and avoiding protracted and expensive legal battles. While highlighting these differences, however, he recognized some pressures for movement toward American-style regulation in Europe. This led him to question whether it was likely that American-style adversarial legalism—with all the costly pathologies that accompany it—might take root in Europe. As Kagan put it succinctly in the title of a 1997 paper, "Should Europe Worry About Adversarial Legalism?"

Kagan answered the question in the negative, emphasizing that entrenched legal institutions and cultures would prevent adversarial legalism from taking root in Europe. Some years later, R. Daniel Kelemen picked up on Kagan's question, but reached the conclusion that a legal style akin to adversarial legalism—one which he eventually termed Eurolegalism—was in fact spreading across the European Union (Kelemen & Sibbitt, 2004; Kelemen, 2006, 2011, 2012, 2013). In a 2007 paper, Kagan responded, challenging Kelemen's arguments by further developing the arguments presented in his 1997 paper "Should Europe Worry About Adversarial Legalism?," again emphasizing that a number of "entrenched differences" would prevent the spread of adversarial legalism in Europe (Kagan, 2007). In a 2011 paper, Francesca Bignami extended the debate in a new direction, drawing on a case study of the data privacy field to suggest that EU regulation may be characterized by a pattern of cooperative legalism rather than adversarial legalism (Bignami, 2011). Together, such contributions have given rise to a lively debate, with a number of other scholars adding empirical studies and theoretical arguments concerning the impact of the EU on national regulatory styles and exploring whether or not, or in which respects and to what extent, aspects of adversarial legalism may be spreading to Europe (see, for instance, Bignami, 2011; Cioffi, 2009; Mabbett, 2011; Meyerstein, 2013; Rehder, 2009; van Waarden, 2009). This debate has helped build analytic bridges across the Atlantic, enabling scholars of the U.S. and Europe to compare trends in regulation in both contexts.

In this chapter we summarize this debate, highlighting the enduring importance of Kagan's conceptual contribution to the study of regulation in Europe. We begin by summarizing Kagan's main arguments about regulatory style in Europe and why U.S.-style adversarial legalism was unlikely to take root in Europe. We then engage in a dialogue, presenting both Kelemen's argument that European integration is encouraging the spread of a variant of adversarial legalism—"Eurolegalism"—and Bignami's argument that distinctive features of national regulatory regimes prevent the spread of adversarial legalism in Europe and instead lead to the spread of an alternative pattern of "cooperative legalism." We conclude by linking the discussion of our own work with other important contributions to the debate on regulation in Europe inspired by Kagan's work.

Kagan on Why Europe Shouldn't Worry About Adversarial Legalism

Kagan famously labeled the distinctive American legal style as "adversarial legalism." He framed the exceptionalism of the American "way of law" by comparison with legal styles in European countries and other advanced industrialized countries. He captured some central elements of the distinction between adversarial legalism and European legal styles in the following passage, which is worth quoting at length:

> Viewed in relation to Western European governments (including the UK), the USA has developed a distinctive "legal style"—by which I mean its way of making, crafting, and implementing laws and regulations, conducting litigation, adjudicating disputes, and using courts. American laws generally are more detailed, complicated, and prescriptive. American methods of litigating and adjudicating legal disputes are more adversarial and costly. Legalistic enforcement is much more prevalent in American regulatory programs. American judges generally are bolder in scrutinizing and reversing governmental plans, regulations, practices, and decisions. Interest groups in the USA, consequently, more often use courts as an alternative political forum for seeking policy goals.
>
> *(Kagan, 2007, pp. 102–103)*

In comparison to this distinctive American legal style, the legal styles that prevailed across European jurisdictions, while each distinct in many respects, tended to be more informal, cooperative, and opaque and less reliant on lawyers, courts, and private enforcement actions. Kagan recognized in his 1997 article that there were new pressures that might encourage adversarial legalism in Europe including international economic competition, competition in legal services, privatization and deregulation, growing political mistrust of government power, the "federalization" of regulation in the EU, and political gridlock (Kagan, 1997, pp. 171–179). Despite the existence of such pressures, however, Kagan concluded in his 1997 article and subsequent work that entrenched institutions and legal cultures in EU member states would discourage the spread of adversarial legalism to European countries (Kagan, 1997, 2007). Moreover, he noted that the very fact that the pathologies of American-style adversarial legalism were well known to Europeans would make them vigilant against the rise of that mode of regulation in Europe. As he put it in his 2007 article, "Globalization and Legal Change: The 'Americanization' of European Law?," six entrenched differences distinguishing the U.S. legal system from its European counterparts would ensure that the latter would not experience "Americanization" of their legal systems. Specifically, he highlighted as crucial enduring differences:

1. the political nature and remedial powers of American judiciaries
2. the pervasiveness of adversarial legalism in the regulatory process
3. the hyperactive American tort law system
4. the more limited rights to social provision in the U.S.
5. the less demanding American tax laws
6. the punitiveness and adversarial legalism of American criminal justice.

Kagan's foray into the study of European legal styles was seminal in that it has stimulated a lively debate about whether, and if so why, legal styles in European countries may be shifting toward something akin to adversarial legalism. Next, each of us presents our own arguments on this question.

Kelemen on Eurolegalism

In a series of articles (Kelemen & Sibbitt, 2004; Kelemen, 2006, 2008, 2012) and in my 2011 book *Eurolegalism: The Transformation of Law and Regulation in the European Union*, I argue that the process of European integration is transforming traditional patterns of law and regulation across EU member states and pushing them towards a European variant of adversarial legalism, which I term Eurolegalism.[2] I argue that European integration is promoting the spread of Eurolegalism through two linked causal mechanisms, one economic and one political.

The first mechanism involves the process of deregulation and juridical reregulation linked to the creation of the EU's single market. As the EU pursued its 1992 single market project, traditional, informal national styles of regulation based on closed insider networks and trust that had prevailed in European countries came to be seen as barriers to market integration. They were dismantled in field after field, sometimes as a result of EU policy initiatives that demanded liberalization and sometimes as the result of European Court of Justice (ECJ) judgments that ruled national regulations to be illegal non-tariff barriers to trade in the single market. But the EU did not stop with deregulation. In order to pursue their policy objectives, EU policy makers also sought to reregulate, to replace problematic national regulatory regimes with pan-European regimes compatible with the functioning of the Single Market. But the new EU regulatory regimes did not resemble traditional European styles of informal, cooperative regulation. Facing a greater volume and diversity of actors in the liberalized market and demands for a level playing field, EU lawmakers rely on regulatory frameworks that are more formal, inflexible, and judicialized. In short, the EU followed a pattern established in other polities whereby the creation of "freer markets" actually requires "more rules" and where deregulation is followed by "juridical reregulation" (Vogel, 1996).

The second causal mechanism stems from the political fragmentation that characterizes the EU's institutional framework. When EU policy makers "reregulate" at the European level, they do so within an institutional structure that generates political incentives to rely on a judicialized mode of governance. Political power in the EU is highly fragmented—divided horizontally between the European Commission, European Council, and European Parliament—and vertically between the EU and member state administrations. The fragmentation of political power in the EU generates principal-agent problems and breeds distrust between lawmakers and the national administrations that implement most EU policy. The EU also has extremely weak administrative capacity, but does have a relatively strong judicial system under the leadership of the ECJ. This combination of political fragmentation, weak administrative capacity, and effective judicial institutions encourages policy-makers to enact laws with justiciable provisions and to encourage the commission and private litigants to enforce them before European and national courts. In other words, EU policy makers seek to harness national and European courts and private litigants to help make up for their lack of central administrative capacity. This decentralized enforcement, backed by enforcement actions taken by the commission before European courts, helps to safeguard the implementation of EU policies across the large and fragmented European polity.

I recognize Kagan's (2007) point that a number of institutions entrenched at the national level in EU states continue to discourage adversarial legalism. He highlights the absence of jury trials, contingency fees, and massive damage awards in European systems of tort law, the lower degree of politicization of European judiciaries, and the existence across Europe of more generous public social and medical services as examples of entrenched institutions that will discourage the rise of adversarial legalism in Europe. Consider, for instance, the fact that decentralized private enforcement of legal norms is an important aspect of adversarial legalism. As Kagan rightly emphasizes, many rules of civil procedure in national legal systems across Europe discourage private enforcement. For example, the absence of contingency fee arrangements and American-style opt-out class actions in most European jurisdictions raises the cost of litigation, while the absence of remedies such as punitive damage awards often reduces the potential rewards of successful litigation. The fact that many potential litigants across the EU face higher costs and lower potential awards discourages them from seeking to enforce their rights under EU law in court.

However, while such impediments continue to channel and constrain the spread of adversarial legalism, they do not block it entirely. A number of the traditional impediments to adversarial legalism in Europe—such as entrenched rules of civil procedure or patterns of organization in the legal profession—are themselves eroding under pressures generated by European integration. Having introduced a voluminous body of EU law—the so-called *acquis communautaire*—that establishes a wide range of rights and other legally enforceable norms, the EU now increasingly emphasizes that European citizens and other legal "persons" (i.e., firms) must enjoy better access to justice such that they can enforce these rights. To this end, the EU is leading a multipronged effort to create a "Genuine European Area of Justice"—improving access to justice and promoting the harmonization of procedural laws across the EU so as to facilitate private enforcement (Kelemen, 2011, p. 58; Hartnell, 2002; Hodges, 2007). EU initiatives and related legal developments in this field have affected various aspects of litigation financing (e.g., legal aid, conditional fee arrangements, and third-party litigation financing) and procedures governing collective (group) litigation.[3] Taken together, these measures are inducing a change in the litigation landscape across Europe that is facilitating the spread of Eurolegalism.

Moreover, my argument that European integration is encouraging the spread of a mode of governance—Eurolegalism—that involves greater reliance on formal law, lawyers, and litigation, does not suggest that EU governance is identical to American-style adversarial legalism. I am not arguing that Eurolegalism mimics American adversarial legalism in all respects or that it has already seeped into every nook and cranny of law and regulation across all EU member states. Rather, to paraphrase Lord Denning's famous description of EU treaty law,[4] I am arguing that Eurolegalism is an incoming tide. It flows into the estuaries and up the rivers. It cannot be held back, and it is transforming governance across a wide range of policy areas. As a result of the sort of institutional impediments Kagan identifies, the European variant of adversarial legalism—Eurolegalism—is and will likely remain more restrained and sedate than the American version and will affect some policy areas and some member states less than others. Despite the reforms mentioned above, persistent differences between civil procedures in the U.S. and EU mean that we will not see the sort of lawyer-driven, contingency-fee financed class actions in Europe that are so common in the U.S. in fields ranging from securities law to product liability. And the increases in private enforcement we are seeing in Europe will vary significantly across policy area, with private parties eager to take up new opportunities to assert their EU rights in court in such fields as securities and antitrust (where potential litigants tend to be well-resourced corporations or investors) than in the field of disability rights (where potential litigants tend to be workers of modest means who have been victims of discrimination).

But such variations across policy areas and across jurisdictions do not take away from the broader point that Eurolegalism is spreading. And the fact that Eurolegalism is not synonymous with American adversarial legalism does not take away from the point that legal style in the EU is shifting in an American direction. In my 2011 book (Kelemen, 2011) documenting the EU's influence on the spread of Eurolegalism, I take the mid-1980s as a baseline for all quantitative measures and case studies and assessing shifts in regulatory style from traditional European forms toward Eurolegalism over the next two decades. I highlight cross-cutting indicators of the shift in legal style, including aggregate data on legal activity, such as litigation rates, spending on legal services and legal expenses insurance. I also look at qualitative changes in the civil and administrative procedures, such as the spread of class action lawsuits and conditional fee arrangements, which reflect and contribute to the spread of Eurolegalism. Finally, I also conduct case studies of particular policy areas in which I trace shifts in legal style toward Eurolegalism in securities regulation, competition law, and disability rights both at the EU level and in the UK, France, Germany, and the Netherlands. In these case studies, I use process tracing to demonstrate that legal and regulatory styles in Europe in these fields have shifted from traditional styles of regulation towards Eurolegalism, and to demonstrate that the causal mechanisms behind these shifts are those anticipated by my theory.

Bignami on Cooperative Legalism

Turning to the argument that, paraphrasing Kagan, Europeans shouldn't worry about adversarial legalism, this section presents evidence from my own research and that of others that supports a different pattern of regulatory change—what I call cooperative legalism. I suggest below that the reason for this somewhat surprising outcome is to be found in the operation of the two causal mechanisms outlined above: the theorization of market liberalization and political fragmentation in Kagan and Kelemen is heavily influenced by the distinctive American experience with these two phenomena, but it turns out that when transposed to a different political and institutional context, they produce quite different outcomes, most significantly a less prominent role for courts in regulatory policymaking.

To understand the nature of regulatory change in Europe, it is helpful to unpack the category of adversarial legalism into the two dimensions identified in Kagan's original typology of modes of policy implementation and dispute resolution. The first dimension captures the extent to which decisions are driven by horizontally situated parties (participatory) or hierarchically superior officialdom (hierarchical). The second captures the degree to which government decisions are based on the rigid application of legal rules and sanctions (formal) or the discretionary exercise of authority (informal). Policy implementation in the United States is classified as "adversarial legalism" because it generally is party-driven (adversarial) and relies on an extensive, formal set of rules and procedures (legalism). In my study of EU data privacy regulation from the mid-1970s to 2010.

I find evidence of adversarial legalism across the four country cases (UK, Italy, France, Germany) only on the formality dimension and not on the party-driven dimension. In all four countries, the law was reworked to contain more extensive investigative and sanctioning powers, and these powers were being used by data privacy regulators, in particular in France and Italy, suggesting a move, as Kagan had predicted, from an informal and consensual style of regulatory enforcement to a more legalistic and punitive approach. I also find, however, a countervailing trend towards more self-regulation, representing continuity for the UK and Germany, systems known for certain neocorporatist practices, but signifying a shift for France and Italy which have a reputation for top-down administration with little role for interest groups. Neo-corporatism involves a significant role for representative interest associations in policy implementation, either alone or in tripartite settings generally composed of labor, industry, and government representatives. Self-regulation, which entails the exercise of regulatory powers by market actors, can be undertaken by the same industry and professional associations that are central to neo-corporatism. Even in those instances in which self-regulation is undertaken by different types of market actors, such as individual firms, the division of public-private power resonates with neo-corporatist institutional arrangements. Although Kagan does not address directly self-regulation, adversarial legalism's second dimension of detailed rules and little administrative discretion, together with its rights-driven model of regulation, suggest that there is little room for the flexible and context-sensitive approaches to implementation that self-regulation is designed to foster. Because of this pattern of continuity (i.e., little litigation) and change in the data privacy case, I conclude that European regulatory systems were converging on a style of "cooperative legalism."

The data privacy case, as well as some of the other empirical work reviewed below (Bellantuono, 2014; Cioffi, 2009; Bastings, Mastenbroek, & Versluis, 2014; Van Cleynenbreugel, 2014; Hodges, 2014; van Waarden & Hildebrand, 2009), point to three difficulties with the theoretical framework of adversarial legalism and suggest ways of refining our understanding of the ongoing phenomenon of shifting regulatory styles in Europe. As described earlier, the adversarial legalism hypothesis is premised on the causal factors of market liberalization and political fragmentation. What these studies suggest, however, is that the logic of these causal factors operates differently in the American and European contexts and therefore some of what is believed to be universal to the phenomena of market liberalization and political fragmentation, in particular adversarial litigation, may be particular to the American historical experience.

The first difficulty with the adversarial legalism hypothesis concerns the market liberalization prong. In his original piece, Kagan suggested that more rules give rise to more legal fights about the rules inside administration and in the courts (Kagan, 1997, pp. 173–175). However, both his comparative typology of modes of policy implementation, which includes the classic Weberian category of bureaucratic legalism, as well as some of the evidence from the European experience with market liberalization, suggest that there is an alternative way of governing with a dense body of rules—bureaucratic administration of rules by government authorities.

For market liberalization to work and for the normative commitments of the rule of law to be met, the rules must be transparent and subject to oversight by an independent judicial body, but they do not necessarily have to be crafted through a long and drawn-out process of adversarial contestation. This, as I briefly review below, is the form of regulatory governance that appears to be taking hold in a number of sectors in the EU.

Similar to the data privacy sector, many of the regulatory schemes introduced with market liberalization and reregulation involve a central role for a newly created (or newly empowered) national regulatory authority endowed with extensive policymaking and enforcement powers: competition authorities (Maher, 2000), telecommunications authorities (Thatcher, 2007), energy authorities (Thatcher, 2007, pp. 209–230; Bellantuono, 2014, pp. 16–17), financial services authorities (Thatcher, 2007, pp. 90–118; Cioffi, 2009, p. 248), and environmental authorities (Bastings et al., 2014, p. 14) among others. Although it is difficult to obtain systematic comparative data on how these new enforcement powers are being used, anecdotal evidence suggests that, as in the privacy field, they are indeed being deployed by regulators, producing a more formal and punitive style of regulatory enforcement (Faure et al., 2008; Bastings et al., 2014). To date, however, there is little evidence that these new regulatory powers have been accompanied by more contestation by the parties and their lawyers in administrative agencies and the courts.[5] It is true that because regulatory authorities now have the power to impose significant administrative sanctions, including heavy fines, they have also had to afford due process rights in the administrative process to regulated parties, and their decisions have been subject to challenge in the courts (Van Cleynenbreugel, 2014, pp. 11–21). But this development should be seen as part and parcel of the transfer of sanctioning powers from the criminal justice system—which in many jurisdictions previously had the exclusive power to impose fines and other types of sanctions for regulatory offenses and which obviously had a highly developed set of guarantees for defendants—to administrative agencies, which are capable of pursuing regulatory offenses in a more single-minded fashion but in many cases do not possess a developed procedural framework. It does not appear that this proceduralization of enforcement has spread to the rest of agency policymaking and rulemaking activities. For instance, financial markets regulators have been under significant pressure from constitutional and administrative courts to improve the rights available to individual firms in the course of their investigations and enforcement proceedings,[6] but their policymaking activities, which often do involve public consultations, are not bound by strict procedural rules. This stands in stark contrast with the regulations issued by the U.S. Securities and Exchange Commission, which are formulated through the adversarial American rulemaking process and are subject to intense and often unpredictable judicial review in the courts.[7]

The second difficulty with the original theoretical framework relates to the causal factor of political structure and the analogy that has been drawn between the EU political system and U.S. federalism. Kagan argued that one of the causes of adversarial legalism in the U.S. was the mismatch between a highly ambitious federal policy agenda and an underdeveloped federal administrative state, which led lawmakers to rely extensively on state and local authorities for implementation, and to write legislation giving litigants the right to go to court, both to monitor and challenge state implementation and to independently enforce federal policy in court. Kagan, as later developed by Kelemen, speculated that since the EU was also marked by a lack of federal administrative capacity and the fragmentation of state power, EU lawmakers would write similar legal rights into EU law (Kagan, 1997, pp. 177–178).

The weakness of the argument is that it mischaracterizes to some extent the nature of the EU lawmaking process. EU lawmaking is called "harmonization" for a reason. When the EU enters a new policy area, it does not regulate from tabula rasa but rather operates in the context of a thick regulatory field, which generally contains a number of highly developed national administrative and legal schemes. In contrast with U.S. lawmaking, which is controlled by elected politicians who write legislation, including the rights-conferring legislation described by Kagan, to produce certain kinds of policies and therefore win votes (Epstein & O'Halloran, 1999), the EU legislative process is structured to include a wide array of actors and incentives. One set of actors that does not have a U.S. equivalent are the national governments represented in the European Council, which are at least partially motivated by the desire to preserve their existing national schemes—and regulatory styles—by uploading them into EU legislation (Börzel, 2002). The older and more powerful member states, like France and Germany, which generally have both policy experience and bargaining clout, are very often able to do so. Following this logic, member states should have little incentive to support a foreign regulatory style in harmonization instruments and can be expected to oppose attempts to introduce elements of adversarial legalism by other legislative actors, most notably the European Commission, which may very well be driven by the same enforcement incentives as U.S. legislators. To the extent the member states seek to control national administrations and overcome the principal-agent problem identified by Kelemen in the previous section, they can use tools that are more congenial to their traditional regulatory styles (and possibly more effective) than private litigants and court. Kagan very rightly anticipated that adversarial legalism would encounter resistance from national legal cultures and political structures, but this analysis suggests that national traditions run even deeper: they undercut one of the critical sources of adversarial legalism, suggesting that it never had a fighting chance to begin with.

The drafting of the first EU directive on data protection is one example of how member states stymied European Commission attempts to improve litigation rights for privacy violations (Bignami, 2011, p. 438). The best illustration to date of legislative resistance, however, is the ongoing effort to introduce a class action for mass consumer torts in the EU. In the consumer protection area, the commission has articulated what Christopher Hodges (2014, pp. 69–70) calls a three-pillar policy of alternative dispute resolution, enhanced authority for consumer protection agencies, and collective redress to obtain compensation in the courts for consumer harms. To date, however, progress has mostly been achieved on alternative dispute resolution and administrative enforcement, while collective redress has lagged behind. The only concrete action that has been produced in over five years of institutional debate is a Commission Recommendation adopted in June 2013 exhorting the member states to introduce some form of collective redress mechanism, and a fairly weak one at that, which repudiates many of the key elements of the American system. One of the reasons for this lack of legislative action is continued opposition from the majority of member states in the European Council, coupled with what Kagan called the "inherent reflexiveness of human political and legal systems," namely the express desire articulated by both the European Parliament and the European Commission to avoid the pathologies of the American experience with class action litigation (Hodges, 2014, p. 83). The result is that the current consumer protection regime hews closely to the regulatory style of cooperative legalism: a significant role for public, administrative enforcement, widespread resort to alternative dispute settlement through the traditional informal institutions of ombudsmen and neocorporatist bodies as well as newer market-based institutions, and relatively little litigation (Hodges, 2014, p. 81).

The third correction suggested by some of the recent empirical work relates to the particularities of the EU legislative process described above. The importance of national regulatory templates for legislative outcomes points not only to the EU's intrinsic hostility to adversarial legalism but also suggests that EU legislation should be conceptualized somewhat differently from U.S. legislation—as a set of compromises between national regulatory models with elements of adversarial legalism inserted, if at all, on the fringes. If this is the case, then it might be more appropriate to conceive of the legalistic elements of EU regulation as a reflection of, or at least consistent with, the regulatory styles of a certain subset of powerful member states, which require change in the direction of adversarial legalism in other, but by no means all, member states. In other words, the degree of transformation of regulatory styles may vary significantly by member state, and the transformations that do occur may reflect not the emergence of a novel, adversarial, and legalistic mode of regulation, but rather convergence on a dominant European style.

To again illustrate with data privacy, among the four countries included in my study, the UK system began as the most informal one, due to a combination of the traditional UK policy style and a foot-dragging approach to the substantive issue of privacy: in the 1980s, the administrative authority responsible for data protection had very few regulatory and enforcement powers and individuals were given virtually no legal rights to sue in the courts. Following the passage of the EU directive, which was largely a hybrid of the French and German models, the UK system was transformed more thoroughly in the direction of adversarial legalism than any of the others in the study. The data protection authority acquired rulemaking powers for the first time and obtained a host of new enforcement tools, including the power to impose stiff administrative fines. In addition, a general right of action was added to the British privacy legislation and therefore individuals became entitled to sue in court for any type of privacy violation. The institutional practices of both the data protection authority and the courts reflected these legal changes.

Other research suggests that the Dutch system as a whole is vulnerable to change because of its extremely informal and pragmatic traditional regulatory style, which has made it an outlier even among European states. For instance, in their study on regulatory enforcement of the EU packaging-waste directive in the Netherlands and Germany, Bastings and her coauthors show that the German system, which was reflected in the directive, remained stable and legalistic, while the previously "passive" Dutch style morphed into a legalistic style (Bastings et al., 2014). More generally, van Waarden and Hildebrand have documented how the Netherlands in the 1970s represented the informal and consensual extreme of the spectrum, especially when compared to countries like Germany and Austria, and how it has since experienced a dramatic rate of growth in lawyers, legal insurance, administrative litigation, and civil litigation, so that it has largely caught up with its neighbors, albeit with distinctively Dutch neocorporatist elements (van Waarden & Hildebrand, 2009).

There is also evidence that for their own distinct national reasons, certain member states may be more litigation-friendly than others. A recent study on the compensation of asbestos victims showed that while the courts played absolutely no role in Belgium, in the UK there were significant levels of personal injury litigation, and in Italy victims sometimes obtained compensation for damages in criminal prosecutions (Boggio, 2013). Similarly, in his otherwise quite muted assessment of how collective redress procedures have been and will be used in national jurisdictions, Hodges (2014, p. 83) singles out the UK and Italy, together with Poland and, for settlements, the Netherlands as potential "hot spots" for consumer litigation.

In sum, although market liberalization and Europeanization have certainly altered national regulatory styles, they have done so more by enhancing deterrence-oriented enforcement of rules by administrative authorities than by increasing contestation in the administrative process or through the courts. While, as suggested by some of Kelemen's analysis, litigation may become more pervasive in domains such as competition law and corporate law, where the financial stakes are high and the impact of market liberalization is particularly significant, it is unlikely to emerge as the dominant force in European regulatory governance. Among the many contributions of Kagan's scholarship, his comparative frame has pushed others to grapple with the question of what is intrinsic to regulation in liberal markets and fragmented polities—undoubtedly global trends that affect not only the EU but jurisdictions throughout the world—and what is exceptional to regulation in the U.S. My own view of the evidence so far is that a certain degree of legalization, largely enforced by administrative authorities, is inevitable but that the pervasive contestation of regulatory policymaking characteristic of the U.S. is the product of a distinctive historical experience with the law and politics of the regulatory state.

Conclusion

The debate provoked by Kagan's comparative insights has by no means been settled. It is possible, however, to identify a number of areas of consensus as to the nature of regulatory change in Europe. First, it is fairly clear that the increasingly dense set of rules coming from Brussels is being applied by special-purpose national regulatory authorities that have acquired new enforcement powers and that have moved towards a more legalistic and punitive style of regulatory enforcement. In doing so, these agencies have experienced significant proceduralization of their enforcement activities: administrative bodies like competition authorities, banking regulators, and data protection agencies have had to create internal divisions responsible for conducting adversarial proceedings that can potentially result in heavy fines and other forms of administrative sanctions and that can be, and often are, challenged in court. Second, in some policy areas, and in some countries, litigation invoking the rights and duties of regulatory statutes has become more prominent. This is the case for policy sectors like competition law and securities regulation where liberalization has had a direct and profound impact on the organization of markets (and market actors with the financial incentives to litigate regulatory claims). This is also the case for countries like the Netherlands, which were previously extremely informal and consensual even by European standards, and countries like Italy, which for distinct domestic reasons have experienced a rise in regulatory litigation.

Of course, we, and the many others engaged in this area of inquiry, also differ in our assessment of the current state of affairs and the likely future trajectory of European regulation. The main point of difference concerns the role of rights and litigation in shaping regulation across the policymaking cycle (from general norms to enforcement of those norms in specific cases) and the policymaking spectrum (across all policy areas). While Eurolegalism takes the view that litigants and courts have already become and will continue to become major players across a wide range of policy areas, cooperative legalism sees the balance of power as remaining in the hands of administrative authorities, especially at the rulemaking phase and in areas involving diffuse interest such as consumers and the environment. Even here, as the labels suggest, there is overlap, since both acknowledge that national institutions and legal traditions constitute obstacles to the diffusion of adversarial legalism. In Kelemen's assessment, however, national traditions are a stumbling block that stands in the way of the advance of adversarial legalism. In Bignami's assessment, on the other hand, national traditions operate as a central element of regulating a liberalized and fragmented policy space. In a number of sectors, European lawmakers have adapted their existing (nonadversarial) legal tool kit to the new realities of European integration, and they are likely to continue to do so going forward, significantly reducing the likelihood that adversarial administrative proceedings and court litigation will come to serve as the dominant mode of policy implementation in Europe.

Settling the debate outlined above will require careful studies of specific policy areas involving accurate quantitative measures of regulatory litigation and covering a wide range of countries. It is an issue of importance, not only for understanding the evolution of regulation in Europe, but also a host of other regions across the globe in which the twin phenomena of the regulatory state and the empowerment of transnational and international bodies are transforming the status quo. At stake are the types of government institutions and public and private professionals that will be empowered to make the resource-distributing and market-stabilizing policy decisions of the regulatory state, with all of the consequences so vividly revealed by Kagan. The difference, put in the starkest terms, is between specialized bureaucracies, on the one hand, and generalist judges and partisan litigators, on the other hand. Which is preferable depends to some extent on how close historically and geographically situated government institutions come to our ideal types of bureaucracies and courts. It also depends on how convincing one finds the normative dimension of Kagan's work.

Another question for further research is the relationship between the increasing legalism of European regulation and informal and flexible modes of regulatory governance. At the same time as Kelemen was documenting the rise of Eurolegalism, a number of other scholars were focusing on the increasing popularity in the EU of "new modes of governance," namely discretionary forms of regulation that allow administrators considerable flexibility in how to interpret regulatory norms and that entrust the regulated parties with significant responsibility for implementing those norms. In cooperative legalism, as illustrated by the data privacy and consumer protection cases, the two forms of regulatory governance—legalistic and self-regulatory—coexist. There is no doubt, however, that this is a somewhat paradoxical development: top-down agency enforcement and cooperative public–private problem-solving are generally pitted as alternative, not complementary, regulatory techniques. Public enforcement implies fixed legal duties with which market actors are asked to comply, whereas self-regulation requires flexible, general public norms that are supplemented through private-sector initiatives.

In response to this puzzle, Kelemen has argued that new modes of governance are a "red herring." He contends that they constitute peripheral experiments in governance that have been much discussed by academics but that have had little impact in practice. He argues that attention to these experiments in new governance detracts attention from the more pervasive shift to more legalistic regulation—Eurolegalism—across the European policy space (Idema & Kelemen, 2006). This certainly is one possibility, but there are others too: some of the research undertaken on efforts to introduce flexible regulation in the American context suggests that hard and soft governance can interact in productive ways (Short & Toffel, 2010), while the literature on institutional change highlights the possibility that old forms of European self-regulation may be retooled without being entirely abandoned (Streeck & Thelen, 2006). Like adversarial litigation, the question of how hard and soft forms of regulation interact over time will require careful case studies, the results of which have implications not only for Europe but for the development of the regulatory state in a number of other regional settings.

The vibrancy of this ongoing debate is a testament to Kagan's influence. Einstein (1938) once said, "The formulation of a problem is often more essential than its solution, which may be merely a matter of mathematical or experimental skill. To raise new questions, new problems, to regard old problems from a new angle, requires creative imagination and marks real advances in science." Throughout his career, Kagan has shown a remarkable knack for asking the right questions—often the vital questions about law and politics that others had not thought to ask. His own work has gone a long way to answering these questions, and he has inspired hundreds of others to take up the questions he poses. This has certainly been the case in the study of European regulatory styles. By posing a trenchant question others had not thought to ask—"Should Europe worry about adversarial legalism?"—Kagan triggered a vibrant debate and inspired a wealth of research that continues to transform our understanding of European regulatory styles and of the impact of the EU on national regulation.

Notes

1 Though our chapter focuses exclusively on the debates Kagan has inspired concerning EU law and regulation, his work has also inspired similar debates about legal developments in Asian countries. See, for instance, Kelemen & Sibbitt, 2002; Johnson, 2003; Nelken, 2003; Ginsburg, 2008; Baharvar, 2006–2007.
2 In fact, the very term "Eurolegalism" was suggested to me by Professor Kagan. I remain deeply grateful for this catchy suggestion.
3 Traditionally, because American-style contingency fees have been prohibited in European jurisdictions, litigants were discouraged by the potentially high costs of litigation. However, a number of recent developments have established new funding schemes for litigation that reduce the costs to plaintiffs. See Kelemen, 2011, pp. 58, 2013.
4 See *HP Bulmer Ltd v J Bollinger SA [1974]* Ch 401 at 418.
5 One exception appears to be certain areas of land-use planning and environmental regulation, where the Aarhus requirement of affording participation in the preparation of environmental impact statements has given rise to the right to participate in and challenge certain types of agency policymaking. See Nadal, 2008.
6 See, for example, *Grandes Stevens et al. v. Italy*, nos. 18640/10, 18647/10, 18663/10, 18668/10, 18698/1, European Court of Human Rights, July 7, 2014.
7 See, for example, *Business Roundtable v. SEC*, 647 F.3d 1144 (D.C. Cir. 2011).

References

Baharvar, D. (2006–2007). "Adversarial Legalism as China's Primary External Model of Legality: What Does It Mean for China's Future? *Chinese Law & Policy Review*, 2, 65.

Bastings, L., Mastenbroek, E., & Versluis, E. (2014). "The Other Face of Eurolegalism: International Convergence on Packaging Waste Enforcement Styles in the European Union." Paper prepared for panel "In Search of Coherence in the Implementation of EU Policies," ECPR Standing Group on Regulatory Governance, 5th Biennial Conference, Barcelona, 25–27 June.

Bellantuono, G. (2014). "The Regulatory Governance of Public and Private Enforcement." Paper prepared for ECPR Standing Group on Regulatory Governance Biennial Conference, IBEI, Barcelona, June 25–27.

Bignami, F. (2011). "Cooperative Legalism and the Non-Americanization of European Regulatory Styles: The Case of Data Privacy." *American Journal of Comparative Law*, 59, 411–61.

Boggio, A. (2013). *Compensating Asbestos Victims*. Farnham: Ashgate.

Börzel, T. (2002). "Pace-Setting, Foot-Dragging, and Fence Sitting." *Journal of Common Market Studies*, 40, 193–214.

Cioffi, J. (2009). "Adversarialism Versus Legalism: Juridification and Litigation in Corporate Governance Reform." *Regulation & Governance*, 3, 235–58.

Einstein, A. (1938). *The Evolution of Physics: The Growth of Ideas from Early Concepts to Relativity and Quanta*. New York: Simon & Schuster.

Epstein, D., & S. O'Halloran. (1999). *Delegating Powers: A Transaction Cost Politics Approach to Policy Making Under Separate Powers*. Cambridge: Cambridge University Press.
Faure, M., Ogus, A., & Philipsen, N. (2008). "Enforcement Practices for Breaches of Consumer Protection Legislation." *Loyola Consumer Law Review*, 20, 361–401.
Ginsburg, T. (2008). "Judicialization of Administrative Governance: Causes, Consequences and limits." *National Taiwan University Law Review*, 3, 1.
Hartnell, H. (2002). "EUstitia: Institutionalizing Justice in the European Union." *Northwestern Journal of International Law and Business*, 23, 65–138.
Hodges, C. (2007). "Europeanization of Civil Justice: Trends and Issues." *Civil Justice Quarterly*, 26, 96–123.
Hodges, C. (2014). "Collective Redress: A Breakthrough or a *Damp Sqibb* [sic]?" *Journal of Consumer Policy*, 37, 67–89.
Idema, T., & Kelemen, R.D. (2006). "New Modes of Governance, the Open Method of Coordination and Other Fashionable Red Herrings." *Perspectives on European Politics and Society*, 7, 108–23.
Johnson, D. (2003). "American Law in Japanese Perspective." *Law & Social Inquiry*, 28, 771.
Kagan, R.A. (1997). "Should Europe Worry About Adversarial Legalism?" *Oxford Journal of Legal Studies*, 17, 165–83.
Kagan, R.A. (2007). "Globalization and Legal Change: The 'Americanization' of European Law?" *Regulation and Governance*, 1, 99–120.
Kelemen, R.D. (2006). "Suing for Europe: Adversarial Legalism and European Governance." *Comparative Political Studies*, 39, 101–27.
Kelemen, R.D. (2008). "The Americanisation of European Law?: Adversarial Legalism *à la Européenne*." *European Political Science*, 7, 32–42.
Kelemen, R.D. (2011). *Eurolegalism: The Transformation of Law and Regulation in the European Union*. Cambridge, MA: Harvard University Press.
Kelemen, R.D. (2012). "Eurolegalism and Democracy." *Journal of Common Market Studies*, 50, 55–71.
Kelemen, R.D. (2013). "Eurolegalism and the European Legal Field." In B. Witte & A. Vauchez (Eds.), *Lawyering in Europe*. Oxford: Hart Publishing, pp. 243–58.
Kelemen, R.D., & Sibbitt, E. (2002). "The Americanization of Japanese Law." *University of Pennsylvania Journal of International Law*, 23, 269.
Kelemen, R.D., & Sibbitt, E. (2004). "The Globalization of American Law." *International Organization*, 58, 103–36.
Mabbett, D. (2011). "A Rights Revolution in Europe? Regulatory and Judicial Approaches to Nondiscrimination in Insurance." LEQS Paper No. 38 (May 30, 2011). Retrieved from http://ssrn.com.
Maher, I. (2000). "Juridification, Modification and Sanction in UK Competition Law." *Modern Law Review*, 63, 544–69.
Meyerstein, A. (2013). "Global Adversarial Legalism: The Private Regulation of FDI as a Species of Global Administrative Law." In M. Audit & S. Schill (Eds.), *The Internationalization of Public Contracts*. Retrieved from https://works.bepress.com/ariel_meyerstein/12/
Nadal, C. (2008). "Pursuing Substantive Environmental Justice: The Aarhus Convention as a 'Pillar' of Empowerment." *Environmental Law Review*, 10, 28.
Nelken, D. (2003). "Beyond Compare? Criticizing 'The American Way of Law.' " *Law & Social Inquiry*, 28, 799.
Rehder, B. (2009). "'Adversarial Legalism' in the German System of Industrial Relations?" *Regulation & Governance*, 3, 217–34.

Short J., & Toffel, M. (2010). "Making Self-Regulation More than Merely Symbolic: The Critical Role of the Legal Environment." *Administrative Science Quarterly*, 55, 361.

Streeck, W., & Thelen, K. (2006). "Introduction: Institutional Change in Advanced Political Economies." In W. Streeck & K. Thelen (Eds.), *Beyond Continuity: Institutional Change in Advanced Political Economies*. Oxford: Oxford University Press, pp. 1–39.

Thatcher, M. (2007). *Internationalisation and Economic Institutions: Comparing European Experiences*. Oxford: Oxford University Press, pp. 168–98.

Van Cleynenbreugel, P. (2014). "*Effectiveness Through Fairness?*: 'Due Process' as Institutional Precondition for Effective Decentralised EU Competition Law Enforcement." Paper prepared for 9th ASCOLA Conference, Warsaw, 2014, on Procedural fairness in competition proceedings, 26–28 June.

van Waarden, F. (2009). "Power to the Legal Professionals: Is There an Americanization of European Law?" *Regulation & Governance*, 3, 197–216.

van Waarden, F., & Hildebrand, Y. (2009). "From Corporatism to Lawyocracy?: On Liberalization and Juridification." *Regulation & Governance*, 3, 259–86.

Vogel, S. (1996). *Freer Markets, More Rules: Regulatory Reform in Advanced Industrialized Countries*. Ithaca, NY: Cornell University Press.

5

COPING WITH AUTO ACCIDENTS IN RUSSIA

Kathryn Hendley

Automobile accidents offer an intriguing arena for studying adversarial legalism in action. The costs of accidents in most polities are usually at least partly socialized through health insurance and disability policies, but in many nations compensation for injuries arising from car crashes also comes from claims made against motorists and their insurers—and those claims often result in disputes that can end up being litigated.

Adversarial legalism decentralizes the enforcement of law, putting it in the hands of everyday citizens. The literature on disputing, though, makes a compelling case that both institutional structures and social attitudes profoundly shape the extent to which citizens mobilize the law. U.S.-based studies have documented the power of insurance companies and their willingness to use their customers' fears of litigating to fashion settlements that favor them (Ross, 1980). Analogous concerns in Japan have contributed to the popularity of mediated settlements (Tanase, 1990).

This chapter focuses on Russia, a setting in which adversarial legalism has not been extensively studied. The many differences in the institutional landscape and history between Russia and most other western countries make it an intriguing case study. The relatively low transaction costs associated with going to court in Russia has made litigating an increasingly popular option, yet my study demonstrates that a host of institutional and attitudinal factors discourage everyday Russians from mobilizing the law.

For much of the 20th century, Russians were spared the tragedies associated with auto accidents because few people had cars. The preference for guns over butter was a defining feature of the Soviet Union. The shortage of cars and other consumer goods was an inevitable consequence. With the collapse of state socialism and the introduction of market mechanisms, cars have become almost as ubiquitous in Russia as elsewhere. The number of accidents has exploded. Indeed, Russia has emerged as a world leader in fatal accidents. On a per capita basis, Russia has almost five times more fatalities than Japan, about three times more than Germany, and about 60 percent more than the U.S. (Belova, 2010).

Like their unfortunate counterparts elsewhere, Russians who have been involved in auto accidents have a range of choices about how to respond. This chapter explores the factors that shape their decisions. I begin with a brief overview of the formal mechanisms available to Russians, laying out their pluses and minuses. I then turn to an analysis of actual behavior, which is grounded in 29 focus groups and 79 follow-up interviews I conducted in five Russian cities (Kushchevskaia, Moscow, Tomsk, Saratov, and Shumerlia) during the summers of 2007 and 2008. These conversations yielded 70 stories about various types of traffic accidents.

In analyzing the experiences of the focus group participants, I make use of the conceptual framework of the "disputing pyramid" laid out by Felstiner, Abel, and Sarat (1980–81). It provides a language and structure for making sense of the process by which people engage (or decline to engage) in adversarial legalism. The first hurdle is "naming," a process of determining whether to recognize an experience as injurious.[1] The second hurdle is "blaming," a process of deciding whether there is a third party who is responsible. The final hurdle is "claiming," a process of deciding whether to seek a remedy from whoever is to blame. This final stage of claiming can be broken into a variety of types of claims. Injured parties may seek out recompense informally in lieu of, or as a prelude to, litigation. The distinctive aspect of adversarial legalism is that the law is only enforced if individuals reach the claiming stage, and only results in formal legal action if the individual is unsatisfied with the outcome of making a claim.

The pyramid is a useful image. The main finding of this body of research is that most disagreements fall away at the base. The value of the model lies in its focus on the reasons why disagreements do or do not grow into full-fledged disputes. While not losing sight of the role played by the nature of the disagreement and the relationship between the parties, Felstiner et al. identify a number of factors that act as transformational agents by facilitating or discouraging the transition of disputes from one stage to another. Key among these is the worldview of the injured parties which, in turn, is influenced by their religion, class, prior experiences with the legal system, and the underlying legal culture. From an institutional perspective, lawyers, who act as gatekeepers, emerge as especially important at the final stage of claiming.

The model of the disputing pyramid was developed with the U.S. in mind, and sociolegal scholarship on the U.S. has used it to good effect (e.g., Calavita & Jenness, 2013; Albiston, 2005; Engel & Munger, 2003; Merry, 1990). The basic logic, however, transcends the U.S. experience. The model has been used to elucidate disputing behavior in Canada (Kritzer et al., 1991), China (Michelson, 2007), and Thailand (Engel, 2005). I have previously employed it in the Russian context to explore disputing behavior regarding overdue payments between industrial enterprises during the 1990s (Hendley, 2001), and the decision-making process of homeowners who were left dissatisfied by home repair projects (Hendley, 2010). Though the basic pyramidal structure of disputing is universal, the motivations for moving forward or abandoning a dispute are deeply contextual. Variation in the structure of legal institutions and in legal culture leads to differences in individuals' willingness to mobilize the law.

The Process of Auto Accident Claiming in Russia

Russian law requires those involved in an auto accident to report it to the traffic police. In contrast to Japan, where such officials have earned a high level of societal respect, the Russian traffic police are uniformly seen as deeply corrupt.[2] Russian websites publish city-specific price lists of the amounts that need to be paid based on the alleged offense (Heofitsial'nye, n.d.).[3] In an effort to curtail bribes, the rules about traffic tickets have been revised. Violators no longer pay the traffic police directly, but are now given a ticket and asked to pay via bank transfer. This reform has done little to curb abuses. Alleged violators are typically offered two prices. If they hand over cash to the officer, then the amount is reduced. But there is no documentary record of the transaction and, not surprisingly, this money goes directly into the officer's pocket.[4] Those who want to abide by the law can insist on getting a ticket and paying it at their bank. Few bother. Not only do they see little value in upholding laws that the police themselves are openly flouting, but doing so requires them to stand in line at their bank (Zernova, 2012, p. 481).

If those involved in an accident wait for the traffic police, then the traffic police will produce a report that details what happened and who was at fault. This report becomes the centerpiece of any formal process, whether the venue is an insurance company or a court. If a driver disagrees with the assessment of the traffic police, he or she has the right to challenge it in court.

But before contemplating litigation, most Russians seek compensation for their losses through their insurance policies. Much like the abundant supply of cars, private insurance companies are a post-Soviet phenomenon. Indeed, Soviet officials were openly hostile to the very idea of liability insurance. They argued that "it would be entirely destructive of the moral functions of civil liability and that a man who insured beforehand his carelessness was either half-intending it or, at least, not trying strenuously to avoid it" (Tay, 1969, p. 15). The elaborate social safety net left the Soviet state as the primary insurer.[5] With the legalization of private property as part of the transition to the market, however, the role of the state has changed. It continues to provide basic medical insurance, but private insurance companies have stepped in to protect property interests. As to motorists, insurance became mandatory in 2003 (Ob obiazatel'nom, 2002). Drivers are required to have a minimal policy for collisions, for which the rates are set by the state, but are free to buy supplemental insurance. Russians' concern about the high incidence of traffic accidents led them to be generally supportive of the move to mandatory insurance.[6]

In their relatively short lives, Russian insurance companies have already managed to follow in the footsteps of their western counterparts by earning the disdain of their clients. Most Russians find insurance companies unresponsive at best, manipulative at worst. Initially, victims of traffic accidents had to seek compensation from the insurance company of the driver at fault, which had little interest in whether these victims were satisfied with their services. In 2009, the rules were changed to allow those involved in accidents to work directly with their own insurance companies.[7] Tales of foot-dragging by insurance companies persist in the Russian press and on web forums, on which people share their experiences and offer advice. More troubling are claims of systematic efforts to minimize claims by co-opting supposedly independent appraisers. When policy holders were asked in 2012 by the National Agency for Financial Research why they had switched insurance companies, concerns with service were a close second behind increases in premiums.[8]

Those who are dissatisfied with the amount recovered from their insurance companies can appeal to the courts. Such cases take several forms. Individuals can sue their insurance companies for violating their policies. Individuals can also take the other driver(s) to court to pursue either civil or criminal remedies. Not infrequently, insurance companies sue each other to recover the amounts they have paid out to their clients.

The persistence of high-profile politicized cases in which the outcome is dictated by the Kremlin rather than the law (e.g., Mikhail Khodorkovsky, Pussy Riot) has compromised the overall independence of the Russian courts. Yet use of the courts has increased markedly in the post-Soviet era. As I have argued elsewhere, Russians are able to distinguish disputes in which litigation is likely to be productive from those in which it is counterproductive (Hendley, 2011). They know that it's pointless to involve the courts in disputes that attract the attention of political leaders, or that concern economic elites. But Russian courts scrupulously follow the law in mundane cases (Hendley, 2017). Claims arising from injuries sustained in auto accidents fall into this category, and the number of cases related to traffic accidents has increased.[9] (See Table 5.1, p. 118.)

This has been facilitated in part by major changes in legal doctrine in the post-Soviet years. Within the Soviet legal system, tort law was a mostly unwanted stepchild. In the heady years following the October Revolution, Communist Party officials saw tort law as a vestige of the past (Hazard, 1952). They believed that comprehensive social insurance would obviate the need for private causes of action.[10] By 1922, cooler heads prevailed, and a chapter on tort law was included in the civil code (chapter 13, 1922 GK). It was drawn from a never-enacted czarist draft that, in turn, had been based on German law. The 1964 civil code made few changes in the area of tort law. Compensatory damages were available when a petitioner could demonstrate harm caused by another. Punitive damages were not allowed; they were seen as a "bourgeois legal institution" that amounted to unjust enrichment (Barry, 1996, p. 183). Driving a car was a fairly unusual activity, and it was deemed to be an inherently dangerous activity that triggered strict liability (article 454, GK 1964). Liability attached to the driver of the car rather than the owner, which was a clever way for the state to avoid liability, given that most cars were the property of Soviet state-owned enterprises (Barry, 1967, p. 76). But tort claims of any stripe were not numerous (Barry, 1979, p. 237).

The elimination of strict liability for auto accidents in the post-Soviet civil code (article 1079, GK RF part 2) opened the door to liability insurance.[11] Insurance companies are only obligated to pay damages in cases of fault. As a result, formal admissions of fault have profound legal consequences. Where neither or both sides acknowledge responsibility, insurance companies often refuse to pay (Arakcheev, 2008). Thus situations where the traffic police are unwilling or unable to determine fault are particularly vexing.

The Soviet-era ban on punitive damages has also disappeared. Though the chapter on torts is silent on this issue, the general provisions of the post-Soviet civil code are amenable to so-called moral damages (article 151, GK RF). Judges have considerable discretion in setting the amount. They are directed to take into account the nature of the plaintiff's suffering and the nature of the defendant's actions. The amounts available are trivial compared to the huge sums awarded by U.S. juries in egregious torts claims.[12]

Responses to Involvement in Auto Accidents

Traffic accidents are, by definition, jarring. It is not surprising that all of the focus group participants who reported accidents recognized the experience as injurious. They have "named" the injury. This stands to reason, given that being in an auto accident is by its very nature upsetting at best and life-threatening at near worst. It is at the next steps of the disputing pyramid that the focus group participants took different paths.

Doing Nothing or "Lumping It"

In 27 of the 70 accidents reported, the victims made no effort to seek a remedy. Doing nothing is a common, but under-studied, response to problems. Even in the U.S., with a populace that prides itself on defending its rights, Sandefur (2007, pp. 123–125) found that many opt for inaction when faced with problems that could be solved by mobilizing the law. She identifies three general reasons for opting out: (1) feelings of shame and embarrassment; (2) an unfavorable balance of power in the parties' relationships; and (3) frustrated resignation. These motivations turn out to be useful categories when analyzing the behavior of my Russian focus group participants.

One subset was stymied because they believed they were partially to blame for the accident, giving rise to a sense of embarrassment about the incident. As a result, they did not feel entitled to blame the driver. The basic fact pattern was the same for all these cases. The victims were hit while crossing the road in an unofficial crosswalk, sustaining serious injuries. A Saratov woman told of an elderly relative with failing eyesight who was killed after being struck by a car in St. Petersburg. Miroslava; a 40-year-old seamstress from Shumerlia, who had been struck when she was in the third grade, still walked with a limp. Neither the focus group members nor the victim-participants themselves felt much empathy. The fact that the victims were mostly children and the elderly, who are universally seen as among the most vulnerable in any society, made their lack of compassion striking. For the most part, the victim-participants took responsibility for their fates.

Intertwined with the shame felt by these victims at their stupidity was a belief that their negligence eliminated any chance of recovery. As a result, they did not allow themselves to ponder who to blame or how to claim. The other members of the focus groups shared this understanding of the law. The most extreme example was provided by Regina, a 55-year old cleaning woman from Shumerlia. Some years ago, her eight-year-old daughter had been hit while crossing the road by two soldiers driving a Moskvich.[13] The soldiers brought her home. They offered to take her to the hospital and to provide monetary compensation for the young girl's injuries. Regina declined, explaining that her daughter had probably not been paying sufficient attention. She understood that the soldiers felt bad, but did not believe they were responsible. As Regina told her story, others around the table nodded in agreement.

In reality, however, the situation was not as straightforward as the focus group participants believed. Russian law embraces comparative negligence (article 1083, GK RF part 2). In theory, this means that even if the pedestrian is found to be partly at fault, the driver might still be liable for some proportion of the pedestrian's injuries. In fact, courts are generally unforgiving when dealing with drivers who hit pedestrians. In such situations, the law reverts back to the Soviet rule for strict liability. Though several of the focus groups included people with legal education, no one spoke up to correct this misimpression. None of them had bothered to consult the law on this question. Yet their confidence in the unavailability of a legal remedy was complete, illustrating that sometimes what people believe the law to be can take on a life of its own (Hendley, 2010; Ellickson, 1991).

Others opted to do nothing, as Sandefur suggests, because their accidents had been with people more powerful and well connected. These participants engaged in blaming, but saw the power differential as blocking any potential for claiming. For example, David, a 25-year-old security guard from Kushchevskaia, was involved in a hit-and-run accident that sent him to the hospital. At the time, he was a soldier doing his mandatory service. Initially he hoped to get the other driver to cover the cost of his medicine. When it turned out that the culprit was the former police chief of a nearby town, the traffic police advised him to drop it. As he told the story, there was an implicit threat that the repercussions of pursuing a claim would be worse for him than for the driver at fault. He took the hint, saying that this sort of outcome was typical for Russia.

A power differential between drivers with no official government connections can play out in the same way. In the wake of the transition to the market, private firms and their leaders have gained great clout (Kryshtanovskaya & White, 2005). Several focus group members shared their difficulties in this regard. Vladimir, a 51-year-old Moscow mechanic, sustained a concussion and was on bed rest for over a month after a 3 A.M. collision with a ZIL 130 truck that belonged to the powerful Mikoyan machine-building factory.[14] The driver admitted to speeding at the time of the accident. Unlike the pedestrian-victims who felt their negligence barred them from seeking a remedy, Vladimir's failure to take action was due to his belief that fighting the factory was "useless." The behavior of the traffic police at the scene only confirmed his sense of the political reality. Their report favored the truck driver. When the other focus group participants said that the driver from the Mikoyan factory had probably paid off the police, Vladimir did not disagree. Indeed, no one in the group faulted Vladimir for not pursuing the case. Several shared their own feelings of impotency. Ida, a 40-year-old Muscovite who worked as a chief accountant for a private firm, spoke for many when she said that Russians "have nowhere to go that guarantees a positive result." A few held out hope that the introduction of mandatory insurance would cure the sorts of difficulties faced by Vladimir, whose accident occurred before the law requiring all drivers to be insured had been passed.

Most accidents involve at least two drivers, and so a decision to do nothing does not necessarily act as a shield if the other driver decides to pursue the matter. When Elvira, a 44-year-old state bureaucrat, was hit while parked on a Saratov street, she resolved to do nothing when she learned that the other driver was the general director of a local furniture factory. She was convinced that he would be able to outgun her in court. To her surprise, the driver claimed that he was the victim and demanded 15,000 rubles, arguing that she opened her door with no warning. Finding this claim absurd, she ignored it, and found herself a defendant in a court case. Much like Vladimir, she saw the bias of the traffic police as fueling the claim. Though all the witnesses said the other driver was at fault, the police report stated that it was mutual fault. This opened the door for the lawsuit. We will return to this incident when discussing how courts deal with claims related to auto accidents. The point here is that doing nothing requires mutual assent.

Many of those who talked themselves out of pursuing a claim feared the possible backlash from more powerful counterparts. Though resignation can sometimes mask deeper anger, this was not the sense conveyed. Neither those directly affected nor others in the focus groups lashed out against the injustice of the system. Rather, there was a collective shrug and a rhetorical "What can be done?"

"Frustrated resignation," Sandefur's phrase, arose from several sources. Some felt that the damage to their car or to themselves wasn't serious enough to warrant further action. In other words, the costs, typically measured in terms of wear and tear on their psyche, outweighed the potential benefits. Others were reluctant to go to war with adversaries that had greater resources, such as municipal authorities or insurance companies.[15] Even when they felt they had been swindled by their insurance companies, few relished the prospect of suing them. The most common refrain was that to do so would be "useless." Some felt stymied due to the boilerplate language buried in their insurance policies. Anatolii, a 51-year-old midlevel manager from Tomsk, told of the aftermath of an accident involving a minivan owned by his wife. The van was used in her business; it was intended to be driven primarily by her employees, one of whom was driving it at the time of the accident. The traffic police found her employee to be at fault. Anatolii and his wife did not dispute this finding. Initially they thought the damage to the van would be covered by insurance. His wife had purchased comprehensive insurance with an eye to just this sort of situation, but learned to her chagrin that her policy did not include other drivers. When they purchased the insurance, no one pointed this out to them. Anatolii attributed this to the negligence of the insurance agent, but admitted that neither he nor his wife had read the policy carefully. This being the case, they felt they had no recourse. The other members of the group commiserated. Some had gone through similar experiences. All agreed that they routinely signed contracts without reading them.[16] The bottom line was that the insurance company had no obligation to compensate them. Anatolii and his wife were left holding the bag. He was resigned to his fate, saying, "Such is life."

Negotiation With the Other Driver

A common response to accidents in Russia is to talk to the other driver in hopes of working out an informal accommodation. It proved popular among the focus group participants, half of whom took this route. Because the parties were almost always strangers, establishing trust was difficult. What all those who sought to negotiate a settlement shared—regardless of whether their efforts were successful or not—was a firm belief about who was to blame, a desire for a remedy, and the willingness to approach a stranger to claim it. Put in terms of the Felstiner et al. typology, they were "claiming" (1980—81). The remedies were not always monetary. Sometimes victims simply wanted an apology or an acknowledgment from the other driver of having been at fault. When money was at issue, the amounts were not exorbitant.

Negotiations suggest a willingness to forgo punishment. In theory, settlement did not preclude criminal charges. But the stories elicited from the focus group participants suggest that the purpose of releases—whether written or oral—was to settle all claims. This, of course, raises an ethical dilemma as to whether a driver should be able to escape criminal liability. When the injuries are minor, moral compunctions tend to be ignored. But when they are life-threatening, some are troubled by allowing the driver to sidestep criminal responsibility.

The discussion in one of the Saratov focus groups is instructive. Filipp, a 22-year-old salesman, told of a recent incident in which several of his friends were badly injured. In the revelry following their university graduation, several of his friends got into a car driven by a young man whom they did not know. All of them were drunk. The driver wrapped his car around a telephone pole. He was not injured, but his passengers were. One young woman was in a coma for eight days. The other had a fractured hip and a variety of internal injuries. According to Filipp, the driver approached the families of the victims with a generous settlement offer. Representatives from the prosecutor's office encouraged settlement, hinting that their drunkenness could complicate any prosecution. Some focus group participants were pragmatic about this story. They said that, were they in the unfortunate shoes of the families, they would take the money, noting that it could be helpful in paying for treatment. More generally, they argued that pursuing criminal sanctions should take a backseat to restoring those injured to full health; they would prefer to spend their time and energy focused on their own recovery or advocating for loved ones rather than badgering the police to go after the other driver. Filipp reported that the parents of these young women were preoccupied with their medical care. On the other hand, despite criticizing his friends for getting into the car, Filipp was unforgiving when it came to the driver: "It seems to me that he's done something horrible—he's endangered the lives of others. One girl may be an invalid for her entire life, if she survives. He's a grown-up and needs to answer for his behavior."

As in the U.S., many of those involved in auto accidents prefer to avoid involving their insurance companies. Unlike in the U.S., however, the rationale is not connected to fears over increased premiums. Most Russians have only the basic policy for which the rates are set by the state, so Russians try to settle on the spot to avoid having to go through the bureaucracy of their insurance companies.

Gennadii, who works as a department head in an industrial enterprise, was traveling in a Volga with several colleagues, one of whom was driving. When they tried to overtake a Moskvich at high speed, the driver lost control and smashed into the other car. The Volga landed in a ditch. According to Gennadii, no one involved had any interest in going the official route due to the inevitable paperwork involved. Neither side called the traffic police, though they showed up, as did a local television news crew. In order to put a stop to any potential claims, one of Gennadii's colleagues simply bought the damaged Moskvich from the other driver. No receipts were exchanged. It was an oral agreement, but everyone left satisfied. The other driver was badly hurt; the payment for his car was presumably intended to cover any incidental medical expenses as well. Gennadii implies that the traffic police and the camera crew were paid to hush up the accident. The other members of this Tomsk focus group were entirely supportive of his handling of the incident.

In situations where physical injuries were profound, the assistance provided by the driver at fault sometimes took a more practical form. Fatima, a 25-year-old student who worked at a charitable organization, saw her life turned upside down when she accidentally hit a teenager crossing a busy street in Moscow. Fatima was stuck in traffic. Next to her was a large truck. As she was inching along in a crosswalk, she failed to see the teen darting through the maze of traffic. The girl sustained a compound fracture of her leg. During the months she spent in the hospital, Fatima was a constant presence, bringing food to sustain her and her mother (who was single with another child to support as well). She also provided over $3,000 to ensure that the girl received first-rate treatment and to cover her tuition for higher education, money that she raised by selling her car. At first, the family refused to talk to Fatima. As she put it, "The mother wanted to strangle me." After four months of apologies and material support, she wore the mother down, but the teenager never wavered. During the frosty period, the family filed a civil suit against Fatima and supported the police in pursuing criminal charges. By the time these lawsuits were set for trial, relations had thawed and the family withdrew its civil claim and asked the court for lenience in the criminal case.

Viktoria, a 44-year-old Tomsk teacher, was hit while crossing a crowded street in 2001. The driver was immediately surrounded by witnesses. Much like Fatima, he said that he never saw her. She was not as badly hurt as the Moscow teen, but did sustain a concussion and later needed surgery to repair her leg. During the three months of her recovery, the driver was vigilant. When she was unable to walk, he carried her in his arms to his car and took her to her treatments. He paid for her treatment. In her words, "He did everything to ensure my recovery and to make amends." After three months, when she was literally back on her feet, he offered her a final payment of 10,000 rubles and asked her to sign a release of liability. She went along. By that time, they had developed what she described as a "human relationship" (*chelovecheskoe otnoshenie*). She had no desire to ruin his life by going to the traffic police and bringing a criminal case that, at a minimum, would cause him to lose his license (which he needed for his job) for a sustained period.

In the discussion of cases like Viktoria's, the focus groups were openly suspicious of the motives of the do-gooders. The groups doubted their sincerity and believed that their help was cynically motivated to ensure that the victims forgo legal action against them. The analysis of failed efforts at negotiation shows that Russia has its share of unscrupulous con men who promise the world only to disappear into thin air. Fatima provides some insight into how this happens. After her accident, she sought out a lawyer to help her sort through her options. He offered to help her create an alibi to avoid liability that would stand up in court. He counseled her against going to see the teenage victim in the hospital and assured her that the girl would be helped with a generous "gift" in due course. The combination of the accident and her encounter with this lawyer gave rise to a "road to Damascus" conversion for Fatima. Raised as a secular Muslim, she converted to Christianity and thereafter devoted her life to charitable work. She fired the lawyer and resolved to do right by the girl.[17] She explicitly linked her choices to her faith, saying that Christians do not bribe their way out of problems: "If a person has forgotten about God, he lives however he wants. If a person is a believer, then he does not budge; he is like stone. Of course, there can be exceptions. But I know of many people who will not betray their beliefs for any amount of money." She had the moral fiber to stand up to temptation, but not everyone does.

A number of participants in the focus groups told of unfulfilled promises. Most common were promises of money that never materialized. When this happened in the wake of a fender-bender, the victim learned a lesson about human nature but was not unduly harmed. More problematic are accidents that give rise to serious physical injuries, where the broken promises undermine the ability of victims to secure first-rate medical treatment. What happened to Anton, a 31-year-old geologist from Saratov, is a tragic example. Several years before, when he was a college student, he was waiting at a railroad crossing when a car came barreling out of a nearby gas station and hit him. He lost consciousness. When he awoke, he was in the hospital with a shattered pelvis. The mother of the other driver, who was also a student, came to see him. She explained that her son had no money, but promised that her family would take care of everything for Anton if he signed a release. Once he signed, the mother and her son disappeared. Anton's initial treatment was botched. He was in and out of hospitals and on crutches for the next three years. In reflecting on what happened, Anton acknowledges that he probably could have pursued the other driver in court, but says that it would have been unlikely to produce a windfall, given that he was a student. His main concern at the time was not punishing the other driver or his mother, but getting better. Though as an agnostic, he does not attribute his behavior to his religious beliefs, like Fatima, he is satisfied that he behaved fairly.

Sometimes it is the victims themselves who are the scam artists. The Russian media is replete with stories of people who make a good living by jumping in front of cars and pretending to be more seriously injured than they are. Examples of ham-handed practitioners of this art can be found on the internet. One goal of introducing mandatory insurance was to discourage this practice. Whether it has succeeded is difficult to know. The desire of many to avoid interacting with their insurance companies leaves them vulnerable. Liubov, a 56-year-old Muscovite who works as the chief accountant at a small factory, was with her husband when they hit an elderly man with their new car. He had been in his own car, but jumped out. He injured his head; blood was everywhere. Liubov and her husband felt bad. When the old man and his daughter called to ask for money and help, they initially gave them money. Her husband also brought food to the man. But as the demands became more frequent and the amounts increased, they grew suspicious. They began to tape his calls. When he asked for $10,000, they played the tape for the police. The investigation was terminated and the requests stopped. No doubt many people lack the common sense and courage exhibited by Liubov and her husband, and so are held hostage to the demands of pseudo-victims. It is likely not coincidental that they were driving a new car when this happened. These con artists target those whom they perceive as rich, assuming they have greater access to money and a strong desire to avoid the criminal courts.

Bribery can color the options available to the parties. When Ida's daughter was hit on New Year's Day in 2006, she sustained an open fracture of her right hip and leg. Ida spoke candidly of how the doctors and nurses told her that they would provide aggressive treatment only if she paid them under the table. Not only did she have to navigate a corrupt medical system, she also felt the consequences of corruption in her treatment by the legal system. Her daughter had been in a *zebra*, a designated crosswalk when she was hit. The driver, who was from Azerbaijan, was speeding and made little effort to brake for her. When Ida met him, his wife offered to pay her $1000 to hush up the incident. It was Ida's understanding that the driver himself did not speak Russian. She refused the money, not because she was squeamish about accepting a payoff, but because she was not yet sure how much her daughter's treatment would cost. In quick order, the Azerbaijani couple vanished along with their offer. The indifferent attitude of the traffic police left Ida convinced that the money had gone to them. Some months later, she coincidentally got a job working for a procurator. He insisted that she hire a lawyer to pursue the case. Proving what happened has not been easy. At the time of the focus group, she was discouraged, saying that she had probably wasted her money on the lawyer. As this suggests, not all failed negotiations end with the victim doing nothing, like Anton. Sometimes such failures are merely a way station on the path to litigation.

Settlement With Insurers

For some auto accident victims an insurance payment resolved their claim. The incidents recounted during the focus groups spanned the time period before and after the imposition of compulsory insurance. There is no question that few Russians bothered to obtain insurance before they were required to do so. Indeed, a majority of Russian drivers continue to flout the law ("Strakhovanie postepenno vozvrashchaetsia," 2012). But for those who did have insurance, most were able to get paid. Not all came away satisfied by the experience, but only one of the focus group participants was sufficiently disgruntled to pursue her claim to the courts.

Not surprisingly, those who had purchased comprehensive insurance (rather than the minimal compulsory policy), were more likely to be content.[18] Yet even this group complained about the endless red tape. Vladislava grumbled about being forced to do the legwork for the insurance company, and was insulted when her agent left her with the impression that she was somehow to blame for the damage to her car, even though she had been hit by a drunk driver. She was also dissatisfied with the amount she received. In her words, "I tried to complain within the insurance company .... But it was to no avail—I was stuck with their procedures. They didn't help me. I came away disappointed in insurance companies generally."

The idea of suing the insurance company was unappealing. "I understood that my health was more valuable and decided not to initiate a lawsuit."

Those who had only compulsory insurance were uniformly dissatisfied, both with the way they were treated and with their payouts. They felt that their insurance companies had co-opted the so-called independent appraisers to underestimate the cost of repairs. Several told of how they got their estimates bumped up by bribing these appraisers. None of them thought it was worth the effort to litigate.

Litigation

Going to court was no one's first choice. It represented a grudging response to an inability to resolve problems through negotiation. Taking on a lawsuit required a strong commitment, regardless of whether the target was an individual or an entity. Despite the clarity of the procedural rules, which opens the door to self-representation, many hired lawyers to help them. Even so, they took on much of the responsibility for assembling the bits and pieces of evidence needed to prevail. Proof problems were the most commonly cited obstacle to going to court—it was a much bigger concern than fears of politicized justice.

Not surprisingly, those who took this route were stubborn characters. Petitioners typically describe themselves as being driven by principle more than money, which makes sense given that the amounts recoverable are rather modest, at least by U.S. standards. Likewise, the targets of these lawsuits use every trick in the book to escape liability. After all, if the parties were open to amicable settlement, the case would not have gotten to court. A somewhat extreme example is the behavior of the driver who hit Katya, a 20-year-old Saratov university student. He plowed into her, sending her car flying across several lanes of traffic, where it was stopped by a tree. He and his family walked away from the incident, but Katya was knocked unconscious and spent several months recovering in the hospital. The traffic police report declared him to be at fault, but he refused to acknowledge responsibility and made no effort to contact her. She tried to get criminal charges brought against him, but because he had not been drunk and she had survived the accident, the police were uninterested. She then resolved "to beat him up financially." For Katya, this was a matter of principle. In her words, "My parents told me to let it go . . . but I have such strong resentment and pain that I had to pursue it."

The lawsuit turned into a soap opera. Acting on the recommendation of friends, she located a lawyer to whom she paid a 20,000-ruble retainer. They agreed that the lawyer would also get 15 percent of any amount recovered. The complaint sought 1 million rubles in moral damages. It is doubtful that she had any realistic expectations of recovering anything close to that amount. Not only are Russian courts disinclined to award such large amounts, but the driver was a schoolteacher with a monthly salary of 4,000 rubles. In addition, anticipating a lawsuit, he had transferred all his assets (including his apartment) into his wife's name. When he received the complaint, he made an abortive suicide attempt and checked himself into a psychiatric facility, where he was beyond the reach of the courts. When we spoke, 18 months had elapsed since the incident, but he was still there. Katya's lawyers had tried to convince the judge of his bad faith. She was sympathetic but told them that the case could not go forward until the defendant was declared legally competent. She ordered an independent psychiatric evaluation, but it was carried out by the same doctor who had been treating the defendant, and came to the same conclusion. Over the months of waiting, Katya's ardor dimmed, but she was reluctant to abandon the case due to the money she had already put into it. Her belief in the ability of courts to right wrongs—which made her a bit of an outlier among the focus group participants—also kept her in the game.[19] But she did not view herself as an exception. As she said, "I think I am not the only person who believes in the law."

Sometimes litigation can be part of a grieving process. Anna, a 40-year-old Moscow real estate agent, was in a horrific accident in which she lost control of her car when a drunk driver darted into her lane of traffic. Her car flipped over several times. Her brother, who was a passenger in the car, had to be cut out of the car by emergency technicians. He died without regaining consciousness. Anna spent six months recovering in the hospital, and was unable to return to work for another several months. The other driver and his family received only minor injuries. They never contacted her to express their regret. Nor did they attend her brother's funeral. Though she had their contact information, she did not reach out. She felt that their behavior telegraphed their character.

No one questioned the responsibility of the other driver. He was prosecuted and received a three-year sentence for drunk driving. But seeing the other driver in jail was not enough for Anna. She brought a civil lawsuit against him in an effort to recover her out-of-pocket expenses for medical care. She had been forced to pay under the table to get needed medications and to ensure she had the best surgeons. Unlike Katya, she did not hire a lawyer. Though she had a law degree herself, she had no litigation experience. In reflecting on the court case, she speculated that she might have done better had she had help from legal professionals, but noted the difficulty of finding reputable lawyers. The experience of her friends left her convinced that good lawyers were very expensive. She explained that any spare financial resources had gone to pay for her brother's funeral and her own medical expenses.

Though Anna won the lawsuit, she received no emotional closure from the experience. It only seemed to intensify her grief over her brother's death. She recovered 5,000 rubles, which was a small fraction of her actual medical expenses. The court took the formalistic position that medical care in Russia is free, thereby placing the burden on her to prove her financial outlays. She found the demands of the court for documentary evidence of her side payments to medical personnel to be unrealistic and humiliating. She felt pressured by the judge to drop the case and believed that the other side had bribed the judge. In contrast to Katya,

Anna did not trust in the integrity of the legal system, arguing that "any judge can be bought." She concluded: "It is sad to live in a state where we are completely unprotected, where we have no hope."

In the focus groups, I heard only one instance of a lawsuit against an insurance company rather than a driver. Kira, a 52-year-old bookkeeper from Tomsk, was a passenger in the family car being driven to the family's dacha by her husband. When they were going through a green light at a traffic intersection, they were hit by a foreign-made car that seemingly came out of nowhere. Their car was totaled. There were four people in the other car, each of whom had been drinking. The other car sped off after the accident, but was quickly apprehended. The traffic police said they were unable to determine who had been driving. Kira believes that this was a subterfuge designed to protect an influential local military official.

In any event, Russian law requires a determination of who was driving before an insurance company is required to pay. The insurance company clung to the letter of the law and refused to make a settlement. Kira and her husband found a lawyer to represent them who was a coworker of their daughter. The lawyer explained what sort of evidence would be needed. Her husband then tracked it down, wooing witnesses to come forward with traditional Russian gifts of wine and candy. Thanks to the help of the lawyer, they prevailed at trial, only to face an appeal, which they also won. In the end, they had to resort to the bailiffs (*sudebnye pristavy*) to recover the judgment of 32,000 rubles. This amount was not sufficient to buy a new car outright. They used a third of it as a down payment on a loan. They used another third to pay the lawyer.[20] The lawyer made no financial demands on them, but they were convinced that they could not have succeeded without her help, and so insisted that she take the money.

Though the experience was not pleasant—the litigation dragged on for 18 months and required them to persist through "terrible red tape"—Kira felt the insurance company gave them no choice. She insisted they were motivated by justice and not by a desire to punish. In her words, they pressed forward because they "decided that the law was on our side. Plus we weren't to blame." In terms of her trust in the legal system, she falls somewhere between the extremes of Katya and Anna. She felt that they got justice from the courts, and did not see their experience as an aberration.[21] The other members of her focus group were generally supportive of her choices. Several chimed in to say that the only way to get an insurance company to pay was to sue. Others said that they too would have sued in Kira's situation, but might have refrained if the amount at stake were less significant. Everyone—including Kira—was bothered by the fact that the identity of the driver was never established.

Of the participants in the focus groups, only Elvira ended up having to go through the full process as a defendant. As I noted earlier, she believed herself to have been the victim and had resolved not to pursue her claim. The status differential was a key factor in her decision. The other driver was the general director of a local furniture factory, whereas she saw herself as a lowly state bureaucrat.

Unfortunately, the other driver viewed himself as the aggrieved party and pursued her as a matter of principle. They met several times. She made him aware that her husband had connections to the local procurator's office in an effort to equalize their status, but he paid no attention.[22] When he would not budge from his initial demand, she said they would have to leave it to the court. Sure enough, he brought a lawsuit against her in the justice-of-the-peace courts.

Elvira felt out of her element in the court. As the case proceeded, she believed that the judge consistently favored the other side, allowing him to go on at length, while cutting her off. She had the help of an "assistant" (*pomoshchnik*), who was a recent law graduate. She met with several more experienced lawyers who specialized in litigating traffic cases, but their price was too steep for her. She did not bring a counterclaim to assert her version of what happened, explaining that she feared the expense of doing so. The decision went against her. Because she lacked the funds to pay the judgment, a portion of her salary was garnished.

In reflecting on the experience, Elvira listed a series of strategic mistakes she had made. Even though she had few assets, her initial instinct had been to give the other driver what he wanted, but her assistant convinced her to stand firm. In her words: "I am sorry that I didn't just give him the money right away because the court hearings were unpleasant. If you go to court, you end up feeling guilty." She did not see the judicial process as being even-handed. She felt that the judge and the plaintiff were part of an insiders' circle to which she was not privy. In her view, "If I had been within this circle, then probably it would have been seen as mutual fault." If she had it to do over, she would make every effort to avoid the courts. If that proved impossible, then she would hire a lawyer, who would "guarantee victory." Put more bluntly, she would find a lawyer who had the backdoor connections needed to bribe the judge. Though not convinced that the judge in her case was bribed, she believed that the law itself was a peripheral issue. In her opinion, the outcome was dictated by connections.

Explaining Russians' Responses to Auto Accidents

On the most prosaic level, the seriousness of the injuries sustained in an accident explains the responses. This is hardly unique to Russia. Regardless of the setting, people tend to have different reactions to minor fender-benders than to crashes in which cars are destroyed and life-threatening injuries are sustained. The evidence from the focus group confirms that Russians are more likely to "lump it" when the damages are insignificant. But there are many other factors at play, both institutional and individual. Many are carryovers from the Soviet past, while some are new to the post-Soviet era.

Thinking more deeply about why some Russians do nothing and others pursue their causes with a Javert-like intensity requires us to return to the theoretical framework of Felstiner et al. (1980–81). They identify a series of possible transformational factors that can have the effect of pushing the problem from one stage to another. Their analysis focuses on the U.S., but many of the factors are universal. The genius of their approach is that it incorporates both individual and social factors.

Worldviews

Felstiner et al. (1980–81) posit that how one looks at the world will have a profound effect on one's approach to problem-solving. As part of the transition away from state socialism, Russians have come to feel increasingly isolated. For many, the collapse of state services in the 1990s shattered their faith in the ability of the state to protect them. Their social support networks frayed as people scrambled to support their families when the Soviet-era practice of featherbedding disappeared with the imposition of market incentives. Inflation evaporated the pensions of the elderly, forcing many of them back onto the job market and leaving them unavailable for their traditional role of assisting with child care. The shattering of longtime norms after the Soviet era has left many unsure of what is right or wrong. I suspect that this effect is more deeply felt among older generations, though the unrepresentative nature of my focus groups does not allow for the testing of this hypothesis.

Whether post-Soviet Russian society has developed a clear set of norms that govern behavior in the aftermath of an auto accident is unclear. As I noted at the outset of the chapter, the proliferation of cars is a relatively recent phenomenon, which means that those who are unfortunate enough to be in an accident cannot think back on how their parents or grandparents handled it. For most, it is an entirely new experience, and many respondents felt as though that they were on their own. They relied on themselves and on immediate family members. Some were frightened by the idea of contacting law enforcement, fearing that doing so would not end favorably. This sense of isolation, which may have been latent in the Soviet era, has become a powerful motivating force in present-day Russia, especially in large metropolises (Shevchenko, 2009).

Self-reliance is a double-edged sword. It can express itself in a single-minded determination that makes all the difference in dealing with bureaucracies. After her brother was killed by a drunk driver, Anna said that "no one wanted to do anything." Many of the focus group participants felt similarly ignored and marginalized by officialdom. Kira knew no one else would help her get the money she was owed by her insurance company, and pressed forward to the court with her claim. But individualism can also express itself as selfishness. Anton's desperate need for help in recovering was ignored. When the mother of the perpetrator was negotiating with Anton, she stressed her son's student status and his consequent lack of resources, conveniently ignoring that Anton was also a penniless student at the time. Such behavior reflects a hardness of heart that may be a quasi-survivalist response to the economic chaos of the 1990s. Katya's case shows how self-reliance can sometimes result in a stalemate. Ignoring her parents' advice to move on, Katya pursued a scorched-earth strategy, filing a million-ruble lawsuit. The other driver responded in kind by transferring his assets to his wife and feigning mental illness.

Although they felt isolated, in fact many of the focus group participants drew on their membership in communities to help them through the experience. These ranged from the family at the micro-level to the community of believers at a more cosmic level. Turning again to Anton's experience, the other driver benefited from being part of a family that was determined to preserve his options in life. Anton's family was no less concerned with his future, but his precarious physical condition took up all their energy. Along similar lines, Ida's identity as a mother led her to do whatever was necessary, including bribing medical personnel, to ensure that her young daughter did not become an invalid. Her priority was her daughter's recovery rather than seeking out and punishing the Azerbaijani couple who were to blame. Some Russians have turned to religion as a way of making sense of their feelings of isolation.[23] In ordering their behavior, these believers are mindful of the Golden Rule of doing to others as you would have them do unto you. Fatima, who grew up as a secular Muslim but embraced Christianity in the form of the Russian Orthodox Church after injuring a teenager with her car, is a good example of how genuine religiosity can lead to remarkably unselfish behavior.

Being an outsider also influenced behavior. For the focus group members, such feelings mostly served as a deterrent to disputing. A number of them did nothing in the wake of their accidents because they felt the other drivers were better connected and that pursuing them would come to naught. Elvira is a cautionary tale. Though she tried to keep her head down when she learned that the other driver was part of the local economic elite, she would not let it go. Once she ended up in court, she believed that her outsider status sealed her fate.

How a person sees herself in relation to her community was important. In the wake of two accidents described in the Shumerlia focus group, the victims decided not to sue because they saw themselves as part of a relatively small and tight-knit community and worried about how an effort to recover damages would be viewed by friends and neighbors. The victims spoke of how everyone knew each other's business in Shumerlia. Recognizing that claiming was not a socially acceptable response, they signed away their rights. Such attitudes are reminiscent of the rural residents Engel studied in Sander County in the United States (1984), who saw injuries as a part of daily life on farms to be endured. He found that newcomers were more likely to pursue damages than were longtime residents and to be ostracized for their behavior. Like their counterparts in Sander County, the Shumerlia feared that pursuing a claim would make them appear petty in the eyes of the community, but were not worried about rupturing its social cohesion. This stands in contrast to the more communitarian motivations of Thai villagers in the wake of accidents. Engel (2001) found that Thai villagers saw compensation, particularly in the form of elaborate and costly funeral ceremonies, as a way to return harmony to the community. His work reminds us of the ways in which different conceptions of community or "reality frames" can play out in terms of post-accident claiming (p. 9).

Rather than worrying about how neighbors and others close will view their behavior, the common thread among the respondents from these larger cities was a concern over what sort of clout the other party to the accident might have. In this we see the lingering effect of the web of personal connections that determined one's ability to survive and thrive in the Soviet era. As the scholarly, literary, and memoir literature remind us, the perennial shortages made coping on one's own impossible (Baranskaya, 1990; Ledeneva, 1998; Young, 1989; Smith, 1977; Voinovich, 1976). The abundance of consumer goods and the beginnings of a service economy has lessened the need to build and maintain personal networks. But all bets are off in the case of unexpected events like auto accidents. Many Russians still believe that law takes a back seat to connections when it comes to getting out of trouble. It is no surprise that the focus group participants preferred informal solutions to litigation. Nor is this attitude unique to Russians. Nelken (2009, pp. 36–37) notes that, in the aftermath of car accidents in Sicily,

> The key question after an accident . . . is not who is to blame but with whom you have to deal. It is important to find out as much as possible about the personal and social background of the person you have been in an accident with, getting information about the reputation of his or her insurance company, the lawyer, garage mechanic, medical expert available to him or her, and in general the person's larger network.

Adversarial legalism relies on individuals to mobilize the law, and so the resources of both plaintiffs and defendants—social, financial, even psychological—profoundly shape the way adversarial legal policies like auto injury tort are implemented.

Corruption

The dividing line between connections and corruption is fuzzy at best. Corruption—both real and perceived—had a significant influence on the focus group participants' behavior at every stage of the post-accident process. There was literally no element of Russian institutional life that they did not view as being susceptible to corruption.

The resignation felt by those who did nothing was often prompted by a sense that any effort to engage the system would be futile due to the willingness of officials to be swayed by bribes. For those who made claims, their efforts to settle reflect their lack of faith in the integrity of the state and private officials who were charged with protecting them. Repeatedly I was told that anyone could be bought. Some experienced this sad reality for themselves. Most acted preemptively based on common wisdom. Teasing out how much faith is placed in such rumors is an impossible task. For my purposes, what is more important is the extent to which my respondents were convinced of the futility of using the formal system and reacted by opting out, either by doing nothing or settling.

Perceptions of corruption were not limited to the legal system. Corruption of the medical establishment, for example, was also taken for granted (Rivkin-Fish, 2015). This explains why those close to victims with severe injuries were rarely able to focus on claiming and, instead, had to devote themselves to advocating for their loved ones in the medical system. Ordinary Russian hospitals provide few creature comforts to their patients. When Fatima brought food to hospital for the teenager she had accidentally injured, she endeared herself to the teen's mother, who otherwise would have had to do this. Many respondents told of having to make side payments to get access to needed treatments and rehabilitation facilities. No one disagreed with these sad realities. Rather, they chimed in with their own examples.

Russian Tort Law

Russia is a late developer of torts, and this colors Russians' understanding of the law. In the West, torts came into their own in the late 19th century as an antidote to the Industrial Revolution and the growth of the railroads (Baker, 2009). As Friedman (1987, p. 53) cogently points out, "For efficiency in mangling people, en masse, there is nothing like the modern machine." Though industrialization was a signature accomplishment of the Stalin period, tort law did not grow apace, but was supplanted by the state as the insurer of last resort. Many were doubtless dissatisfied with the compensation provided, but political constraints (both formal and informal) prevented them from taking further legal action.

The post-Soviet changes to tort law would seem to make it easier for injured parties to recover damages. The Soviet-era approach of imposing strict liability on drivers has been abandoned in favor of comparative negligence. Yet comparative negligence remains poorly understood by the Russian public, especially when it comes to accidents involving pedestrians. As I noted earlier, many who were injured while jaywalking assume that their malfeasance makes them ineligible for damages. Determinations of contributory negligence are made on a case-by-case basis. Whether the victim was in a *zebra* would be relevant to the analysis. Although it is theoretically possible that a pedestrian–victim could be barred from recovering damages, it is highly unlikely. As a general rule, drivers are held strictly liable when they hit pedestrians. A good example is the teenage victim of Fatima. She was darting through traffic at a busy Moscow intersection as cars were inching through. She must have known that she was not visible as she ran out of the shadow of a large truck into Fatima's path. Yet because she was in a *zebra*, her mother felt justified in pursuing legal remedies. By contrast, those whose children were injured when crossing the road without the protection of a designated crosswalk felt they had no recourse. Worse, they blamed themselves and felt embarrassed by their foolishness. This confirms the role of law as a gatekeeper. A belief that the law is receptive to their situation is a necessary, but not sufficient, condition for Russians to make the leap from naming one's injury to blaming and claiming.

Lawyers

Confusion about the substance of the law is hardly unique to Russia. Lawyers might be expected to pick up some of the slack. But this assumes that people are comfortable bringing their problems to lawyers. Few of my respondents bothered to consult with a lawyer to learn their rights before deciding how to proceed. The focus group participants assumed the cost of legal services would be beyond their means. Few had friends or acquaintances who were lawyers and so they did not know how to assess the qualifications or integrity of lawyers. Fatima initially ended up with a lawyer she described as a "bandit." She was horrified by his matter-of-fact advice to cover up her involvement. Others were less squeamish. In the aftermath of an accident on an icy road that injured an elderly woman, Zinaida, a 30-year-old Saratov doctor, did not hesitate to hire a lawyer who had worked for many years as a *gaishchnik* (traffic police officer) to help her and her husband through the system. He gave them advice about how to minimize their potential liability and helped them recognize that the seemingly helpless elderly woman was a scam artist who supplemented her income by putting herself in harm's way and bilking unsuspecting drivers.

Lawyers mostly came into the picture for the focus group participants when they were seriously contemplating litigation. Though my sample is small and unrepresentative, it is nonetheless interesting to note that those who had professional assistance did better than those who eschewed help.[24] Recall Anna, who fought to recover damages from the driver who killed her brother and left her

TABLE 5.1 Information About Cases Involving Traffic Accidents Brought to the Russian Courts, 2008–2011

	All cases related to traffic accidents	*Traffic accident cases as % of all civil cases*	*Win rate for traffic accident cases*	*Win rate for all civil cases*	*Delay rate for traffic accident cases*	*Delay rate for all civil cases*
2008						
All courts	96208	0.9	70.6	90.4	15.2	3.5
JP courts*	52065	0.6	72.4	91.5	14	2.8
2009						
All courts	126525	0.95	76.3	88.8	10.4	1.9
JP courts	81915	0.8	78.6	93.4	8.6	1.2
2010						
All courts	155043	1.1	80.1	88.3	7.7	1.6
JP courts	84221	0.8	83	94	6.9	0.8
2011						
All courts	190340	1.7	82.6	86.1	6.2	1.6
JP courts	98683	1.1	86	92.2	4.9	0.8

Sources: Otchet (2008, 2009, 2010, 2011); Otchet—JP Courts (2008, 2009, 2010, 2011).
**Justice-of-the peace courts.*

badly injured. Despite having a law degree and having previously worked in the administrative structure of the courts, she was all thumbs when it came to assembling the requisite evidence. She devoted a great deal of time to the case but ended up with a pittance. Yet she had no regrets. She told me of friends who had hired expensive lawyers and had come away empty-handed. By contrast, Elvira, who economized by hiring a recent law school graduate whom she referred to as her "assistant," felt she would have stood a better chance had she retained one of the expensive lawyers she met with. Though she did not use Galanter's (1974) language, she was making his point about the advantages shared by courtroom veterans in terms of their understanding of the formal and informal rules of the litigation game. As a first-time litigant—Galanter's proverbial "one-shotter"—she felt out of her element against the general director who was a "repeat player," someone who was at home in the courtroom and traveled in the same social circles as the judge.

Judges

Table 5.1 highlights several notable features of cases dealing with traffic accidents that help explain injured parties' distaste for going to court. These cases tend to take longer than the average case and petitioners are less likely to prevail. This simply reveals that these are cases that require full-fledged hearings on the merits; they do not lend themselves to expedited procedural mechanisms. Over the four-year period, only nine cases were resolved using a summary procedure that avoids a hearing on the merits of judicial orders.[25] The higher-than-average delay rate along with the lower-than-average win rate makes it tempting to conclude that these cases are deeply contentious and that parties fight to the bitter end. No doubt this describes some cases, but conversations with Russian judges, buttressed by my observations in the courts, lead me to believe it is not the norm. Judges report that the results in most traffic-related cases are foregone conclusions. They grumble about the tendency of insurance companies to use every trick in the book to drag out the proceedings in order to avoid having to pay, indicating that the tactics associated with adversarial legalism are beginning to emerge in Russia.

The lower-than-average win rates are more of a puzzle. The focus group participants complain about the difficulty of assembling the requisite documents.[26] Some are overwhelmed by the task and abandon any plans to pursue a claim. It may be that those who do go forward tend to fall short. The positivism reflected in the procedural codes and the expectations of judges lead them to be unforgiving about missing documentary evidence. This may contribute to petitioners' losses. Unlike individual claimants, insurance companies are generally represented by legal professionals in court. Whether this gives them an edge is unclear. Judges complain about the poor quality of lawyering for insurance companies, attributing it to the low wages paid and the consequent high turnover rate in their legal departments. Unfortunately, the way the data have been collected do not allow me to determine whether individuals or insurance companies are more successful.[27]

This penchant for documentary evidence helps explain why the reports (*protokoly*) of the traffic police take on such importance. All understand that the determination of fault in the *protokol* usually dictates the outcome in any court case. At a minimum, it establishes a presumption of liability that must be overcome by the other side. It also casts a heavy shadow in any negotiations between the parties, whether conducted on the side of the road or when the dust has settled. Insurance companies rely on it, as Kira learned to her detriment. If the police report does not identify a culprit, then insurance companies generally refuse to pay absent a court decision. Those dissatisfied with the substance of a *protokol* rarely succeed in disproving the substantive account of what happened. Judges are predisposed to believe the police. Savvy courthouse players (whether lawyers or litigants) understand that the key to undermining a police report is to show that some element of procedure was violated in completing the report.

Protokoly and other documentary evidence may be sufficient to educate judges as to what happened in simple fender-benders, but do a poor job of capturing the details of the more serious accidents that tend to end up in court. Witnesses are needed to flesh out the story. Sadly, those involved in the accident are not always able to fill in the gaps. As the stories shared above indicate, concussions and loss of consciousness are not uncommon. This leaves bystanders. Tracking them down can prove arduous.[28] The skepticism of judges towards witnesses makes it unclear whether it is worth the trouble. A number of focus group participants abandoned the fight at the outset due to fears of being unable to find eyewitnesses.

Russian judges' expectations as to documentary evidence can be problematic. Requiring receipts for any payments for which compensatory damages are sought would seem to be uncontroversial. Yet in a society in which side-payments are routine, demanding written evidence of such outlays is unrealistic. Anna's lawsuit is a good example. She was unable to recover the amounts that she paid to medical personnel to get access to newer medications recommended by her doctor that were otherwise unavailable to the public. The judge was not bothered by the bribe-like character of the payments. Instead, Anna's efforts to recover were torpedoed by the lack of written substantiation.

This sort of formalism can lead judges to give a cold shoulder to claims for services from private clinics. Once again, Anna's experience is instructive. Like many Russians, she was skeptical of the quality of the medical care provided free of charge and opted to go to a private clinic for rehabilitation. The court refused to countenance these charges, telling Anna that she could have obtained treatment at no charge. Even though Anna had been educated as a lawyer and understood the inherent positivism of the system, she came away from the experience frustrated by the court's unwillingness to deal with the real-life challenges she faced. Others in the focus groups echoed her concerns. Demanding the impossible marks the courts as out of touch with reality. Judges take no responsibility; they point to the codes and say their hands are tied. In reality, however, the codes—both procedural and substantive—provide a considerable amount of wiggle room. The risk-averse nature of Russian judges makes them wary of exercising discretion.

The Traffic Police

Russia is far from unique in treating police reports as determinative. In his study of the Japanese system, Tanase (1990, p. 673) notes that "the police report is accorded such weight that the facts as recorded are hardly ever challenged later in court." It is not just the authority and integrity of the police that give their reports such weight, it is also that the police work with those involved in the accident to "hammer out a consensual story as to what happened to which the parties agree and formally endorse by signing" (p. 674). This approach limits their ability to come to court and put forward alternative narratives.

What makes the Russian courts' practice of giving credence to the reports of traffic police problematic is the low esteem in which the public holds this branch of law enforcement. Despite its questionable integrity, the courts accept its reports at face value, much as in Japan. In essence, the *protokol* creates a rebuttable presumption of accuracy. In the justice-of-the-peace court hearings I observed, although those who had been cited for traffic violations often quibbled with the version of events laid out, I witnessed no successful efforts to rewrite history. To do so would require a credible witness to buttress the self-serving claims of the driver. A personal friend of mine succeeded in challenging his ticket for reckless driving thanks to his wife's testimony, which the judge believed. It helped that the traffic officer who issued the ticket had only a vague recollection of the incident. An easier route to overturning a traffic violation is to harp on technical shortcomings in the report.

The experiences of the focus group participants with the traffic police help us understand why this institution is widely distrusted. Arkadii, a 29-year-old psychologist from Kushchevskaia, captured the feelings of many when he said: "I don't bother going to the police anymore. It is a waste of time. Forgive me for saying this, but they work as prostitutes. Whoever pays them more makes out." Concrete illustrations were plentiful. The involvement of those with political sway was routinely hushed up. Unlike the courts, where mundane cases are typically processed according to the law, the malfeasance of the traffic police spilled over into their everyday activities. Respondents readily admitted to making side payments to the traffic police when threatened with the loss of their license. As in the Japanese case, the Russian police negotiate the content of the report with those involved in the accident. But rather than working towards a narrative that reflects what happened, *gaishchniki* are thought to be willing to skew the *protokoly* to whoever pays them more. Such stories were told in every focus group. Some told of draft reports that were written to fudge fault in an effort to solicit a bribe. When the initial report downplayed the icy conditions that led her husband to lose control of their car on a Saratov street, Zinaida hired a second expert, who supported her position that her husband was not to blame. She was advised to do this by the former traffic policeman turned lawyer whom she hired to help them. He knew how to beat his former colleagues at their own game. Respondents felt that their lack of respect for the *gaishchniki* was reciprocated. They reported waiting hours for someone to show up. When they did, victims described their attitude as "boorish" (*khamskoe*), and said that they were left feeling as if they were criminals rather than hapless victims.

Every once in a while, the traffic police rose to the occasion. Timofei, a 25-year-old Moscow lawyer for the tax inspectorate, told of an incident from his adolescence when several drivers, including his father, were spooked by a horse and crashed into one another. The traffic police officer determined that all involved had been negligent and brokered an amicable settlement. Several others related similar stories, but these were the exception rather than the rule.

Insurance Companies

In contrast to the traffic police, whose presence in Russians' lives dates back to the Soviet era, insurance companies are a new institutional player. Before liability insurance was mandated in 2002, few drivers bothered with it. Despite its now compulsory character, over a third of Russian drivers remain uninsured. As I noted earlier, Russians are skeptical of the commitment of insurance companies to their clients' interests. These attitudes were reflected in the focus groups. In all locales, I heard complaints about the tendency of insurance companies to use loopholes to avoid paying claims. They were described as "greedy" (*zhadnye*). There was a consensus that suing them was an uphill battle.

In Russia, as elsewhere, insurance companies are more experienced than most of their clients in dealing with auto accidents. To put it in the language of Galanter's seminal 1974 article, they are "repeat players," who understand how to maneuver through the system, whereas their clients are "one-shotters," who have no previous experience and tend to treat any accident as a one-time event rather than as a learning opportunity. They take advantage of the fact that those who were injured (or whose family members suffered injuries) are preoccupied with recuperation and the universal desire of those involved to put these mishaps behind them. They make it easy to get an estimate of property damage through appraisers of their choosing. Without exception, the focus group participants saw these mechanics as in the pocket of the insurance companies despite their claims to be independent. No doubt the mechanics understood that continued cooperation was contingent on lowballing their estimates. Though clients have the right to get their own estimate, this takes time and insurance companies drag their feet in reviewing such estimates. Indeed, some found that bribes were required to get mechanics to provide a realistic estimate. The reputation of mechanics has been sullied as a result of these practices. In my time at the justice-of-the-peace courts,

I saw countless cases in which an individual or her insurance company was seeking to recover the difference between the original estimate and the actual cost of repairing the car.

Some countries have introduced alternatives to court for resolving disputes with insurance companies. Japan, for example, has both private and state-sponsored alternatives (Tanase, 1990). As to the latter, court-annexed mediation has proved to be a popular option. Though the amounts received through mediation tend to be lower than court awards, mediation is quicker. As to the former, a network of traffic accident dispute resolution centers was established in the 1970s as a nonprofit corporation and was financed by profits from compulsory insurance. These centers offer private adjudication services. As to both, disputes that prove resistant to solution are forwarded to the courts. When writing about the Japanese system, Tanase pointed to these managerial solutions as a key element of the reason why only one in 100 disputes arising from auto accidents ended up in court, as compared to 21.5 out of 100 in the United States (p. 651). Russia has not followed this example, though the experiences of the focus group participants suggest that the Japanese solutions might be helpful. But these institutional innovations in Japan arose in an environment in which the traffic police are beyond reproach and public corruption is minimal. Lacking these starting conditions, any new tribunal might quickly "go native" and be driven by bribes rather than the law. Moreover, the tentative steps Russia has taken towards encouraging mediation have been met with public indifference (Hendley, 2013b).

Conclusion

Victims everywhere are reluctant to go to court, preferring to negotiate settlements informally. This gives adversarial legalism its characteristic irony: While in theory it promises everyone a mechanism for vindicating their rights, in practice few proceed to the top of the disputing pyramid. Fundamental to the politics of adversarial legalism, then, is the attitudinal and institutional factors that induce some individuals to mobilize the law.

In Russia, the disinclination to press claims stems from a general skittishness about officialdom, both private and public. Bilateral negotiations between those involved in accidents allowed victims to bypass insurance companies as well as the traffic police and the courts. This distaste for formal channels among Russians is well known. This study of behavior following auto accidents simply provides yet another illustration.

Those who have the misfortune to crash—literally—into people who they perceive as being more powerful are equally as likely to "lump it." Power is a fluid term. It extends to those who hold political office or have immense wealth as well as those who have strong connections to such individuals. When they stumble into this world, many ordinary Russians view themselves as outsiders who cannot penetrate these networks of power and influence where a quiet word may be determinative. Others worry that decision-makers will be bribed to look the other way. At the heart of these fears is a lack of power of law to trump connections and corruption.

Yet in disputes between ordinary citizens there is reason to believe that Russian courts operate relatively well. Judges in such cases are able to apply the law without fear of political repercussions. This finding would likely come as a surprise to ordinary Russians themselves. Judging by the focus groups, few of them see the courts as inviting. Indeed, they mostly see the entire system as stacked against them, from the unresponsive and insolent attitudes of the traffic police in the immediate aftermath of accidents to the bureaucratic maze required to recover through insurance companies to the courts. They complain bitterly about the time required to assemble the evidence required to substantiate their claim and about the emotional energy needed. The outsiders' assessment of the several months needed to complete a case as speedy is not shared widely among Russians, who regularly vent on the internet and in the press about the slow pace of justice in the justice-of-the-peace courts. As a result, their hesitancy to take their claims to the courts is entirely understandable.

Notes

1 In their comparative study of the tendency to seek out compensation for various types of injuries in Canada and the U.S., Kritzer et al. (1991, p. 501) develop a slightly different vocabulary. They identify the barriers to moving from one stage to another. Initially, victims must overcome a recognition barrier. They argue that some view what happened as part of daily life and not as an injury. Victims then face an attribution barrier. Blaming someone else "requires a combination of information and a willingness to externalize the cause of an injury." Seeking out the person at fault requires them to triumph over a confrontation barrier. At the final stage, victims must confront a litigation barrier. Following the lead of Felstiner et al., much of their analysis is devoted to the role of lawyers.

2 When asked about corruption within law enforcement agencies, Russians consistently identify the traffic police as highly problematic. A survey fielded by the Foundation for Public Opinion in 2008 put the traffic police in first place in terms of corruption (Rimskii, 2012). In a December 2010 survey by the Levada Center, the traffic police also came in first, with 56.8 percent of respondents listing it as the most corrupt. Russians are skeptical about efforts to rein in the traffic police. When asked about the likely impact of the plan to increase oversight over the traffic police in a March 2007 poll by the Levada Center, only 30 percent felt it would decrease bribery. A solid majority (58 percent) was sure it would have no impact. About the same number believed that increasing fines for traffic violations would lead to bigger bribes for traffic policemen (Levada, 2008, p. 72). The polling results on the police more generally paint a dismal picture. In surveys carried out regularly from 2004 through 2012, over 80 percent of respondents saw lawlessness and arbitrariness within the police as a serious problem (Zorkaia, 2012, p. 104). The efforts to remake the police by renaming them as *politsia* rather than *militsia*, along with a series of deeper institutional changes, was dismissed by respondents as ineffective (p. 106). As part of this reform, salaries for policemen were tripled in an effort to de-incentivize the practice of taking bribes (Robertson, 2013, p. 170).

3 www.vashamashina.ru/bill.php#g1
4 When surveyed in 2006 and 2007 by the Levada Center, only 20 percent of respondents said that the efforts of Russian police are mainly devoted to protecting citizens. Over 60 percent viewed police as being mostly interested in protecting their own interests. The remainder of the sample declined to respond (Levada, 2008, p. 72).
5 For a thorough analysis of Soviet insurance law, see Rudden (1966). For a primer on contemporary Russian insurance law, see Belykh (2009); Moudrykh (2002).
6 In a survey conducted by the Independent Research Center ROMIR in the spring of 2004, 85 percent agreed that something needed to be done to protect victims of traffic accidents. Nearly half, or 48 percent, of respondents viewed the law requiring insurance for drivers as necessary (Nuzhno, n.d.). A survey carried out in the spring of 2005 by the All-Russian Center for the Study of Public Opinion documented the support of two-thirds of those polled for having the rates for mandatory insurance set by the state (VTsIOM, 2005).
7 Russian insurance companies lobbied vigorously against the new rules, and managed to delay their introduction for a year. Critics argue that insurance companies continue to exploit loopholes to avoid paying claims or to minimize them (Zinenko, 2009). Industry spokesmen defend their record (Nikoforov, 2009).
8 Respondents were allowed to check multiple reasons. The most common response was increase in premiums at 36 percent. The several responses related to service (dissatisfaction with the amount paid out for a claim, poor response to a claim) attracted a quarter of the respondents (Pochemu, 2012).
9 While the raw numbers have almost doubled over this four-year period, they remain a relatively minor part of the civil docket, accounting for about 1 percent of all civil cases. The amount at issue determines where the case is brought. Before 2010, the justice-of-the-peace courts handled all claims under 100,000 rubles. This jurisdictional limit is now set at 50,000 rubles (Federal'nyi, 2010).
10 Tay (1969, p. 8) quotes P.I. Stuchka from the 1922 meeting of the All-Union Central Executive Committee of the Bolsheviks: "It is undignified for the Worker-Peasant Government to initiate disputes in court to determine whether a man was injured on the railway track intentionally or by accident." Reflecting on this, she concludes that "a socialist government should be concerned with social harm, an objective social concept, and not with fault, a subjective individual one."
11 The list of inherently dangerous activities, set forth in article 1079 of the 1996 Civil Code, is not exhaustive. Means of transportation are explicitly included, but the last sentence of the article clarifies that liability for harm caused by the collision of two or more cars is not covered by strict liability. On the other hand, the Russian Supreme Court, in a 2010 decree, clarified that drivers who hit pedestrians can be held strictly liable (Postanovlenie, 2010).
12 For example, in a 2004 case decided by a Saratov district court, the victim of a car accident initially sought 155,000 rubles in moral damages, but was awarded only 18,000. By contrast, the court awarded the full amount requested for compensatory damages, which were grounded in documentary evidence (*Iliasov v. Lapin*, 2004).
13 The Moskvich was a compact passenger car manufactured during the Soviet era.
14 A ZIL 130 is a large dump truck. The Mikoyan factory assembled MIG fighter jets. For a history of ZIL (*Zavod imeni Likhacheva*) see Siegelbaum (2008, pp. 10–35).
15 Those who were injured by buses or other means of public transportation uniformly did nothing. Not only were they confused about what entity would bear responsibility, but they were convinced they would be unable to gather the necessary evidence. These accidents often happened during rush hour when witnesses were hustling to and from work. Tracking them down to corroborate what had happened seemed overwhelming, especially given their injuries. Some thought about hiring a lawyer, but did not follow through because they assumed it would be prohibitively expensive. As a rule, those who

fell into this category received medical care at no charge which may have dimmed their ardor for seeking damages.

16 This was a common theme in all the focus groups (Hendley, 2010). It mirrors what sociolegal scholars have observed about the U.S. (Macaulay, 1963).

17 Fatima reported that when she refused the services of this lawyer, her tires were slashed.

18 Many Russian banks require comprehensive insurance as a condition of providing a loan. This explains why both Dmitrii and Vladislava had this type of policy. Few opt for it voluntarily.

19 Skeptics might assume that she was new to the judicial system. In reality, however, she had been involved in a Dickensian case brought by her father's ex-wife to get the title to an apartment that was owned by Katya and her father. Perhaps her faith was stoked by the fact that the court shared her view of her former stepmother's claims as bogus.

20 They put the remainder aside as a rainy day fund. Both Kira and her husband had latent health issues that they worried could flare up at any time.

21 Kira had very different reactions to the trial and appellate courts. She felt validated by the trial court, where she and her husband were allowed to share their stories. By contrast, she found the appellate hearing off-putting because the three-judge panel had no interest in them, but only wanted to query their lawyer about technical details.

22 This was an empty threat. Her husband had no legal training; he was not a procurator himself. He had previously worked as an assistant in the section of the procurator's office that handles environmental claims. He was unable to help her once the case ended up in court.

23 According to periodic polling by the Levada Center, the segment of Russian society that identifies itself as Russian Orthodox grew from less than 20 percent in 1989 to about 80 percent in 2012. The percentage of nonbelievers took a precipitous nosedive during this period, dropping from over 70 percent to about 12 percent (Zorkaia, 2012, Figure 16.1, p. 165).

24 Several (e.g., Katya, Kira, and Irina) even praised their lawyers.

25 In straightforward cases, judicial orders (*sudebnye prikazy*) are used to expedite decisions. Judges decide such cases on the basis of the pleadings, without a hearing on the merits. Disgruntled defendants can force a hearing on the merits simply by notifying the court of their dissatisfaction. They need not submit any proof of their position. Relatively few defendants (less than 10 percent) challenge judicial orders aimed at them. For more on judicial orders, see Hendley (2013a).

26 The rules governing what documents must be presented to an insurance company are set forth in densely worded government regulations, which are difficult for laymen to parse (Postanovlenie, 2003).

27 As a general rule, plaintiffs tend to win their cases in the justice-of-the-peace courts. Regardless of whether individuals are suing legal entities or vice versa, plaintiff win rates are well over 90 percent. Somewhat incongruously, the only group that has a poor track record is the state, which wins about two-thirds of the cases it initiates against individuals (Otchet, 2011).

28 A number of Russian forums exist on the internet in which people involved in accidents seek out eyewitnesses to their misfortune.

References

Albiston, C.R. (2005). "Bargaining in the Shadow of Social Institutions: Competing Discourses and Social Change in Workplace Mobilization of Civil Rights." *Law & Society Review*, 39(1), 11–49.

Arakcheev, D.D. (2008) "Dogovory OSAGO: slozhnye sluchai." *Zakonodatel'stvo*, 10.

Baker, T. (2009). "Liability Insurance at the Tort-Crime Boundary." In David M. Engel, & Michael McCann (Eds.), *Fault Lines: Tort Law as Cultural Practice* (pp. 66–79). Stanford, CA: Stanford University Press.

Baranskaya, N. (1990). *A Week Like Any Other: Novellas and Stories*. (Pieta Monks, Trans.). Emeryville, CA: The Seal Press.

Barry, D.D. (1967). "The Motor-Car in Soviet Criminal and Civil Law." *International and Comparative Law Quarterly*, 16(1), 56–85.

Barry, D.D. (1978) "Soviet Tort Law." In Ralph A. Newman (Ed.), *The Unity of Strict Law: A Comparative Study* (pp. 319–39). Brussels: Établissements Émile Bruylant.

Barry, D.D. (1979). "Soviet Tort Law and the Development of Public Policy." *Review of Socialist Law*, 5(1), 229–49.

Barry, D.D. (1996). "Tort Law and the State in Russia." In George Ginsburgs, Donald D. Barry, & William B. Simons (Eds.), *The Revival of Private Law in Central and Eastern Europe* (pp. 179–92). The Hague: Martinus Mijhoff Publishers.

Belova, T.N. (2010). "Statistika dorozhno-transportnykh proisshestvii v kontekste natsional'noi idei." *Voprosy statistiki* (10), 28–33.

Belykh, V.C. (2009). *Strakhovoe pravo*. Moscow: NORMA.

Calavita, K., & Jenness, V. (2013). "Inside the Pyramid of Disputes: Naming Problems and Filing Grievances in California Prisons." *Social Problems*, 60(1), 50–80.

Ellickson, R.C. (1991). *Order Without Law: How Neighbors Settle Disputes*. Cambridge, MA: Harvard University Press.

Engel, D.M. (1984). "The Oven Bird's Song: Insiders, Outsiders, and Personal Injuries in an American Community." *Law & Society Review*, 18(4), 551–82.

Engel, D.M. (2001). "Injury and Identity: The Damaged Self in Three Cultures." In David Theo Goldberg, Michael Musheno, & Lisa C. Bower (Eds.), *Between Law and Culture* (pp. 3–21). Minneapolis: University of Minnesota Press.

Engel, D.M. (2005). "Globalization and the Decline of Legal Consciousness: Torts, Ghosts, and Karma in Thailand." *Law & Social Inquiry*, 30(3), 469–514.

Engel, D.M., & Frank W. Munger. (2003). *Rights of Inclusion: Law and Identity in the Life Stories of Americans with Disabilities*. Chicago: University of Chicago Press.

Federal'nyi zakon ot 11 fevralia 2010 g. No. 6-FZ. (2010). "O vnesenii izmenenii v stat'iu 3 Federal'nogo zakona 'O mirovikh sudakh v Rossiiskoi Federatsii' i stat'iu 23 Grazhdanskogo protsessual'nogo kodeksa Rossiiskoi Federatsii," *Rossiiskoi gazeta* (31), February 15. Retrieved from www.rg.ru/2010/02/15/miroviye-dok.html

Felstiner, W.L.F., Abel, R.L., & Sarat, A. (1980–81). "The Emergence and Transformation of Disputes: Naming, Blaming, Claiming. . . " *Law & Society Review*, 15(3–4), 631–54.

Friedman, L.M. (1987). *Total Justice*. Boston: Beacon Press.

Galanter, M. (1974) "Why the 'Haves' Come Out Ahead: Speculations on the Limits of Legal Change." *Law & Society Review*, 9(1), 95–160.

Grazhdanskii Kodeks Rossiiskoi Federatsii, chast' pervaia. (1994). [GK RF]. Retrieved from www.consultant.ru/document/cons_doc_LAW_5142/.

Grazhdanskii kodeks RSFSR. (1964). [GK 1964]. Retrieved from www.tarasei.narod.ru/kodeks/zx4.txt.

Grazhdanskii Kodeks Rossiiskoi Federatsii, chast' vtoraia. (1995). [GK RF part 2]. Retrieved from www.consultant.ru/document/cons_doc_LAW_9027/.

Hazard, J. (1952). "Personal Injury and Soviet Socialism," *Harvard Law Review*, 65(4), 545–81.

Hendley, K. (2001). "Beyond the Tip of the Iceberg: Business Disputes in Russia." In Peter Murrell (Ed.), *Assessing the Value of Law in Transition Economies*. Ann Arbor: University of Michigan Press, pp. 20–55.

Hendley, K. (2010). "Mobilizing Law in Contemporary Russia: The Evolution of Disputes over Home Repair Projects." *American Journal of Comparative Law*, 58(3), 631–78.

Hendley, K. (2011). "Varieties of Legal Dualism: Making Sense of the Role of Law in Contemporary Russia." *Wisconsin International Law Journal*, 29(2), 233–62.

Hendley, K. (2013a). "Too Much of a Good Thing? Assessing Access to Civil Justice in Russia." *Slavic Review*, 72(4), 802–27.
Hendley, K. (2013b). "What If You Build It and No One Comes? The Introduction of Mediation to Russia." *Cardozo Journal of Conflict Resolution*, 14(3), 527–58.
Hendley, K. (2017). *Everyday Law in Russia*. Ithaca, NY: Cornell University Press.
Heofitsial'nye shtrafy GAI. (n.d.). http://www.vashamashina.ru/bill.php
Iliasov v. L. (2004). Delo No. 2–299, Leninskii raionnyi sud. Saratov, April 15. Retrieved from http://sud-praktika.narod.ru/12.vred/Lapin-Ilasov.doc
Kritzer, H.M., Bogart, W.A., & Vidmar, N. (1991). "The Aftermath of Injury: Cultural Factors in Compensation Seeking in Canada and the United States." *Law & Society Review*, 25(3), 499–543.
Kryshtanovskaya, O., & White, S. (2005). "The Rise of the Russian Business Elite." *Communist and Post-Communist Studies*, 38(3), 293–307.
Ledeneva, A.V. (1998). *Russia's Economy of Favours: Blat, Networking and Informal Exchange*. Cambridge: Cambridge University Press.
Levada Center. (2008). *Russian Public Opinion 2007*. Moscow: Levada Center. Retrieved from www.levada.ru/old/books/obshchestvennoe-mnenie-2007
Macaulay, S. (1963). "Non-Contractual Relations in Business: A Preliminary Study." *American Sociological Review*, 28(1), 55–67.
Merry, S.E. (1990). *Getting Justice and Getting Even: Legal Consciousness Among Working-Class Americans*. Chicago: University of Chicago Press.
Michelson, E. (2007). "Climbing the Dispute Pagoda: Grievances and Appeals to the Official Justice System in Rural China." *American Sociological Review*, 72(3), 459–85.
Moudrykh, V. (2002). *Russian Insurance Law*. Moscow: RDL.
Nelken, D. (2009). "Law, Liability, and Culture." In David Engel and Michael McCann (Eds.), *Fault Lines: Tort Law as Cultural Practice* (pp. 21–38). Stanford, CA: Stanford University Press.
Nikoforov, V. (2009). "Novye uslovie vyplaty kompensatsii po OSAGO." February 20. Retrieved from www.samru.ru/society/gost/44299.html.
"Nuzhno li OSAGO." (n.d.). Retrieved from http://prosmibank.ru/marketinsurance-1.html.
"Ob obiazatel'nom strakhovanii grazhdanskoi otvetstvennosti vladel'tsev transportnykh stredstv (OSAGO)." (2002). From April 25, 2002, No. 40-FZ, with amendments through December 25, 2012. Retrieved from www.consultant.ru/popular/osago/
Otchet o rabote sudov obshchei iurisdiktsii po pervoi instantsii o rassmotranii grazhdanskikh del za 12 mesiatsev 2008 g. (2008). Retrieved from www.cdep.ru/index.php?id=5.
Otchet o rabote sudov obshchei iurisdiktsii po pervoi instantsii o rassmotranii grazhdanskikh del za 12 mesiatsev 2008 g.—Svodnyi otchet po vsem mirovym sud'iam v Rossiiskoi Federatsii (Otchet—JP Courts 2008).
Otchet o rabote sudov obshchei iurisdiktsii po pervoi instantsii o rassmotranii grazhdanskikh del za 12 mesiatsev 2009 g. (2009). Retrieved from www.cdep.ru/index.php?id=5.
Otchet o rabote sudov obshchei iurisdiktsii po pervoi instantsii o rassmotranii grazhdanskikh del za 12 mesiatsev 2009 g.—Svodnyi otchet po vsem mirovym sud'iam v Rossiiskoi Federatsii (Otchet—JP Courts 2009).
Otchet o rabote sudov obshchei iurisdiktsii po pervoi instantsii o rassmotranii grazhdanskikh del za 12 mesiatsev 2010 g. (2010). Retrieved from www.cdep.ru/index.php?id=5.

Otchet o rabote sudov obshchei iurisdiktsii po pervoi instantsii o rassmotranii grazhdanskikh del za 12 mesiatsev 2010 g.—Svodnyi otchet po vsem mirovym sud'iam v Rossiiskoi Federatsii (Otchet—JP Courts 2010).

Otchet o rabote sudov obshchei iurisdiktsii po pervoi instantsii o rassmotranii grazhdanskikh del za 12 mesiatsev 2011 g. (2011). Retrieved from www.cdep.ru/index.php?id=5.

Otchet o rabote sudov obshchei iurisdiktsii po pervoi instantsii o rassmotranii grazhdanskikh del za 12 mesiatsev 2011 g.—Svodnyi otchet po vsem mirovym sud'iam v Rossiiskoi Federatsii (Otchet—JP Courts 2011).

"Pochemu strakhovanie ne rasprostraneno." (2012). September 13. Retrieved from http://nacfin.ru/novosti-i-analitika/press/press/single/10599.html

Postanovlenie Pravitel'stva RF ot 7 marta 2003 g., No. 263. (2003). "Ob utverzhdenii Pravil obiazatol'nogo strakhovaniia grazhdanskoi otvetstvennosti vladeltsev transportnykh sredstv, with amendments through December 1, 2012." *Rossiiskaia gazeta*, March 13. Retrieved from www.rg.ru/oficial/doc/postan_rf/263-03.shtm

Postanovlenie Plenuma Verkhovnogo Suda Rossiiskoi Federatsii ot 26 ianvaria 2010, no. 1. (2010). "O premenenii sudami grazhdanskogo zakonodatel'stva, reguliruiushchego otnosheniia po obiazatel'stvam vsledstvie prichineniia vreda zhizni ili zdorov'iu grazhdanina." *Rossiiskaia gazeta*, February 5. Retrieved from www.rg.ru/2010/02/05/sud-dok.html

Rimskii, V.L. (2012). "Rezul'taty sotsiologicheskikh issledovanii ispolneniia gosudarstvom pravookhranitel'noi funktsii: otsenki grazhdan i neogkhodimye reformy." Komitet grazhdanskikh initsiativ, Moscow: Fond INDEM.

Rivkin-Fish, M. (2015). "Bribes, Gifts and Unofficial Payments: Rethinking Corruption in Post-Soviet Russian Health Care." In Dieter Haller, & Cris Shor (Eds.), *Corruption: Anthropological Perspectives* (pp. 47–64). Ann Arbor: Pluto Press.

Robertson, A. (2013). "Police Reform and Building Justice in Russia: Problems and Prospects." In Kay Goodall, Margaret Malloch, & Bill Munro (Eds.), *Building Justice in Post-Transition Europe? Processes of Criminalisation within Central and East European Societies* (pp. 158–75). New York: Routledge.

Ross, H. L. (1980). *Settled out of Court: The Social Process of Insurance Claims Adjustment* (2nd ed.). New York: Aldine.

Rudden, B. (1966). *Soviet Insurance Law*. Leyden: A.W. Sijthoff.

Sandefur, Rebecca. (2007). "The Importance of Doing Nothing: Everyday Problems and Responses of Inaction." In Pascoe Pleasence, Alexy Buck, & Nigel Balmer (Eds.), *Transforming Lives: Law and Social Process* (pp. 112–32). London: HMS.

Shevchenko, O. (2009). *Crisis and the Everyday in Postsocialist Moscow*. Bloomington, IN: Indiana University Press.

Siegelbaum, L.H. (2008). *Cars for Comrades: The Life of the Soviet Automobile*. Ithaca, NY: Cornell University Press.

Smith, H. (1977). *The Russians*. London: Sphere Books Limited.

"Strakhovanie postepenno vozvrashchaetsia." (2012). July 11. Retrieved from http://nacfin.ru/novosti-i-analitika/press/press/single/10584.html

Tanase, T. (1990). "The Management of Disputes: Automobile Accident Compensation in Japan." *Law & Society Review*, 24(3), 651–91.

Tay, A.E. (1969). "The Foundation of Tort Liability in a Socialist Legal System: Fault Versus Social Insurance in Soviet Law." *University of Toronto Law Journal*, 19(1), 1–15.

Voinovich, V. (1976). *The Ivankiad*. (David Lapeza, Trans.). New York: Farrar, Straus and Giroux.

"VTsIOM: Rossiane ne khotiat pol'zovat'sia OSAGO." (2005). July 19. Retrieved from http://top.rbc.ru/society/19/07/2005/91417.shtml.
Young, C. (1989). *Growing Up in Moscow: Memoirs of a Soviet Girlhood.* New York: Ticknor & Fields.
Zernova, M. (2012). "The Public Image of the Contemporary Russian Police: Impact of Personal Experiences of Policing, Wider Social Implications and the Potential for Change." *Policing,* 35(2), 216–30.
Zinenko, Il'ia. (2009). "Novye pravila OSAGO budut rasprostraniat'sia ne po vse." February 25. Retrieved from www.rb.ru/article/novye-pravila-osago-budut-rasprostranyatsya-ne-na-vseh/5694787.html.
Zorkaia, N. (2012). "Obshchestvennoe mnenie—2012." Moscow: Levada-Tsentr.

6

OVERCOMING THE DISCONNECT

Internal Regulation and the Mining Industry

Neil Gunningham

Adversarial legalism depends on private parties to activate the law by pursuing their individual rights and remedies. Compliance is driven from the bottom up, usually in an ad hoc way by uncoordinated litigants scattered across the polity. Regulation, the subject of this chapter, is quite different because it does not depend on either private parties or litigation to mobilize the law. Regulation is centralized—this is why it falls under the category of "bureaucratic legalism" in Robert Kagan's typology—so that regulatory officials have complete control over enforcement. They can deploy the law strategically using a variety of tactics, many less combative and resource-intensive than litigation.

Of course, finding the ideal combination of enforcement strategies, tactics that would encourage the targets of the law to comply with their commands with a minimum of fuss, is far from straightforward. For decades, regulatory theorists, policy analysts, and others have grappled with how best to induce corporations to comply with social regulation. The focus of their attention has been on various "external drivers" of corporate behavior, whether instrumental, normative, or social. There is, for example, a continuing debate about whether compliance stems from fear of legal sanctions or from a sense of social or legal obligation, and about the importance of corporate social responsibility and the "social license to operate": the expectations of social stakeholders—such as local community members, organized activists, and voters—towards a regulated business (Gunningham, Kagan, & Thornton, 2003, pp. 35–36). Regulatory practitioners continue to grapple with the related issue of what instruments (or combination of instruments) are best capable of achieving compliance, and what roles might best be played by incentives, management-based approaches, and informal mechanisms of social control (Gunningham & Grabosky, 1998).

Much of Robert Kagan's research on regulation moves away from the sole focus on regulators and their tactics. In this line of research, Kagan and other sociolegal scholars examine the effects of regulation from the receiving end, through fieldwork that probes how organizations respond to regulatory commands. For example, in *Shades of Green*, the book I coauthored with Kagan and Dorothy Thornton (Gunningham, Kagan & Thornton, 2003), we found that external pressures could explain some, but not all, of the response of firms to environmental regulation. To fully understand the variation in response to regulation among firms, then, we had to go inside the organizations.

Regulatory theories sometimes treat organizations as unitary rational actors. Once one studies what goes on inside organizations, however, this simplification becomes untenable. Tensions within organizations themselves can be an important factor in regulatory response. Irrespective of what regulatory and social pressures a company is facing, or what public policy instruments it must respond to, a firm has the challenge of ensuring that the objectives and priorities established by senior management at its head office are successfully communicated to *and implemented by* its various operations. This is no simple matter. Corporations have considerable difficulty in ensuring that their various far-flung operations behave as corporate headquarters would wish them to, and in making commitments adopted at the center work at the edges. Put differently, aligning corporate social goals with those of managers, supervisors, and workers at individual sites is a substantial, and largely unresolved, organizational challenge, and there is often a substantial "disconnect" between head office goals and facility-level commitment and performance.

As regards profit maximization, this is hardly new, and successful corporations have become relatively refined in their techniques for ensuring that their various operations "make their numbers." But achieving their social goals has been much more problematic, for reasons that relate in substantial part to the tensions between social and profit-making goals, to the opportunities for signals and incentives to be received and interpreted in different ways at different levels of the organization, and to the problems of overcoming bounded rationality.[1] Indeed, the limited evidence available suggests that aligning corporate objectives with those of their (often distant) operations remains a major and unresolved challenge for many issues of social regulation and corporate social responsibility. For example, it seems that multiple-facility firms do worse when it comes to issues such as environmental protection than do single-facility firms (King & Shaver, 2001, p. 1070), which is counterintuitive given that the former benefit from considerable economies of scale, and suggests that overcoming the head office–facility disconnect may be a considerable challenge. This is also a reasonable conclusion to draw from Gray and Deily's finding that single-plant firms are more likely to be in compliance, notwithstanding that they had "expected multi-plant firms to have a greater incentive to invest in a reputation for firm-wide compliance" (1996, p. 96). Similarly, it seems that foreign firms (in the United States at least) lag behind their local counterparts in preventing waste, a result attributed "to the difficulty that foreign firms face in managing complex and contingent improvement processes (like pollution prevention)" (King & Shaver, 2001, p. 3).

This large gap between corporate intentions and behavior at site level is in no way peculiar to the area of environmental regulation or specific to the United States. It is also evident in the case of occupational health and safety (OHS) in Australia. For example, a government inquiry into a large explosion at an Exxon facility causing loss of life and extensive property damage found serious failings at site level, notwithstanding relatively extensive efforts at corporate headquarters to prevent such an occurrence (Hopkins, 2000), as did a 2004 inquiry into fatalities at work sites in western Australia (Ritter, 2004). Only a few months later, the New South Wales *Mine Safety Review* identified as a central finding the "disconnect" between the sorts of OHS systems and protections put in place by corporate headquarters, and what happened "at the coalface" (Wran & McClelland, 2005).

Notwithstanding the seemingly widespread and serious nature of this disconnect, far less attention has been given to the instruments, mechanisms, and strategies through which a firm that is committed to achieving given social outcomes (whether prescribed by regulation or otherwise) may best succeed in doing so—what we might term *internal regulation*[2] (Black, 2002)—than has been given to the various external drivers of corporate social behavior.

Those limited studies that have been conducted on internal regulation have focused very largely on the application by firms of various "management based" strategies. Those strategies rely on internal planning and management practices such as management systems and standards, and form the cornerstone of internal regulation in most large companies. While this literature makes a valuable contribution in exploring this approach, it still leaves many important questions unresolved. For example, although it has done much to identify the particular instruments, mechanisms, and strategies that constitute management-based regulation and has provided some preliminary assessment of their effectiveness, much work remains to be done in understanding how this form of internal regulation works in practice, in identifying the obstacles to its successful implementation and in determining whether, to what extent, or in what circumstances it is capable of institutionalizing corporate social objectives across the firm. In short, there is much that is still not known about the capacities, strengths, and limitations of internal regulation.

One intriguing finding is that companies in very similar situations (and using much the same management tools) sometimes react very differently to the same external stimuli (Gunningham et al., 2003). This suggests the possibility that "management style" matters much more than management systems and that effective internal regulation may be about much more than the formal management-based tools companies have at their disposal. It was that insight that was a substantial motivator for engaging in the present project.

In the remainder of this chapter, internal regulation will be examined through a case study of one company and the behavior of its managers, employees, and contractors at a number of individual sites with regard to one area of social regulation. The case involves BHP Billiton (hereafter BHP), Australia's largest company and arguably an exemplar of modern management techniques, and the study concerns the manifest disconnect between the ambitious occupational health and safety strategies, systems and standards established by the head office, and the actual behavior of individual managers, employees, and contractors at site level in its various mining operations in the Pilbara region of western Australia. While the case is confined to one social issue in one jurisdiction, the lessons it provides are of much broader application, and have implications for the internal regulation initiatives of complex organizations in diverse areas of social regulation.

There are, of course, limits to a case study approach, and dangers in seeking to generalize from specific cases drawn from particular contexts. But at an early stage in the development of a field, such studies may provide substantial insights and address questions which quantitative studies are ill-equipped to answer. Given that there are currently no large-N studies addressing the central concerns of this paper, individual case studies have considerable virtues. They can provide in-depth qualitative analysis of firm or facility-level behavior, of corporate and managerial motivations, and of the connection between motivations and management-based strategies. There may be particular value in studying behavior at different facilities in the same company since this approach enables one to hold constant a number of variables (as where the company seeks to impose the same form of management-based regulation on all its facilities) while enabling variation in others (such as differences in site-level culture) to form the focus of study.

The chapter proceeds as follows. First, I describe the circumstances of the Australian mining industry and OHS performance at BHP. Second, I show how BHP's commitment to achieve the high standards of OHS was in tension with production imperatives, contractor-related issues, and an adversarial industrial relations agenda. Third, I explain the implementation failures though an analysis of the role and limitations of OHS safety management systems, incentives structures, and its ideological agenda, suggesting that a failure to take account of workplace culture served to undermine many of the company's safety initiatives.

The Mining Industry, OHS, and BHP

The mining industry is of considerable economic importance to Australia, contributing some 9 percent of total earnings and approximately 33 percent of total exports of goods and services. However, the industry also has exceptionally high levels of occupational injury and disease—over twice the national average. And while safety performance has improved considerably over recent years, mining is still an exceptionally dangerous occupation. In western Australia, for example, mining accounts for only 5 percent of the workforce but is responsible for about 25 percent of total workplace deaths (Ritter, 2004).

The mining industry includes a number of large companies with multiple operations and facilities. It is these that have the greatest need for internal management–based regulation and which are the focus of this article. Such companies are

> faced with a pattern of low credibility and social opposition, which drives from a general perception that mining is a dirty business . . . The image of abandoned mines, tailings dumps, waste-rock piles, and abandoned communities has significant resonance with the general public.
>
> *(Joyce & Thomson, 1999 p. 441)*

Fatalities and serious injuries contribute significantly to that negative image, and BHP has struggled to maintain its legitimacy and social acceptance.

The importance of maintaining their reputation is now widely recognized by major mining companies (Yakoleva, 2005). Such enterprises are inclined to view regulation as merely a baseline, a minimum standard beyond which they will seek to go, to the extent that they believe this is necessary to reduce risk and achieve their broader OHS goals. For the most part, such companies now aspire to go "beyond compliance" and have their own internally determined targets. As such, their managers and agents are likely to be influenced to a much lesser extent by external drivers such as regulation and far more by the company's own internal goals and aspirations.

BHP falls squarely within this group. It is a large player, highly visible and vulnerable to external pressure, with an international reputation to protect. Like many other major mining companies, it has come to regard occupational health and safety as a high priority, for which there is now a compelling "business case." Mining injuries can cause serious disruption of the production process, escalate already punitively high workers' compensation costs, increase staff absences, and threaten the company's "social license." For all these reasons, BHP has set itself ambitious "beyond compliance" OHS targets.

At the corporate level, perhaps what is most striking about BHP's approach to OHS in its western Australian mining operations, as elsewhere, is the very great effort that it had devoted to this issue, particularly in terms of policies, systems, standards and procedures, employee involvement, communication, expert advice, and auditing (Ritter, 2004, p. 63). Not only does BHP have a set of values and a set of corporate OHS goals, it has a charter, a health, safety, community and environment (HSEC) policy, comprehensive management standards, company-wide HSEC guidelines and procedures, business-based HSEC management systems, and operational HSEC procedures. At the core of this elaborate framework are 15 corporate OHS standards and a very detailed and sophisticated OHS management system. The overall corporate goal in terms of OHS is stated to be "zero harm" meaning "managing risks so no injuries to employees, property damage, environmental impact or community harm occur while doing work" (Ritter, 2004, p. 62).

But in May 2004, in the Pilbara region of western Australia, there were three deaths at sites owned and/or operated by BHP subsidiaries: BHP Billiton Iron Ore Pty Ltd (BHPBIO) and Boodarie Iron. Three deaths in the space of a month, in unrelated incidents, was a matter of major concern even in a high-risk industry like mining. Perhaps unsurprisingly, it prompted a Ministerial Inquiry (to which the writer was OHS advisor)[3] whose ensuing report provides considerable insights regarding the difficulties of aligning corporate social goals with those of managers, supervisors, and workers at individual sites, and regarding the limitations of internal and management-based regulation.

That report suggested that the three deaths were symptomatic of wider failings, and that BHP's sophisticated management system and its various other initiatives at corporate level identified above had manifestly not ensured adequate levels of OHS at particular work sites in the Pilbara. Indeed, when the inquiry took evidence from a variety of workers and others in the Pilbara, it became apparent that there were serious matters of concern at site level that this elaborate corporate OHS apparatus had done little to address. Some of these matters will be examined in detail later in this chapter, but a flavor can be gleaned from the following examples, taken from the Inquiry Report:

- Allegations of minimal employee involvement in preparation of Job Safety Analyses (JSAs), with employees just being told to look at and sign these documents (Ritter, 2004, p. 148), and a perception among witnesses "that management consider they lost too much production time if employees discuss and prepare JSAs together."
- Allegations that "although pre-start checks are required by safety policy, if an employee finds a fault and subsequently raises it as an issue they are called a 'whinger'" (Ritter, 2004, p. 149), and a perception amongst witnesses "that management want employees to perform pre-start checks but in practice there is an inadequate amount of time given to do the checks, sending an inconsistent message to employees" (Ritter, 2004, p. 149).
- Problems with the local safety culture. According to the minutes of a 2003 workshop, participants pointed to a lack of accountability, the use of shortcuts, a reluctance to report problems and incidents, a can-do culture with a high tolerance for risks, a large number of contractors, high contractor turnover, and treatment of contractors as second-class citizens (Ritter, 2004, p. 271).

In trying to explain this gap between corporate intentions on the one hand and on-site outcomes on the other, the inquiry invoked the metaphor of a cascade. It suggested that:

> the corporate visions, policies and standards of BHPBIO can be imagined to be a body of water which cascades down a waterfall and, for successful implementation, needs to carry people and information with them and

> reach and be 'lapped up' by BHPBIO sites further down the body of water. If the health and safety systems are not 'lapped up' by the sites, there is an element of 'spillage'. The 'spillage' which occurs will have an impact upon the extent to which the body of visions, policies and standards is successfully implemented at site level. If there is a large amount of 'spillage' it will substantially undermine the effectiveness of the systems.
>
> *(Ritter, 2004, p. 97)*

But while this may be a colorful way of describing what happened, it falls far short of an adequate explanation. Developing such an explanation, based on the evidence provided to the Ministerial Inquiry, is the concern of the following sections.

What Went Wrong: Tensions Between Competing Agendas

From the detailed evidence provided to the inquiry by a variety of witnesses at the various BHP operations, it became apparent that, at site level at least, BHP's commitment to OHS was not unqualified, and that corporate claims of an "overriding commitment" to safety at all levels were not substantiated in practice. On the contrary, when OHS clashed with other implicit corporate priorities, beliefs, goals, and ideologies, then it often came off second best. The following section examines how tensions between a commitment to achieve high standards of OHS on the one hand, and (i) production imperatives, (ii) contractor-related issues, and (iii) the company's industrial relations agenda, on the other, served to substantially derail the OHS agenda at site level.

Safety Versus Production

The alleged tension between safety and production—or more crudely, between safety and profit—is at the heart of debates about the appropriate roles of law and regulation in OHS policy. Numerous academics, trade union officials, and others have pointed to evidence demonstrating that, at least in the short term, there is frequently a conflict between maximizing production and maximizing safety, and that in these circumstances, the latter is usually sacrificed to the former.

For example, when a large group of chief executive officers in the United States were asked some years ago what prevents their companies from doing a better job on health, safety, and environmental issues, over 50 percent cited the pressure to achieve short-term profits as the main reason (Rappaport & Flaherty, 1991). Because corporations are judged by markets, investors, and others principally on short-term financial performance, they have difficulty justifying investments in OHS improvement with primarily long-term payoffs.

However, many companies, particularly in reputation-sensitive industries such as mining, would argue that the above is an outdated analysis, and that whatever might have been the case in past decades, today there are compelling reasons of enlightened self-interest (risks of disruption of the production process, escalating workers compensation costs, and threats to the company's "social license" described above), not only for taking a proactive approach to OHS, but also for giving it priority, even when to do so conflicts with production pressures. Certainly various BHP corporate documents suggest that safety takes a high priority in all the company's policies, with an "overriding commitment" to health, safety, environmental responsibility, and sustainability listed first in the company's values defined by the BHP Billiton Charter (BHP Billiton Iron Ore, 2004, p. 22).

However, notwithstanding the setting of ambitious corporate targets, a strategy based "on the development and maintenance of a safe workplace with good systems, leadership and workforce commitment" (BHP Billiton Iron Ore, 2004, p. 6) and the introduction of a series of demanding corporate OHS standards, there is considerable evidence that the corporate "safety comes first" message did not permeate the site level in the Pilbara. For example, following a serious incident in 2001, the QEST Consulting Group was commissioned to undertake an engineering report under section 45 of the Mines Safety and Inspection Act. This report noted that the BHP Boodaree Plant has had "severe difficulties in meeting its production specifications and operational parameters since construction leading to a reduction in management focus on safety within the operations. *This led to a production first culture throughout the operations*" (Qest, 2002; emphasis added).

While there may have been a "renewed focus on safety" following that incident, any such focus was not apparent to the Ministerial Inquiry in 2004, and a variety of sources gave evidence to the contrary. According to one long-term employee: "The behaviour of our senior staff has left few people in doubt that production at all costs is the real agenda here . . ." (Ritter, 2004, p. 189). There were numerous reports that reductions in staff numbers (in the interests of greater productivity) increased OHS risks, "as when a worker may have conflicting duties to both get on with their own work and supervise that of an apprentice" (Ritter, 2004, p. 140), and of some supervisors "push[ing] production ahead of safety, involving safety shortcuts. There are operational issues which affect this attitude, including production requirements and lack of staffing levels" (Ritter, 2004, p. 292).[4] A safety survey conducted by BHPBIO in mid-2004 (following a series of presentations on "zero harm" which in themselves may have skewed the results) also suggested cause for concern. In response to a question as to whether respondents believed "the business puts safety before production" it appears (based on the inquiry's mode of analysis) that "30% of the recipients believed that the business does not put safety before production. This is of a total of about 800 respondents. It is a significant figure, in the opinion of the Inquiry both in absolute terms and proportionally" (Ritter, 2004, p. 90).

Perhaps the most graphic illustration of the continuing nature of the problem was the series of large posters which were produced and put up at one operation, with the slogan "Aim high, Move fast" and an exhortation to achieve a specified production outcome. As the inquiry pointed out, "[I]t is noteworthy that nowhere on this poster is contained any message about safety, unless the small reference to Operating Excellence implicitly includes a subtle safety message" (Ritter, 2004, p. 92). Employees themselves also reported to the inquiry that production came first, in myriad different ways. For example, "supervisors in various areas were pushing production, even where it was not at all times safe to do so" (Ritter, 2004, p. 291). Following the May 2004 fatalities, the use of the posters was discontinued.

Relationship With Contractors

BHP made substantial use of contractors in its Pilbara operations, and some of its most dangerous operations were subcontracted. Because contractors traditionally have an exceptionally high incidence of work-related injury and disease, the relationship between BHP and its contractors could have considerable implications for the safety of the broader workforce engaged in the Pilbara.

At the corporate level, considerable efforts were made to ensure high OHS standards amongst contractors. These included a requirement for contractors to demonstrate commitment to and compliance with the BHP HSEC Management Standards and the development of tender documentation incorporating various OHS requirements, including the submission of a safety management plan (SMP), which meets 14 occupational health and safety processes and objectives. Once a contractor has been engaged, a risk assessment or audit is undertaken to ensure that appropriate controls are in place prior to operations commencing, and a detailed SMP must be submitted shortly after operations begin. Each contract mine has an appointed BHPBIO Site Representative who is responsible for ensuring that the contractor complies with the contract conditions, including managing contractor compliance with the SMP. As part of the SMP, the contractor is required to implement an effective inspection, audit, and review process to determine compliance, assess relevance of the information contained in the SMP, and promote continuous improvement.

However, once again the evidence given to the inquiry suggested that there was a substantial disconnect between the requirements established at corporate level and actual practices at individual sites. For example, witnesses suggested that BHP did not allow sufficient time for contractors to do work safely and meet contractual conditions. Concern was expressed that key performance indicators are time-based and that this could create an economic disincentive to perform a job steadily and safely. Indeed, "some contractors commented that key performance safety indicators are seen as being a numbers and economic exercise rather than being used to assist in achieving positive safety behaviour and culture" (Ritter, 2004, p. 224). This led the inquiry to conclude that exhortations to contractors to work safely are "hollow if the economic and supervisory relationship between [BHP] and contractors is counter-productive to the effective resolution of OHS issues" (Ritter, 2004, p. 229).

Similarly, obstacles were put in the way of effective OHS reporting (especially incident reporting) by contractors, thereby seriously reducing available information concerning potential OHS hazards. The central problem was that contractors were not willing to disclose OHS issues to BHP safety management for fear that it would slow down the job and put them in breach of their contractual commitments. However, there was also evidence that contractors were singled out for minor safety breaches, an attitude that "discourages the reporting of near miss accidents or injuries. Incidents are not being reported because of the reactions of these managerial staff" (Ritter, 2004, p. 224). Beyond this, there was considerable evidence provided to the inquiry that the OHS performance of some contractors left much to be desired (Ritter, 2004), notwithstanding BHP's concern to ensure that "contractors have the same type of systems that mesh with our systems" (Goodyear, cited in Ritter, 2004, pp. 222–223).

Tension Between Safety and Industrial Relations

Almost all analyses of OHS best practice conclude that genuine worker participation is absolutely essential (Walters et al., 2005), but such participation at site level was made very difficult, and perhaps impossible, by a simmering and long-term battle between BHP and the relevant trade unions over the use of nonunion labor. Approximately 80 percent of BHP's workforce in the Pilbara is engaged under individual contracts (workplace agreements), with the remaining 20 percent currently employed under union collective arrangements. The unions are strongly opposed to the introduction of workplace agreements and have campaigned against them. BHP, in turn, is strongly opposed to the trade union awards and prefers to negotiate individual workplace agreements. And all this takes place against the backdrop of a long history of industrial conflict and antagonism between the company and the workforce in the Pilbara.

As a result, consultation and communication procedures for OHS were fraught with difficulty. It was alleged that BHP failed to effectively communicate and consult with award employees, or with their elected representatives on OHS; failed to involve appropriate people in accident investigation processes; failed to allow elected OHS representatives the opportunity to accompany the Employee Inspector on inspections; and failed to consult on safety policy prior to its introduction (Ritter, 2004, Appendix 4, pp. 12–13). Indeed, the key trade union involved, the Construction, Forestry, Mining and Energy Union (CFMEU), maintained that "BHP's anti-unionist and anti-collectivist industrial relations agenda is driving and shaping its approach to safety" (Ritter, 2004, Appendix 4, p. 13). The company rejected this view, asserting, among other things, its commitment to flexibility as distinct from an opposition to collectivism.

While it is difficult to make a judgment on the merits of the various conflicting views expressed by BHP and the CFMEU, what *is* clear is that there were important and unresolved industrial relations issues at BHP sites in the Pilbara that could seriously undermine the integrity of BHP's approach to safety management (Ritter, 2004, p. 57). Moreover, BHP provided very little evidence that it had made efforts to overcome these antagonisms, or to find ways of quarantining OHS from the broader and adversarial industrial relations context. Thus the inquiry pointed out not only that "strikingly absent from the [BHP submission to the inquiry] is any serious examination of the role of trade unions, or the impact of industrial relations issues on employee involvement" (Ritter, 2004, Appendix 4, p. 12) but also that "there does not appear to be any indication of a clear plan to steer the way towards the successful implementation of health and safety systems and practices with a workforce of whom a significant number had strong opposition to a key management strategy" (Ritter, 2004, p. 125). Finally, the inquiry found that there was "a real issue about fear of recriminations if occupational health and safety issues are raised. The recriminations may not be demonstrative, but there is a concern at the very least about subtle repercussions—possibly affecting future employment or payments made under contracts of employment" (Ritter, 2004, p. 290).

The depth of these industrial relations problems and their cultural underpinnings may be gauged from the fact that even four years after the inquiry, and notwithstanding everything discovered by the inquiry and by BHP's internal investigations, it was reported that 200 nonunionized workers on Australian Workplace Agreements (AWAs) at one of the Pilbara mines had signed a petition claiming that AWAs promote a culture of compromised safety. A media report said workers at the Mount Whalebank site had complained of an atmosphere of "intimidation and victimization" and warned "a serious safety incident is inevitable unless the culture changes" (OHS News, 2007).

Discussion

The above account suggests that BHP had in place a set of formal structures for addressing issues of internal compliance that, for the most part, approximated best management practice. Yet what is most strikingly revealed by the Ministerial Inquiry is that those formal structures were manifestly inadequate to achieve adequate levels of OHS at its Pilbara operations, or to prevent three deaths within the space of a single month. The substantial cause, so it would appear, was a "disconnect"—or rather a series of disconnects—between Head Office edicts and aspirations, and behavior "at the coalface."

The Corporate–Mine Site Disconnect

The most obvious disconnect revealed by the Ritter Report was between corporate and mine site management. Whereas corporate management appeared to have a strong commitment to high standards of OHS, mine management self-evidently did not. At mine site level, production came first, safety an extremely poor second. The Inquiry Report documents a variety of ways in which mine management's failure to "walk the talk" and their single-minded commitment to production served to relegate OHS to the periphery.

How can this disconnect between corporate aspirations and mine site behavior be explained? One possibility is that there simply was no disconnect. It is, after all, hardly unknown for corporations to develop impressive-looking policy statements and websites for public relations purposes rather than because of any genuine commitment to improving their social performance. Some companies make the calculated decision that it will be possible to protect their social license by cosmetic means rather than by investing in the often-expensive mechanisms necessary to bring about substantial and genuine change on the ground. On this view, mine management was simply following corporate management's real agenda in relentlessly pursuing production and profit at the cost of OHS.

While researchers (or government inquiries) can rarely penetrate the corporate boardroom or be sure beyond doubt of corporate motivations in particular circumstances, nevertheless there is considerable evidence that for the most part, the larger, reputation-sensitive mining companies that dominate the market have a substantial corporate commitment (driven by "the business case" described earlier) not only to meet, but also to go substantially beyond, the minimum OHS standards prescribed by legislation. This is not to suggest any newfound altruism on the part of senior management in the private sector. Rather, in reputation-sensitive industries with a high public profile, there may be compelling reasons of corporate self-interest for aiming high and going "beyond compliance" with what the law requires (Kagan, Gunningham and Thornton, 2003).

In the case of the mining industry majors, including BHP, there is substantive evidence to confirm that a genuine and not merely a cosmetic change in their approach to OHS has taken place over the last decade or so. The downward trend in injuries and fatalities over that period is an impressive one, and greater than in other industry sectors, although it has slowed in recent years. While injury incidence or frequency rates data can certainly be manipulated, this is not the case with fatalities, which show a similar downward trend (Gunningham, 2007). Galvin (2005) suggests that in the past two decades there has been "around a 90% reduction in lost-time injuries and fatalities in the Australian minerals industry," and government data since the late 1990s confirms a continuing downward trend in the rate of fatalities and injuries.[5] BHP's performance has improved broadly in line with the industry trend.[6]

While the Ritter Inquiry was not privy to BHP's internal decision-making processes or to boardroom discussions, the documents that it did obtain, and its own investigations, suggested that BHP's corporate commitment to ambitious OHS targets was a genuine one. It has powerful reasons of corporate self-interest to protect its social license and had articulated a compelling "business case" for placing a high priority on OHS. Its range of OHS management tools approximated international best practice[7] (Ritter, 2004, Appendix 4, p. 33), and in some respects (as in its development of fatal risk protocols) it had established international leadership.

So what went wrong? Why in particular were the elaborate and sophisticated mechanisms of internal regulation that the company put in place to ensure that OHS was adequately addressed at site level not sufficient? In part, it may be that BHP's internal regulation mechanisms, while extensive and sophisticated, nevertheless did not pay sufficient attention to the need to explicitly align site-level management with corporate objectives. This is apparent in two respects. First, it is doubtful whether BHP provided OHS incentives to mine management of sufficient specificity and strength as to counter the traditional emphasis that line management places on production. Certainly the company provided incentive payments based on a range of business performance metrics including OHS (which is also included in the BHPBIO "Road Map" Performance Score Card). However, it is not clear how influential the OHS criteria are in practice, as compared to traditional production-based incentives. The latter were both quantifiable and substantial (emphasizing ends, not means, in terms of dollars per ton of production) as contrasted with only broad and qualitative OHS incentives. It may well be that one unfortunate result was to send both a direct financial message and a subliminal broader message about the relative priorities of the company.

Second, and closely related, there was arguably insufficient emphasis on accountability mechanisms at mine site level. For example, individual managers might have been assigned particular safety action items that would have to be certified as completed by a more senior manager. Of course, such forms of architectural internal regulation have their limits. Bardach and Kagan pointed out many years ago that "the risk of [pushing] accountability requirements into the farthest reaches and deeper recesses of social life is that, in the long run, everyone will be accountable for everything, but no one will take responsibility for anything" (Bardach & Kagan, 1982, p. 321).

The challenge, as Bardach and Kagan recognized, was for regulators (whether internal or external) not simply to impose controls (or, we might add, management systems) "*but to activate and draw upon the conscience and the talents of those they seek to regulate*"(Bardach & Kagan, 1982, p. 31; emphasis added). Without such commitment, then the problem will remain: Managers and workers who lack commitment to safety will undertake safety precautions only when they are being watched and evaluated. But comprehensive oversight is simply not possible, so what is required to achieve such commitment is the nurturing of a "safety culture."

According to James Reason's (1997) classic analysis, an organization with an effective safety culture has a safety information system that collects, analyzes, and disseminates information from incidents and near misses, as well as from regular proactive checks on the system; has a reporting culture where people are prepared to report their errors, mistakes, and violations; has a culture of trust where people are encouraged and even rewarded to provide essential safety-related information, but also in which the line between acceptable and unacceptable behavior is clear;

has flexibility, in terms of the ability to reconfigure the organizational structure in the face of a dynamic and demanding task environment; has the willingness and competence to draw the right conclusions from its safety system; and has willingness to implement reform when it is required.

There is not space in this chapter for an extended discussion of the safety culture literature, which can be found elsewhere (Reason, 1997). However, one of its most important findings is that an improvement in safety culture will be far more effective than increased accountability, sophisticated management-based regulation, or (more controversially) behavior-based safety (Reason, 1997, p. 293). Reason argues that an organization's safety culture takes on a profound significance at the point where accident rates reach a "plateau," that is, at the very point the mining industry has now reached (Reason, 2000). It is argued that to advance beyond this "low but (seemingly) unassailable" plateau and to continue improvement in safety performance, "it is necessary to address the hearts and minds of the management and workers" (Lee, 1998, p. 217). It may well be that this plateau is often reached after requirements for safety "hardware and software" (i.e., barriers and management-based requirements) have been met (Reason, 2000, p. 65).

The Worker–Management Disconnect

In terms of shaping the OHS behavior of their workforce, BHP's internal regulatory focus relied heavily on the management-based tools described earlier. In particular, although workers were not expected to have close acquaintance with the OHS management system as a whole, they were expected to comply with the specific parts of it that apply "at the coalface." These include job safety analyses and specific controls relating to issues such as personal protective equipment, fall protection/safe working from heights, hazardous substances, housekeeping, lifting gear, machine guards, confined space entry, permit to work, and a variety of other identified safety concerns.

To a lesser extent, BHP also relied upon a controversial approach known as behavior-based safety, which assumes workers' unsafe behavior is the cause of most work-related injuries and illnesses. Most commonly, it seeks to achieve behavioral change by requiring "frontline staff to conduct behavioral safety observations on their colleagues" (The Keil Centre, 2002, p. 10). These observations are then fed back to the relevant workers in an effort to both draw attention to and change the undesirable behavior (Geller, 2001, p. 66). BHP's particular version relied heavily on the DuPont STOP program, a central tenet of which is that if you can change behavior, then values will follow. For example, BHP had experimented with techniques such as "Safe Act Observation" and emphasized the critical importance of positive safety behaviors, which involved focus on the people factors of workplace safety. Trade unions perceive this approach to be underpinned by a "blame the worker" philosophy, which they see as obfuscating the true cause of work-related injury and disease: the relentless pursuit of profit.

In any event, neither of these strategies was markedly successful in preventing a disconnect between the BHP's workforce on the one hand and corporate and mine site management on the other—with mine managers being the "human face" with whom workers interacted from day to day. There were a number of reasons for this, probably the most important of which was that neither internal management–based regulation nor behavior-based safety can be effective without worker cooperation and buy-in.

The literature overwhelmingly suggests that genuine workplace participation and involvement in OHS issues will be crucial to improved OHS performance, especially "empowerment of workers and encouraging their contribution to innovation, and a sense of control and autonomy by workers" (Bluff, 2003, p. 78). In the absence of such cooperation, workers pay lip service to OHS requirements, but their impact on behavior is very limited. For example, the independent engineering report undertaken by QEST Consulting in 2002 identified:

> *the lack of discipline in the maintenance workgroups whereby personnel do not always follow the WIN, JSA or standard work practice. As a result, incidents have occurred where the hazard had been previously identified and where control measures had been put in place.* This was more to do with the culture in some work groups and less to do with training and education.
>
> *(QEST, 2002, p. 15; emphasis added)*

Such a culture may be a product, at least in part, of past management behavior. Workers take their cue from senior management and coworkers with the result that where management tolerates certain traits (cutting corners on safety to increase profitability), they are likely to become reinforced and over time—entrenched. According to Pitzer and McGurkin, "Employees develop a perception of what is expected and 'permissible'—in the way they see others (peers, supervisors and managers) behave around them. This is the 'work environment' of employees and it has a powerful influence on risk-taking in the organisation" (Pitzer et al., 2000, p. 46). In the Pilbara, the inquiry documented numerous examples of mine management demonstrably failing to "walk the talk" when it came to safety and failing to put safety before production.[8]

A fundamental cause of lack of cooperation and of an adversarial workplace culture, so a number of official reports have demonstrated, is lack of trust between workers and management. The 2005 New South Wales Mine Safety Review identified a "debilitating mistrust between the members of the tripartite process" (Wran & McClelland, 2005, p. 7) as a principal obstacle to improved OHS in the mining industry. Consistent with the broader literature on workplace safety, the role of mine management in creating trust (or mistrust) is particularly important.

Management sets the priorities, establishes the values, and provides the resources that substantially shape mine management and workforce responses. Messages conveyed by senior management, particularly as to whether and how much they value safety and the well-being of the workforce, are part of the composite picture that workers develop as to the company's motivations and behavior. As Conchie et al. point out in their overview of the trust literature, "A good organisational safety culture typically relies on good safety leadership [that] promotes shared values and commitment to an organization's safety policies" (Conchie et al., 2006, p. 1152). For the workforce, the critical level of management is not at the head office (of whom they often have only the vaguest awareness) but senior management personnel at site level with whom they interact.

At BHP in the Pilbara, a lack of trust was both deep seated and long-standing. For example, the QEST Consulting report of 2002 pointed out that "the workforce had the perception that decisions made at management level are purely for the benefit of the management group and to placate the regulator or public opinion and not to seriously address site issues and hazards" (QEST, 2002, p. 19). At some operations (with regard to both BHP and its contractors), the evidence suggests that management behavior bred particular cynicism and mistrust. One worker told the Ritter Inquiry:

> [Y]ou only have to look at the minutes of the safety committee to see the same things repeated over the years . . . we have no way of enforcing anything without the drastic step of informing the Department and nobody wants to be responsible for that, the fallout would not be worth it. . . . The minutes of our Safety Committee meetings are too brief and "sanitised" so they appear better in print. When pursued it is hard to know what happened.
>
> *(Ritter, 2004, p. 189)*

Worker cynicism was encapsulated in a common response to management "safety before production" notices: "Safety is only an option if it is convenient." A number of witnesses gave evidence in a similar vein (Ritter, 2004).

Relations between management and trade union members were particularly poisoned as a result of BHP's adversarial industrial relations policy described earlier. BHP's ideological commitment to eradicate collective bargaining and trade unions led, at mine site level, to a range of behaviors that served to further undermine trust between workers and management. Moreover, even those who had (often under pressure) taken up individual contracts of employment commonly perceived themselves as vulnerable to exploitation and especially (as the more recent incident at Mount Whalebank illustrates) to "intimidation and victimisation" (OHS News, 2007, p. 1). The result was that BHP's internal management-based regulation and behavior-based safety initiatives barely touched the surface of work site culture at individual work sites.

There is evidence to suggest that these experiences are not confined to BHP but are pervasive within the Australian mining industry. One of the most important findings of Pitzer's cultural survey of the industry was that

> most organisations and the industry as a whole have been very successful in communicating the "safety message." Despite this powerful message the "value" of "Care about employees" that underpins the achievement of a positive safety culture seems lacking in the industry . . . the pervasive message employees connect with is that management does not "value" employees . . . [this is] also suggested by trends on linked factors: high levels of job insecurity; low credibility of senior management; high levels of dissatisfaction with safety management systems; and diminishing value of the traditional safety committee.
>
> *(MCA, 1999, p. 36)*

Again, what is needed is not so much to refine the tools of management-based regulation or greater emphasis on behavior-based safety but to change the mindset of the workforce. And this brings us back to the importance not of systems but of nurturing a positive safety culture, which in turn will be almost impossible in the face of mine site management with a blatant disregard for safety and an adversarial industrial relations policy of the kind being rolled out in the Pilbara.

The Contractor Disconnect

A third disconnect arose between BHP management (primarily at corporate level) and contract workers as a result of the pressure the company placed on contractors to meet production deadlines and quota. This increased their tendency to cut corners and to avoid raising safety issues for fear of slowing or stopping production. In cases where responsibility for an entire mining operation was contracted out, corporate management additionally specified production targets (including tonnages and dates). Although BHP also required compliance with their OHS standards, there remained considerable pressures on contractors to focus on meeting these production targets, which often trumped OHS considerations. While these pressures were exacerbated by the strong production orientation of mine management and their failure to embrace a strong OHS commitment, the greatest pressure on contactors was a direct product of the pressures imposed upon them as a consequence of BHP corporate-level policies.

Earlier it was argued that BHP, like a number of other mining majors, believed that there was a compelling business case for reducing levels of work-related injury and disease *within* the company—driven in substantial part by the need to protect the corporate reputation. However, unless fatalities and injuries of contractors in some indirect way serve to damage BHP's own reputation (of which there is little evidence), then the business case for improving the OHS performance of its contractors is considerably weaker.

It was about the same time as the Australian mining industry began to focus on improving its own levels of OHS that it also substantially increased its use of contractors. Not coincidentally, those contractors have been disproportionately used to address many of the most dangerous mining operations (Johnstone, Mayhew, & Quinlan, 2001, p. 351). In the case of BHP, the net effect of corporate policy was that, through the use of contractors, not only was BHP management able to outsource production, it was, in effect, also able to outsource OHS responsibility as well, substantially avoiding the reputational damage that might follow from a high incidence of work-related injury, disease, and death but without adversely affecting profitability.

Consistent with this approach, in its relationship with contractors, BHP's priority was very clearly production, as evidenced by the extent to which production objectives were clearly specified in contracts with contractors in a way that OHS was not. For example, although BHP quantified specific production targets, any contractual obligation in respect of OHS process and/or outcomes was far less sharply defined (e.g., a general exhortation/requirement to abide by BHP OHS standards), and importantly, there was often no comparable financial incentive/penalty for failing to meet OHS expectations. While this might plausibly have been an oversight—identifying quantitative OHS performance indicators, as discussed earlier, is not easy—it was coupled with a policy that effectively precluded contractors from attending to OHS issues and delivering on production objectives within relentlessly tight time lines. It is hardly surprising, therefore, that contractors respond in kind by making OHS subservient to production. In this respect BHP at corporate level clearly did not place safety first and corporate rhetoric was not matched by OHS practice. Here, the skeptic's view that, notwithstanding appearances, there was in fact, no disconnect between corporate policy and OHS outcomes has considerable substance.

Conclusion

A single case study cannot of course provide a definitive answer to the any of the questions addressed above. But at the very least, there is reason to believe that the sorts of tensions experienced by BHP and the broader regulatory and policy issues it raised may not be atypical. In a number of other well-documented cases, the implementation of a comprehensive mechanism of internal management–based regulation have also failed to achieve their intended goals and in some cases have failed to prevent disaster (Hopkins, 2000; Gunningham, 2007).

Many large companies have placed faith in management-based internal regulation as the principal means of ensuring that their social objectives are achieved at facility level. In the case of work-related injury and disease, particular reliance has been placed on the capacities of OHS management systems, audits, and standards to perform these functions.

But as evidenced by BHP Billiton's performance in the Pilbara, the existence of a formal OHS management system and the other manifestations of management-based regulation tells one very little about whether or to what extent production targets took precedence over safety, production pressures led to risk taking, or workers are constrained from reporting their OHS concerns. And depending on the auditing process,[9] it may not reveal how often safety meetings actually took place, or if they did, whether they engaged with serious safety issues or were tokenistic in nature, or whether worker representatives were constrained from bringing certain safety issues before them. Similarly, the fact that BHP required its contractors to adopt a system comparable to its own tells us very little about how that system operated in practice.

To understand the implementation failure in this case, one needs to get within the organization and observe the gap between how the system purported to operate and what actually happened when workers and site managers were confronted with a variety of implementation challenges.[10] At BHP's operations in the Pilbara, those challenges related to unresolved tensions involving production pressures, adversarial industrial relations, and the time and production requirements BHP imposed upon its contractors. BHP's and its contractors' internal regulation mechanisms proved manifestly inadequate to meet these challenges or to achieve their OHS objectives.

In substantial part, culture lay at the heart of many of these implementation failures. The unwillingness of mine site management to put safety first made corporate commitments sound like empty rhetoric and bred cynicism and mistrust within the workforce. This was compounded by an adversarial approach to industrial relations that also bred acrimony and led workers to doubt that management had any genuine commitment to workplace safety. BHP was not entirely unaware of the importance of shaping the behavior of the workforce and had experimented with various behavior-based safety initiatives. But these did not even touch upon the underlying causes of a mistrustful workplace culture, nor did they go to the roots of risk-taking behavior.

One lesson of this case study is that even the existence of advanced and sophisticated tools of internal management regulation cannot guarantee improved OHS outcomes. Formal systems of internal control need to be complemented by informal structures that serve, in Joe Rees' terms, to "institutionalize a fragile value like safety, particularly where it may conflict with a much more powerful value such as meeting production objectives" (Rees, 1994, p. 4; see also Selznick, 1992). What is needed, so the literature suggests, is to inculcate a state of "mindfulness," a willingness and capacity to question safety failures (Weick, cited in Maxwell, 2004, p. 148), and a state of trust between workers and management that enables blame-free reporting of incidents and near misses (Reason, 2000, p. 65). All of these are manifestations of safety culture (or safety climate) that are barely touched upon by either management-based internal regulation or behavior-based safety initiatives.

A second lesson is that major blockages to cultural change may lie with the management of individual facilities rather than (as mainstream management literature implies) with corporate leadership. While the latter is undoubtedly important, at BHP it was the absence of leadership at site level that largely rendered management-based regulation ineffective. Workers took their lead from site management, and accepted the subliminal message that production came first. A range of unsafe practices, documented by the Ritter Inquiry and described above, followed inexorably. This suggests that a crucial ingredient of the complex process of changing workplace safety culture is mine site management's willingness to "walk the talk." They must, for example, be ready, willing, and able to halt production if safety is seriously compromised. Without such commitment, little progress can be made. But it will be equally important for mine site management to develop mechanisms that serve to break down mistrust, to build a cooperative relationship with the workforce, and to obtain worker buy-in to management-based initiatives.

However, while culture and ideology plays a very large part in this story, other factors also played their part. In particular, the performance indicators and benchmarks that BHP used to assess production performance were much clearer and more quantifiable than those used to assess OHS performance. The result, intended or unintended, was to send an economic signal that the former were more important than the latter. The lesson here is that where management or contractors lack the incentives to engage seriously in systematic OHS management, the outcomes are likely to be disappointing (Coglianese & Nash, 2006).

For the BHP workforce, safety incentives were only one of a number of influences affecting behavior, and there is no evidence to suggest that their role was a critical one. Nevertheless, the provision of more sharply focused incentives for improved OHS performance at site level, coupled with other mechanisms intended to ensure greater accountability and transparency, would have supported initiatives to change the safety culture itself (Howard-Grenville, Nash, & Coglianese, 2008, p. 73). But ultimately, in terms of the disconnect between workers and management and between corporate and mine site management, it was the absence of a safety culture at site level that thwarted the implementation of management-based internal regulation. The principal lesson of this case study is that the tools and techniques of internal management–based regulation are only as good as the culture into which they are received.

In the case of contractors, the performance indicators and incentives that BHP specified were fundamentally important. A failure to meet those indicators would, as all sides were well aware, have profound economic implications, and might result in breach of contract and economic penalties. Both contractors and BHP were well aware that those incentives were such that any trade-off between safety and production would inevitably be settled in favor of the latter. BHP stood to benefit economically from such an outcome, and there was no "business case" built around reputation risk or social license pressures for changing their present practices. This analysis suggests that government regulation will continue to be the principal and perhaps the only source of regulation capable of protecting the OHS of contract workers and other forms of contingent employment. That regulation, moreover, should not rely primarily upon contractors' adopting safety management systems and other "process-based" mechanisms, for these are likely to be more honored in the breach. Rather, various forms of prescriptive or performance-based regulation imposing quantifiable obligations on contractors, coupled with broader-based general duties on those who engage them, will be essential.

These findings have application across a range of other social issues where large companies must protect their reputation and demonstrate their corporate social responsibility to external audiences. These areas include food safety, environmental protection, rail regulation, sustainable forestry, toxic chemical reduction, and trade practices (Coglianese & Lazer, 2003, p. 691). In all of these areas, there is heavy reliance on tools of internal management–based regulation such as management systems, audits, and standards. At least where human factors play an important role, then the findings of this study suggest that a heavy reliance on the tools of management-based regulation, to the detriment or exclusion of cultural considerations, is likely to render those initiatives much less effective.

Third, the findings also have implications for various forms of external regulation. To return to Coglianese and Nash's (2006) classification of management-based strategies, not just companies but also government regulators have placed increasing faith in management-based regulation and incentives over the last decade. A growing and substantial number of incentive-based mechanisms are based on very much the same principles: if one can make (or incentivize) large corporations to put in place sophisticated management-based tools and strategies, then improved social performance should follow. But our findings suggest that such expectations may be overly optimistic, and that management-based regulation ("regulating from the inside") may be insufficient to solve these problems, unless it is used in conjunction with operations-specific cultural initiatives. In sum, both corporate management and government policy makers are in danger of putting too many of their eggs into what may turn out to be a very flawed basket.

Finally, and most broadly, the story of BHP and the disconnects between its stated safety goals and its results provide an object lesson in the usefulness of the approach to studying regulation pioneered by Kagan and his colleagues. As a methodological matter, Kagan stresses the importance of careful case studies, especially in the early stages of a research agenda. This case study reinforces that point, as the details of BHP's response to the law defy any simple set of proxies; they require close study. Only when we study the process by which the organization responds to regulations can we truly understand how the centralized commands of bureaucratic legalism are translated into social practices—or, in this case, fall short.

Notes

1 While some have framed these issues in terms of the principal-agent framework (where the challenge is to align the behavior of self-seeking agents with corporate goals), this is of doubtful value because the conduct of the agents at site level may be undertaken at least in part to benefit the organization (for example, by maximizing production even if this compromises social goals such as safety, health, or environmental protection). See, e.g., Krawiec (2005).

2 Regulation, following Black's (2002) definition, is "a process involving the sustained and focused attempt to alter the behaviour of others according to identified purposes with the intention of producing a broadly identified outcome or outcomes which may involve mechanisms of standard-setting, information-gathering and behavior-modification"(p. 170). As such it need not involve state actors or legal mechanisms.

3 It must be emphasized that all the material upon which the present article relies is drawn from various aspects of the Ministerial Inquiry report (Ritter, 2004) or material otherwise in the public domain, and in no way relies upon any confidential information to which the author was privy.

4 While this is not accepted by BHPBIO, the inquiry accepted the information of people with direct knowledge of the issue (Ritter, 2004, p. 292).

5 National data prior to 1997–98 was incomplete and is not available for some jurisdictions, so time series data prior to this is unreliable. See Safety Performance in the Western Australian Minerals Industry, Accident and Injury Statistics, 2014–2015, p. 5, Western Australia, Department of Minerals and Petroleum, 2015, available at: www.dmp.wa.gov.au/Documents/Safety/MSH_Stats_Reports_SafetyPerfWA_2014-15.pdf (accessed 1 Aug 2016).

6 BHP and Billiton merged in 2001. The principal metric with regard to work-related injury is time lost from injuries. These have broadly declined. However, BHP Billiton has used different metrics to measure time lost from injuries over the past decade, so it is hard to attain a consistent trend prior to 2001–02. Between 2001–02 and 2006–07, the Classified Injury Frequency Rate (CIFR), which represents the number of classified injuries per million hours of work, decreased by almost a third, from 6.8 (approx) to 4.3 (BHP Billiton, 2007). Although fatalities have varied considerably over the past decade or so, they too have broadly declined (BHP Billiton, 2007, p. 174).

7 When evaluated against a set of 10 criteria widely recognized as being central to systematic and effective OHS management, the BHP approach scores very well. Indeed, there is evidence that BHP's broad-based and sophisticated OHS system incorporates the key characteristics necessary to enable positive OHS performance.

8 See the examples listed as bullet points in this chapter.

9 In principle, any major failings in the OHS management system will be identified in the course of regular internal and external audits, which provide the key oversight mechanism intended to keep the management system "on track." However, there is now a strong body of evidence to suggest that audits, across a diversity of areas of social and economic concern, have such serious limitations that they are unlikely to fulfil this oversight role effectively. See the special issue of *Law and Policy 25* (2003).

10 For a review of the evidence, see Saksvik and Quinlan (2003). Paper compliance, insufficient inspectoral oversight, overreliance on management and inadequate worker input are identified as particular problems. See also Nytrö, Saksvik and Torvatn (1998) and Saksvik, Torvatn and Nytrö (2003).

References

Bardach, E., & Kagan, R. (1982). *Going by the Book: The Problem of Regulatory Unreasonableness*. Piscataway, NJ: Transaction Publishers.

BHP Billiton. (2007). *BHP Billiton Full Sustainability Report*. Melbourne: BHP Billiton.

BHP Billiton Iron Ore. (2004). Submission to the Ministerial Inquiry into BHP Billiton Iron Ore Occupational Health and Safety Systems and Practices, Parts 1-3, September.

Black, J. (2002). "Regulatory Conversations." *Journal of Law and Society*, 29, 163–70.

Bluff, L. (2003). *Systematic Management of Occupational Health and Safety*. Retrieved from www.ohs.anu.edu.au.

Coglianese, C., & Lazer, D. (2003). "Management-Based Regulation: Prescribing Private Management to Achieve Public Goals." *Law and Society Review*, 37, 691–730.

Coglianese, C., & Nash, J. (2006). *Beyond Compliance: Business Decision Making and the U.S. EPA's Performance Track Program. Regulatory Policy Program Report RPP-10*. Cambridge, MA: Mossavar-Rahmani Center for Business and Government, John F. Kennedy School of Government, Harvard University.

Conchie, S.M., Donald, I.J., & Taylor, P.J. (2006). "Trust: Missing Piece(s) in the Safety Puzzle." *Risk Analysis* 26(5), 1097–104.

Galvin, J.M. (2005). "Occupational Health and Safety Acts—Performance and Prosecution in the Australian Minerals Industry." *Mining Technology: Transactions of the Institutions of Mining and Metallurgy: Section A*, 114 (4), 251–6.

Geller, E.S. (2004). "Behavior-Based Safety: A Solution to Injury Prevention: Behavior-Based Safety 'Empowers' Employees and Addresses the Dynamics of Injury Prevention." *Risk & Insurance*, 15(12), 66.

Gray, W.B., & Deily, M.E. (1996). "Compliance and Enforcement: Air Pollution Regulation in the US Steel Industry." *Journal of Environmental Economics and Management*, 31(1), 96–111.

Gunningham, N. (2007). *Mine Safety: Law and Regulation*. Annandale, N.S.W: The Federation Press.

Gunningham, N., & Grabosky, P. (1998). *Smart Regulation: Designing Environmental Policy*. Oxford: Clarendon Press.

Gunningham, N., Kagan, R., & Thornton, D. (2003). *Shades of Green: Business, Regulation and Environment*. Stanford, CA: Stanford University Press.

Hopkins, A. (2000). *Lessons From Longford: The Esso Gas Plant Explosion*. North Ryde, N.S.W: CCH Australia.

Howard-Grenville, J., Nash, J., & Coglianese, C. (2008). "Constructing the License to Operate: Internal Factors and Their Influence on Corporate Environmental Decisions." *Law & Policy*, 30(1), 73–107.

Johnstone, R., Mayhew, C., & Quinlan, M. (2001). "Outsourcing Risk? The Regulation of OSH Where Contractors Are Employed." *Comparative Labor Law and Policy Journal*, 22(3), 351–94.

Joyce, S., & Thomson, I. (1999). "Earning a Social License to Operate: Social Acceptability and Resource Development in Latin America. *Mining Journal*, 11 June, 441–3.

Kagan, R., Gunningham, N., & Thornton, T. (2003). "Regulatory Regimes and Variations in Corporate Environmental Performance: Evidence from the Pulp and Paper Industry." *Law and Society Review*, 37(1), 51–90.

Keil Centre for the Health and Safety Executive. (2002). *Contract Research Report #430: Strategies to promote safe behaviour as part of a health and safety management team*. Colegate, Norwich: Her Majesty's Stationery Office.

King, A., & Shaver, J. (2001). "Are Aliens Green? Assessing Foreign Establishments' Environmental Conduct in the United States." *Strategic Management Journal*, 22(11), 1069–85.

Krawiec, K. (2005). "Organisational Misconduct: Beyond the Principal-Agent Model." *Florida State University Law Review*, 32(2), 571–615.

Lee, T. (1998). "An Assessment of Safety Culture at a Nuclear Reprocessing Plant." *Work and Safety*, 12(3), 217–37.

Maxwell, C. (2004). *Occupational Health and Safety Act Review*. State of Victoria, Australia.

Minerals Council of Australia (MCA). (1999). "Australian Minerals Industry Safety Culture Survey Report." Retrieved from www.minerals.org.au/__data/assets/pdf_file/4923/safety_survey_report_jul99.pdf.

Nytrö, K., Saksvik, P.Ö., & Torvatn, H. (1998). "Organizational Prerequisites for the Implementation of Systematic Health, Environment and Safety Work in Enterprises." *Safety Science*, 30(3), 297–307. doi:10.1016/S0925-7535(98)00050-2

OHS News. (2007). "OWS to Look at BHP Safety Culture." *Occupational Health News.*

Pitzer, C., Adam, M., & McGurkin, P. (2000). "Safemap at BHP Cannington Mine." Retrieved from www.qrc.org.au/_files/docs/conferences/QMC_2000/conf_pitzer.pdf.

QEST. (2002). *Safety and Risk Study for BHP DRI Plant.* Melbourne: Quest Consulting Group.

Rappaport, A., & Flaherty, M. (1991). *Multinational Corporations and the Environment: A Survey of Global Practice.* Medford, MA: Center for Environmental Management, Tufts University.

Reason, J. (1998). "Achieving a Safe Culture: Theory and Practice." *Work and Stress*, 12(3), 293–306.

Reason, J. (2000). "Beyond the Limitations of Safety Systems." *Australian Safety News.*

Reason, J.T. (1997). *Managing the Risks of Organizational Accidents.* Aldershot, Hants, England; Brookfield: Ashgate.

Rees, J.V. (1994). *Hostages of Each Other: The Transformation of Nuclear Safety Since Three Mile Island.* Chicago, IL: University of Chicago Press.

Ritter, M., & Western Australia Department of State Development. (2004). "Occupational Health and Safety Systems and Practices of BHP Billiton Iron Ore and Boodarie Iron Sites in Western Australia and Related Matters." Retrieved from www.premier.wa.gov.au/docs/features/BHP_Ministerial_Inquiry_Vol1.pdf.

Saksvik, P.Ö., & Quinlan, M. (2003). "Regulating Systemic Occupational Health and Safety Management." *Industrial Relations*, 58(1), 33–59.

Saksvik, P.Ö., Torvatn, H., & Nytrö, K. (2003). "Systematic Occupational Health and Safety Work in Norway: A Decade of Implementation." Safety Science, 1(9), 721–38. doi:10.1016/S0925-7535(02)00020-6

Selznick, P. (1992). *The Moral Commonwealth: Social Theory and the Promise of Community.* Berkeley: University of California Press.

Walters, D., Nichols, T., Connor, J., Tasiran, A.C., & Cam, S. (2005). *The Role and Effectiveness of Safety Representatives in Influencing Workplace Health and Safety* (Research Report 363). Health and Safety Executive.

Wran, N., & McClelland, J. (2005). "NSW Mines Safety Review: Report to the Hon Kerry Hickey MP Minister for Resources." Retrieved from www.dpi.nsw.gov.au/minerals/safety/mine-safety-initiatives/wran-mine-safety-review/.

Yakoleva, N. (2005). *Corporate Social Responsibility in the Mining Industries.* Corporate Social Responsibility Series, Farnham: Ashgate.

7

DEVOLVING STANDARDS

California's Structural Failures in Response to Prisoner Litigation

Malcolm M. Feeley and Van Swearingen

Adversarial legalism is a double-edged sword. It can cut through seemingly impenetrable complexities to isolate problems, but it can also lead to endless quagmires (Kagan, 2001). And it can do both at the same time. Both the strengths and the weaknesses of adversarial legalism are found in litigation concerning prison conditions and inmate rights. The federal courts have been perhaps the single most important source of improvements in prisons in the United States over the past 50 years, but litigation has failed to institutionalize many of its most important victories. This chapter considers the continuing challenges confronting legislators, administrators, judges, lawyers, and other policymakers as they think about how to institutionalize structural reforms pressed by the courts. Interestingly, in the areas of concern of this study, it is not the courts that have generated the problems of hyper-legalism that correctional institutions now confront. Rather, it is the prisons' own failure to adopt strong institutional structures that allow them to escape the debilitating and seemingly endless cycle of protracted litigation. The California prison system has managed to defang some of the more powerful and heroic aspects of adversarial legalism while retaining or even exacerbating its most troublesome features. Moreover, it has failed to diffuse down to each individual prison a coherent system of operating rules—a failure of bureaucratic legalism within the prison system itself.

The California Department of Corrections and Rehabilitation (CDCR) is the nation's largest correctional agency. This chapter focuses on two policies that weaken CDCR's ability to extract itself from the pathologies of adversarial legalism. One deals with the department's decentralized inmate grievance procedures, the other with the department's delegation of its rule-making authority to individual prisons. To reduce its exposure to litigation as well as to minimize the burdens of existing court oversight, CDCR must employ a strong centralized administration that allows for routine problems to be identified early, resolved authoritatively, and monitored continuously. However, in both of the issues we examine, CDCR has decentralized where it should have developed centralized authority. The results exacerbate the problems and increase the likelihood of continued litigation. In constructing its inmate grievance procedures, CDCR has created a system that does little to resolve grievances but much to foster cynicism and alienation. And in developing policies to anticipate and respond to court-ordered reforms, CDCR has fostered local discretion and institution-specific policies when it should have strengthened central administration.

CDCR has long promoted its goals of reducing litigation, complying with federal court orders, and working towards the termination of judicial oversight. Indeed, these are now formal institutional commitments, pursued by departmental staff including the Office of Audit and Court Compliance as well as the Liability Assessment and Litigation Management Team within the Office of Legal Affairs. The 2005 CDCR Strategic Plan included as one of its seven priorities the need to more competently comply with court orders and to identify and respond with greater clarity and success to potential litigation threats. Similar ambitions were expressed in CDCR's Strategic Plan for the period 2010–15. Indeed, practically each year, CDCR can be expected to publicly articulate some desire to reduce its exposure to litigation.

This quest began in the 1980s, if not before, when prison administrators first felt the brunt of litigation challenging conditions of confinement. CDCR staff responded by developing standards based on regulatory law, internal and external audit reports, environmental health surveys, prior litigation, inmate appeals, and the like. Initially, the strategy worked; CDCR embraced "litigation avoidance management," and committed itself to develop stronger administrative oversight, and it was able to settle cases and at times convince courts to dismiss some complaints by pointing to its own internal standards and promising to correct "isolated" abuses. But many of the promised changes did not materialize. They may have been sidetracked by the explosion in the prison population of the 1980s, undercut by the recession in the early 1990s, lost sight of in the bitter "war against drugs," or swamped by the overwhelming power of the prison guards' union. Whatever the precise reasons, both the state's and CDCR's commitment wavered, and the department settled into a sustained period of weak leadership with little interest in or capacity to effect structural administrative reforms.

This chapter examines those failures with respect to two issues. Part I examines the inmate grievance procedure and shows how it is fundamentally flawed in both design and operation. Part II examines CDCR's practice of developing prison-specific or "local rules" rather than system-wide polices that are embedded in the state administrative process and departmental regulations. In the conclusion, we argue that CDCR's stated goal of reducing litigation exposure, at least in the areas we examine, cannot be achieved without more centralization, stronger leadership at the top, a greater capacity to monitor practices in individual correctional institutions, and an expansion of involvement by neutral parties. Until CDCR embraces these concerns, it will continue to face ineffective administration and unnecessary litigation.

Part I: The Failure of the Inmate Grievance Process

In 1973 the California legislature adopted a comprehensive grievance procedure for prison inmates. Although statutorily authorized, the California Department of Corrections[1] shaped the implementing regulations and the administration of the procedure. At the time it was adopted, the grievance procedure was a model of good prison administration. It anticipated developments that were subsequently embraced by other states, imposed on still others by federal court orders, and still later pressed on the states by the Prison Litigation Reform Act (PLRA) of 1996.

California's grievance procedures allow inmates to appeal "any policy, decision, action, condition, or omission by the department or its staff" claimed to have an adverse effect upon their welfare by filing a CDCR Form 602 (Inmate/Parole Appeal Form).[2] This 602 appeals process, as it has come to be known, provides prisoners with a seemingly efficient opportunity to voice their complaints heard through grievance procedures administered by prison staff, and then appealed through various levels of administration within CDCR. At the same time, it is designed to limit costly and time-consuming litigation: inmates must exhaust the internal grievance procedure appeals process before they can file a state court petition for a writ of habeas corpus or a federal lawsuit regarding prison conditions.[3] California's regulations provide for four levels of review: an informal inquiry reviewed by line staff, a First Formal Level review by an Appeals Coordinator, a Second Formal Level review by an Appeals Coordinator, and a Third Formal Level review by the CDCR Chief of Inmate Appeals.

At first glance this process looks impressive. It was pioneering. Its provisions exact higher standards than do the grievance procedures required by many other states. It requires that inmates have the right to be informed in writing of their rights, and that they have a meaningful opportunity to voice their grievances. At one level, CDCR meets these requirements. Signs detailing inmate rights and describing how and where to file grievances are posted in open spaces throughout the states' prisons. 602 grievance forms and collection boxes are placed in accessible places throughout institutions. So, prisoners do learn of their rights, have access to grievance petitions, and have a convenient way to file them. In theory and in institutional structure, CDCR's grievance process appears to be capable of informing inmates of their rights, receiving inmate complaints, holding hearings, rendering judgments, and providing remedies not available from cumbersome and expensive courts.

There is no question that this process is active and functioning. Inmates generate vast numbers of complaints; many are trivial or without significant merit, but clearly a large number are both serious and substantial. CDCR does not publish the numbers of all annual claims, but by all accounts the total number of complaints is significant and concerning. For example, for the majority of fiscal year 2003–04, the Inmate Appeals Branch processed over 3,100 Third Formal Level appeals each month (Office of the Inspector General, September 2004), and during fiscal year 2005–06, CDCR disposed of 15,836 grievances at the third level (Calavita & Jenness, 2014).

Despite all this, CDCR's inmate grievance process cannot be judged a success. Once one looks beyond its façade, the process is found wanting. In what is sure to become the definitive assessment of CDCR's grievance process, Kitty Calavita and Valerie Jenness point to two near-fatal features of the process: First, they report that during fiscal year 2005–06, inmates' appeals were granted (in part or in full) only 4.9 percent of the time (grants in full represented a minuscule .02 percent of all appeals), and were denied outright 94 percent of the time, figures they claim in fact *overstate* inmate victories (Calavita & Jenness, 2014).

Second, as they explored these figures and the grievance process with both CDCR officials and inmates, Calavita and Jenness found a surprising agreement on the ineffectiveness of the process. Correctional officers characterized inmates as hyper-sensitive, and willing to file complaints at a drop of the hat. Accordingly, they maintained, the low success rates were to be expected. To put it bluntly, most officials they interviewed regarded the appeals process as something of a joke. For instance, at least one Inmate Appeals Coordinator (IAC) reported that she routinely reported that the appeal had been "granted in part" simply because she had read it (Calavita & Jenness, 2014, p. 47). Inmates were equally skeptical of its effectiveness. They reported indifference, pervasive insult, and abuse, and were well aware that virtually no appeals were granted. When asked why they continued to file grievances under such conditions and with little likelihood of vindication, inmates typically responded that it was a matter of principle (Calavita & Jenness, 2014).

Still, in discussions with 602 IACs, Calavita and Jenness reported frequent expressions of sympathy with the plight of inmates in general, but almost never in particular. And so, the low rate of inmate success. Indeed, when the researchers asked IACs to describe a situation in which they had granted an inmate appeal, they were often met with blank stares. Such grants were so rare, they reported, that IACs had to dig deep into their memories to come up with even a single example (Calavita & Jenness, 2014).

Inmate Appeals Coordinators' characterizations of their jobs were reinforced by the physical description of their offices. Calavita and Jenness describe a visit:

> The overwhelming nature of the officials' task as we interrupted their work flow to interview them was constantly apparent to us. The stacks upon stacks of paperwork in the Sacramento filing room, where shelves of appeals six feet high lined walls fifty feet long and snaked up and down the

central aisles, were constant physical reminders to both interviewers and staff respondents of the challenging and hapless task at hand.

(Calavita & Jenness, 2014, p. 189)

One gets an impression of Robert Kagan's worst nightmares about adversarial legalism or, alternatively, a newly discovered story by Franz Kafka.

Of course no one knows for certain what portion of the complaints have merit, but there is more than the indirect evidence presented above to suggest that many grievances that do have merit are not granted. For example, since 2001, CDCR has been involved in a massive system-wide suit dealing with its failure to provide adequate medical care to inmates.[4] This litigation has produced a library of graphic reports documenting accounts of widespread—indeed, system-wide and systemic—failures on a massive scale, failures that had serious, at times fatal, consequences. Lawyers for the inmates produced the first studies, and for the most part CDCR officials did not dispute them. Later, after a consent decree was signed, court-appointed monitors and then a receiver produced still more detailed reports documenting widespread failure, prompting the district court to conclude that "the California prison medical care system is broken beyond repair. The harm already done in this case to California's prison inmate population could not be more grave, and the threat of future injury and death is virtually guaranteed in the absence of drastic action."[5] For the most part, CDCR did not contest these findings; indeed, CDCR readily acknowledged the shortcomings and offered as its defense overcrowding.[6]

Additional information reinforces this impression. Shortly after a consent decree promising better medical care had been signed, Matthew Cate, then the Inspector General of the Prisons and later Secretary of CDCR, told one of the authors that he thought that on average one person a week was dying of medical malpractice in California's prisons, and that the situation was so dire that he was reluctant to take a week's vacation. Similarly, shortly after the state appealed the district court's ruling to reduce the prison population so that it could manage the medical crisis, the court-appointed receiver for the prison system told one of the authors that the department's medical records were in such disarray that prison officials were unable to access inmate medical records in order to respond in meaningful ways to requests for services.[7] These problems were not confined to one or two of the state's three dozen prisons, or restricted to complaints related to esoteric diseases or complicated diagnoses. They were run-of-the-mill problems: unfilled prescriptions, untreated toothaches, broken prosthetics, lost eyeglasses, untreated fevers, lack of nurses on duty—as well as asthma attacks, ruptured appendices, broken limbs, pus-filled abscesses, kidney problems, and the like.

These various indicators all point to the same conclusions: For decades the state failed to provide adequate medical care for inmates, and even when officials learned of this problem, they were unable or unwilling to respond. Despite the public scandal, despite acknowledgment of the problem, despite protracted litigation and intense monitoring by the courts, and despite the fact that medical issues constituted the single largest type of complaints filed by inmates, CDCR complaint handlers acknowledged and granted only 0.02 percent of the complaints filed by inmates (Calavita & Jenness, 2014, p. 39). So, at least in one area—providing medical services—there is overwhelming evidence that California's grievance procedure amounted to an utter failure.

Discussion

Rather than being a pioneering alternative dispute resolution process that effectively corrects errors and clarifies rules, and thus helps avoid cumbersome and expensive litigation, California's grievance procedure is something of a Potemkin village. It provides a façade of an institution but lacks depth and substance. This problem is not unique to the CDCR; it is common for grievance procedures structured as this one is. Below, we examine this phenomenon and then turn to the distinctive features of the CDCR grievance process.

Alternative dispute resolution (ADR) is a common response to some of the more troublesome aspects of adversarial legalism. While advocates of ADR processes claim they are more efficient and more effective than the courts, these processes are usually purchased at a high price. They retain some resemblance to formal courts, but ADR systems dramatically alter the nature of the complaint process that differentiates them from formal courts. Foremost are the lack of legal criteria in decision making: clear rules, traditional remedies, sufficient procedural protections, and trained arbiters. Certainly all these defects are built into the 602 appeals process.

If these were the only problems, the CDCR grievance process might be amenable to reform. ADR systems can be upgraded through more clearly defining rules and processes, assuring complainants an opportunity to make charges without fear of retaliation, and appointing competent and neutral decision makers. But the CDCR process has other, less tractable defects. As we have seen, the system is structured to favor the institution. CDCR defines the rules that give rise to the dispute, is a party to the dispute, and then has its staff adjudicate the dispute. Thus the CDCR process is fundamentally one-sided.

Almost all students of prisons emphasize that they are landscapes pervaded by loathing and mistrust between guards and inmates. Ann Chih Lin warns that "prisoners are confined involuntarily, and the prison staff are the ones keeping them there. The resulting bitterness, resentment, wariness, and contempt would seem to preclude the trust and mutual respect necessary for effective . . . counseling" (Lin, 2000). A library of research on prison culture, beginning with Samuel Jan Brakel's 1982 review of grievance procedures in Illinois prisons, substantiates this claim (Brakel, 1982). Indeed, it requires heroic assumptions to imagine that prison personnel can transform themselves from control agents into neutral third-party arbiters. Certainly, any grievance procedure designed to provide justice for convicted felons confined to prisons has an uphill battle to win the hearts and minds of its ostensible beneficiaries. And one administered by prison officials themselves faces an even greater challenge.

Indeed, such systems have a tendency to shift focus away from an inquiry concerned with wrongdoing and rights of the petitioner to a focus on institutional prerogatives (Swearingen, 2008). In prisons, inmates have limited rights to begin with, so any grievance procedure staffed by prison officials has the potential to further skew its concerns to institutional interests. Even discounting career concerns with their employer, prison personnel are not suited to act as impartial complaint handlers. As Lon Fuller quietly noted in a quite different context, "Obviously, a strong emotional attachment by the arbiter to one of the interests involved in the dispute is destructive of that participation" (Fuller, 1978, p. 391). Calavita and Jenness' book amply documents the failing in a process where arbiters have strong emotional attachments to one of the parties (Calavita & Jenness, 2014, pp. 151–181).

The problem goes well beyond outcomes that favor the institution. It involves the power to shape rules and procedures for the long run. Although each case is distinct to one-shot inmate complainants, for institutional repeat players, each case can be a building block for long-term consideration of rules and procedures that favor the institution. This problem is compounded if courts defer to the rulings, as well as the procedures, fact finding, and rulemaking established by these internal dispute resolution institutions. When this occurs, it is as if the grievance procedure of the CDCR has become an internal compliance structure, an institutional form of negotiated governance. The courts in effect delegate their oversight responsibilities to the agency itself. The regulated become the regulators.

A burgeoning body of literature on what Lauren Edelman has called "internal dispute resolution" (IDR) focuses precisely on these concerns and examines them in a variety of settings. Edelman and her colleagues have examined IDR employment discrimination complaints in corporations (Edelman, 2016; Edelman, Erlanger, & Lande, 1993). Focusing on corporate responses to antidiscrimination laws, Edelman and colleagues have found that while businesses may be responsive to an employee's assertion of rights, the internal grievance procedures they adopt often serve as little more than "window-dressing" (Edelman, Uggen, & Erlanger, 1999). Edelman and colleagues have consistently found that in that portion of the corporate world that is most responsive to claims of employment discrimination, the task of developing and administering the grievance process is delegated to human resource departments. Almost by the definition of their jobs, she suggests, human resource personnel are selected for their abilities to reduce the friction in organizations, make them run smoothly, and protect institutional prerogatives. As such they are widely seen by their institutions as ideal complaint handlers. Accordingly in these roles, she finds, human relations/complaint hearing officers consistently reinterpret legally defined rights into vague notions of justice, and arbitrate employee grievances in forums that allow discontented employees the opportunity to express their *feelings* rather than to vindicate their *rights* (Edelman et al., 1993, pp. 503–505). In some settings such an approach may work well for both the grievant and the institution, but it is not likely to work well in a "total institution" where power relations are lopsided and distrust pervasive. Under such conditions, it is difficult to imagine any wholly internal process that could overcome these problems, address *legal* rights, and provide remedies that would be accepted as just (Edelman et al., 1999, pp. 503–504).

Lauren B. Edelman, Kimberly D. Krawiec (Krawiec, 2003, pp. 487, 491), and others have written extensively about the problems of institutionalizing rights through IDR in still other settings (Edelman et al., 1999; Edelman & Patterson, 1999; Edelman & Suchman, 1997). They focus on different subjects, but their conclusions are much the same. IDR processes offer few resources and protections for vulnerable petitioners in institutional settings, where structures, rules, and procedures are likely to be shaped for the long-run benefit of the institution. Most worrisome for Edelman, Krawiec, and still others is that judges now routinely defer to companies that appear to have "effective" IDR procedures in place, without ever questioning their adequacy (Edelman et al., 1999, pp. 408–409, 447). And Krawiec has shown how, in a variety of legal settings, courts unwittingly reduce or eliminate liability for organizations that appear to embrace respect for individual rights of their employees or members by establishing internal compliance structures (Krawiec, 2003, p. 487). Charles Epp has shown much the same thing for grievances against the police as well (Epp, 2009). In the prison setting, the situation is even worse; if a state has any sort of internal grievance procedures, federal law all but instructs federal judges not to inquire into its adequacy, and to defer to it.[8]

The new IDR polices have institutionalized a Catch-22. In an effort to reduce litigation, both Congress and the Supreme Court have embraced a policy of "judicial retrenchment" by making it more difficult for vulnerable individuals to gain access to court. The rationale for this new policy is that since Congress and the appellate courts have insisted upon the establishment of meaningful grievance procedures within organizations, which are ostensibly designed to be faster, fairer, and less expensive where issues can be handled at the local level, there is no need for more cumbersome proceedings in the federal courts. At first glance, this argument is appealing: IDR processes suggest an institutional commitment to the rule of law and a grievance procedure that is easily accessible and tailored to institutional context. Not surprisingly, such compliance structures have gained great popularity in recent years, and are often cited as models of public/private cooperation—shared governance between the regulator and the regulated (Krawiec, 2003, p. 487). But as Edelman and Krawiec point out, such arrangements unwittingly lead government to effectively delegate its legal and regulatory powers to the dominant institutional party. Furthermore, they emphasize, courts are likely to embrace this delegation so long as the organization has made a formal commitment to the substance of the law and established a dispute resolution process. With such procedures in place, courts then defer to the judgments of these

IDR institutions without bothering to make independent judgments as to the soundness of their decisions (Staszak, 2015, pp. 207–208, 219–220).

This same type of power sharing can be extended beyond the public/private realm to involve arrangements between branches of government. Such is the case at hand. Corrections departments eager to avoid the costs of litigation adopt policies and procedures that decrease the likelihood that inmates can gain access to the courts (Schlanger, 2003, pp. 1681–1682). If accepted, courts in effect delegate their powers to these adjunct institutions, which not only find facts and issue rulings, but in the process make law (Feeley & Swearingen, 2004, pp. 433, 436–439). Krawiec identifies the conditions necessary for this transformation: a written code communicated to employees, a monitoring or auditing system designed to detect prohibited conduct, a reporting system allowing people to report violations, and a high-level officer within the organization who has responsibility to determine compliance with the code (Staszak, 2015, pp. 495–496). These features are all, to varying degrees, incorporated in CDCR's and most other prisons' complaint handling procedures. On the surface they may be appealing, but a closer look shows that all too often there is no meaningful hearing, no access to justice.

Edelman, Krawiec, and others have traced the rapid rise of the IDR movement and have assessed its impact to date. Although internal compliance structures are used with increasing frequency and deferred to by the courts, there is little evidence that they actually reduce the incidence of the conduct they purport to regulate (Feeley & Swearingen, 2004, pp. 491–492). They find that these compliance structures are costly and fail to deter undesirable conduct, and yet legitimize organizational practices that allow them to avoid legal liability (Feeley & Swearingen, 2004, pp. 491–492; Adlerstein, 2001).[9] Moreover, they find that repeat players succeed in using them to shape rules to benefit the institution (Feeley & Swearingen, 2004, pp. 491–492). Calavita and Jenness offer similar observations about the CDCR.

The consequences of IDR systems are, these observers suggest, even more debilitating than many questionable ADR programs established since the 1970s. The earlier ADR movement, at least in theory, emphasized the ideal of an independent arbiter, and much ADR activity involves freedom of choice through contractual arrangements. In contrast, IDR is likely to be *imposed* on especially vulnerable individuals ensconced in institutions and with limited alternatives. Certainly, prison inmates are captive clients with limited alternatives.

Reforming the Process

The portrait painted above is bleak, but it is supported by research on IDR in a variety of settings, including within CDCR. Research on IDR reveals a disappointing record in any number of areas where it has been used. Consistently, it appears that IDR neither resolves particular problems effectively nor generates a meaningful regulatory regime that heightens a sense of concern for legal rights in the organizations in which it is embedded. The CDCR grievance process fits this pattern and suffers from the same near-fatal, if not fatal, design flaws. Indeed, CDCR's internal grievance procedure offers something of a worst-case analysis. In cases of employment discrimination, disappointed petitioners may be able to change jobs or seek transfers within the organization. In schools, students can change teachers, and teachers can change schools. Citizen complaints about the police are closer to our concerns, but even there a disappointed grievant can take steps to avoid the police in the future or move out of the jurisdiction. But total institutions are total, and the options for inmates severely restricted.

Although court orders in California and elsewhere have made a tremendous difference in the administration of prisons in the United States since the 1970s, the most important differences have been to increase resources, expand programming, and provide more effective administrative structures. All but the most ideological opponents of judicial activism have to admit that the evidence showing these benefits is overwhelming (Feeley & Rubin, 1998; Kagan, 2001). This does not mean that courts have changed the fundamental nature of American prisons since the 1970s, but it does mean that they have embraced the conventional standards endorsed by the correctional establishment itself, and translated them into constitutional law.

As significant as these developments are, they have taken prison reform only so far. For the most part, court orders have not penetrated deeply into the nature and structure of grievance procedures in prisons. On those occasions when the courts have addressed the issue, they have been content to rely on formalism, and appear to be satisfied if a system has set out the rights of prison inmates in writing, established a formal grievance procedure, and designated a specific office or unit to handle the appeals. Neither the Civil Rights of Institutionalized Persons Act (CRIPA), nor the Prison Litigation Reform Act (PLRA), nor court-ordered structural reforms have done much to alter this. Although both statutes purport to reduce frivolous and expensive litigation and stem what they see as a tide of *pro se* prisoner petitions that clog the courts by encouraging the establishment of internal grievance procedures, these statutes do not develop criteria to assure meaningful reviews of prisoner petitions. They do not create a more effective alternative as much as they stifle existing alternatives. They must be seen as part of the "retrenchment" of access to justice that Sarah Staszak has written about (Staszak, 2015, pp. 118–164).[10] Once a federal judge might have been moved to respond to an occasional petition by a prisoner or a handful of prisoners and commence a meaningful inquiry, but following the PLRA such opportunities have shrunk markedly.

Ironically, while hardly ideal, the system that permitted direct petitions to the federal courts was probably faster, fairer, less expensive—and more effective—than the elaborate and cumbersome internal bureaucratic review process now in place in prisons in California and elsewhere. It may be that one form of adversarial legalism has been replaced by another even more complicated system that only appears to be better because it is less visible to federal officials who routinely defer to it. Certainly most heads of most state prison systems are wiser, and embraced written rules and established at least nominal grievance procedures, enough to stave off the federal courts. In most instances, they are little more than fig leaves, but nevertheless they are sufficient to cover the most embarrassing parts of state correctional systems.

If this is the case, what then are the alternatives? Edelman favors reducing reliance on IDR and encouraging greater access to the courts. With respect to prisons, we agree, at least in part. Trying to fix the broken internal 602 appeals process in California is a nonstarter. As we have demonstrated, it is failure not only in delivery but in design. Successful reforms depend upon the capacity to develop and sustain an impartial system that can resist the gravitational pull of organizational bias and interests identified above. But we are not persuaded that a return to the old order with easier access to federal courts would be a panacea. Although the avalanche of prisoner petitions once allowed judges to reach out and develop an occasional institutional reform case, most petitions were summarily handled more or less like 602 appeals petitions are now treated in California. Direct access to the federal courts did not lead to the development of a meaningful system of regulation through litigation that many hoped it would. So the question remains, what are the alternatives or complements?

Anecdotal evidence suggests that there can be and are effective dispute resolution arrangements, even in the face of great power imbalances (Talesh, 2012). There may even be such arrangements for handling prison grievances. The prison systems in Hawaii, Iowa, and Nebraska all have well-regarded grievance procedures. It is not clear whether their reputations are well deserved, but we note that they all employ *independent* ombudsmen external to the corrections department to handle inmate grievances (Alarcon, 2007, pp. 591, 599). Obviously more evidence would have to be adduced to assess claims of effectiveness. But they bear scrutiny, and certainly the effort to construct independent hearing officers is a first step in any meaningful reform effort. One big question, of course, is whether external hearing officers have enough authority to act independently in finding facts and issuing rulings. Another is, do they have the power to affect their rulings, and to engage in meaningful oversight? California already has a correctional ombudsmen's office, but it lacks independence; unlike Hawaii's, Iowa's, and Nebraska's, this office is part of the CDCR and responsible to the CDCR director. Thus it does not appear that it provides the basis for a new and different grievance procedure. Something more substantial is required.

We are not the first to suggest such an arrangement. Senior Judge Arthur L. Alarcon of the United States Court of Appeals for the Ninth Circuit, who is probably all too familiar with the problems in California's prisons, has developed a proposal for increasing the procedural integrity that overcomes the concerns raised by Edelman, Krawiec, and others (Jacobs, 2004, 277; Tibbles, 1972; Silberman, 1988, 522; United States Ombudsman Association, 2003, 11). Judge Alarcon proposes that an independent ombudsman handle inmate complaints, and that her authority include the power to investigate inmate claims and determine "whether the administrative action under investigation is unlawful, unreasonable, unjust, oppressive, improperly discriminatory, factually deficient, or otherwise wrong" (Alarcon, 2007, p. 598). He has gone so far as to draft proposed legislation for an independent California prison ombudsman, institutionally separate from the CDCR, arguing that such a body would enhance confidence and integrity in the system, decrease litigation, reduce costs, more responsively address inmate complaints, and provide the CDCR with effective guidance on how to comply with constitutional standards (Alarcon, 2007, pp. 602–621). Similarly, Andrea Jacobs has outlined the desired characteristics of an independent ombudsman's office in an article that sets out a model grievance system to act on inmate claims (Jacobs, 2004, pp. 299–301).

Developing a robust and independent ombudsman's office to respond to complaints and oversee departmental compliance with its findings is hardly a cure. The federal courts have not been especially effective in addressing individual inmate complaints, and ADR systems in many areas have been found to compound and complicate problems rather than resolve them. Any of a number of problems could derail an ombudsman's office for inmate grievances even before it got started: lack of funding, a cozy relationship with the CDCR (say, by retired CDCR officials), lack of remedial powers, lack of authority, lack of ability to develop rules, as well as the powerful norms and culture internal to the corrections department. Still, the problem of inmate grievances is substantial, and the need for dealing with them equitably and developing meaningful oversight of prison operations is pressing. However, it is our belief that there are not likely to be any substantial and long-lasting reforms unless organizational structures are aligned with institutional needs. To date these structures are woefully misaligned. This suggestion is not wishful thinking. There can be and are robust alternative dispute processes that in fact deliver on the promise of faster, fairer, and more effective justice. But they must be carefully calibrated and designed.

Shauhin Talesh has examined two specialized grievance procedures that have been designed to deal with a well-defined set of issues: complaints about "lemons," new cars whose owners claim are plagued with an endless series of problems (Talesh, 2012, pp. 463–492). In the aggregate, the problem was significant enough that consumer groups mobilized to press for legislation to create a specialized means of redress for the problem. Talesh's study assesses the responses of two states to this groundswell. Both created a specialized ADR (or modified IDR) system; in one state, roughly one-third of those bringing complaints receive some form of substantial relief; in the other, virtually no one does. In California, where relief is practically nonexistent, automobile dealers lobbied effectively to shape the legislation that established the system, and in so doing guaranteed that the industry would dominate the hearing process by supplying its own experts, shaping the rules of procedure and evidence, training hearing officers, producing manuals for hearing officers, and hosting hearings in their own facilities. In contrast, Vermont's law was consumer friendly and had protections and independence baked in. Throughout the legislative process, the automobile industry was kept at arm's length, and the resulting law provided for a balanced process including panels of experts to examine the automobiles and independent arbiters to resolve the issues.

Talesh's study is important for two reasons. First, it demonstrates that it is possible to create an ADR process that is both more efficient and effective than the courts. This is no mean achievement, since the ADR movement has generated a huge corps of skeptics who are convinced that it cannot work. Second, his comparative study contrasting California and Vermont delineates the conditions likely to lead to success and to failure. Although he offers no blueprint that can be duplicated with ease, he does identify important and obvious factors—most notably, a dedication to independent oversight that translates into *real* independent oversight—that can and do make a difference. In short, his article is a convincing statement that specialized, institutionally focused grievance procedures that work *can be* and *have been* constructed. And he has identified the relevant factors, well within the control of public authorities, that can be used to make a difference. One hopes that his work will inspire not only consumer advocates seeking to tame abuses in the marketplace but also public officials seeking to increase the responsiveness and fairness within the public sector, including prisons.

Part II: Local Rules and the Lack of Bureaucratic Oversight

Our second case study of administrative policies that undermine CDCR's ability to adequately address underlying problems deals with procedures by which the department adopts rules and regulations that govern prison management.[11] The bureaucratic effectiveness of the department depends largely upon the rules it adopts to govern its employees, inmates, and institutional management. In general, CDCR is responsible for promulgating system-wide rules. This network of rules defines the bureaucratic structure by which centralized leadership can oversee its sprawling enterprise and through which it can maintain control. In theory this is an excellent idea. The organization internalizes reforms and adopts them as its own through a rule-making process rather than having them imposed from the outside—from a judge, the governor's office, or the legislature, a process that, according to Charles Epp in his book *Making Rights Real*, has been effective, at least to some considerable extent, in big city police departments. Seemingly this could work for corrections in California as well, but in that state, individual prisons have the discretion to adopt "local rules" to deal with "institution-specific" issues.

While recognizing the need to adopt flexible policies to handle unique prison-specific issues, widespread adoption of "local rules" is also a double-edged sword. When each separate prison facility crafts its own manner of addressing problems that are common to many or all California institutions, system-wide accountability is undermined. The resulting lack of uniformity in rules prevents CDCR from establishing and enforcing consistent policies in accordance with its stated risk management goals. This is more than a theoretical possibility; it is an established practice, if not policy.

Below, we describe the statutory requirements for promulgating regulations in California, including those requirements specific to CDCR. Then we turn to examine the implications of the overuse of local rules. We conclude with recommendations to better monitor the use of local rules so that they are used only appropriately in occasional and unique situations.

Agency Rulemaking and the Administrative Procedures Act

In California, as elsewhere, as a standard feature of good government, state agency rules and regulations must be adopted in accordance with the state's Administrative Procedure Act (APA) provisions that allow for public notice, comment, and review, to ensure the regulations are clear, necessary, and legally valid. California rulemaking requirements prohibit any state agency, including CDCR, from issuing a rule of general applicability unless the rule complies with the APA and has been reviewed and approved by the California Office of Administrative Law (OAL).[12] If a state agency adopts a rule in violation of APA requirements, a so-called underground regulation, the OAL has the authority to nullify it.[13] On numerous occasions, OAL has determined that CDCR adopted an underground regulation, and rendered it invalid. For example, in 2014, OAL invalidated a CDCR internal memorandum prescribing rules to exclude prisoners with a history of arson or possession of an explosive device from serving their term in a minimum custody facility, such as a conservation camp in a rural area, because the rules failed to comply with the APA.[14]

There are two important exceptions to this general principle of rule-making: in certain circumstances, agencies can enact "emergency regulations" or "local rules." Emergency regulations are temporary responses "to avoid serious harm to the public peace, health, safety, or general welfare," and for good cause are excepted from the standard APA notice and comment procedures for up to 180 days.[15] However, unlike other state agencies, CDCR does not need to show an actual emergency in order to adopt an emergency regulation; instead, the secretary of the CDCR can provide written certification, reviewable by the Office of Administrative Law, stating that "operational needs . . . require adoption of the regulations on an emergency basis."[16] The second exception, local rules, are policies that apply solely to a particular prison or other correctional facility, and are completely exempted from APA rulemaking requirements.[17] The local rule exemption exists to provide flexibility in addressing the unique needs of particular institutions. Unlike emergency rules that are temporary, local rules are permanent. And, as we will see, all too often they fly below the radar of central administration.

Implications of System-Wide Overuse of Local Rules

The local rule exception is sensible, a means of coping with distinctive problems at a single institution occasioned by structural design, specialization, or weather. However, vast numbers of local rules promulgated by dozens of individual institutions across the state suggest that they are used for the sake of convenience, to avoid the cumbersome process required by the APA. Whatever benefits they may yield are offset to some degree by the fact that they reduce CDCR's capacity for meaningful oversight. Local rulemaking frustrates those at the top from seeing the big picture, developing strong bureaucracy, and exercising decisive leadership. Indeed, so far as we were able to tell, there is no centralized repository for local rules, and CDCR management is largely unaware of institutional differences in local rules.[18] There is no authoritative count of the number of such rules nor assessment of their nature and scope.

To the extent that CDCR responds to reform efforts, whether induced by court orders or other reasons, through local rules, it runs the risk of exacerbating the very problem that led to the reform in the first place. Over the past four decades, federal courts have confronted a host of problems in prisons: failures in medical services (including mental health), crowding, classification, abuse, Americans with Disabilities Act and rehabilitative accommodations, food services, staff training, and the like, and have moved forcefully to ameliorate inadequate conditions. Even at the earliest stages of prison conditions litigation, judges who spearheaded prison reform were acutely aware that one of the sources of the problems was the failure of organizational accountability, both within individual prisons and in the correctional system as a whole. The worst prison systems in the South were pre-bureaucratic in structure, and most others lacked strong centralized leadership and oversight, so a central though often unstated objective of the early structural reforms was to enhance bureaucratization—to create a centralized system with a consistent set of internal controls and regulations—that would both repair the broken system and institutionalize the changes (Feeley & Rubin, 1998, pp. 271–290; Feeley & Swearingen, 2004, pp. 466–475).[19] In case after case, judges sought to assure permanent change by chipping away at the local autonomy and expanding centralized bureaucratic authority, capacity, and accountability.[20]

Stated in terms of public administration, the objectives of reform-minded courts in seeking centralization were fourfold:

1. to foster judicial compliance by mandating that all institutions internalize the constitutional norms set forth by the courts
2. to enhance administrative efficiency by providing a common standard by which to train prison guards and other staff
3. to facilitate due process by recognizing a common standard by which to evaluate an individual inmate's behavior
4. to promote risk management objectives by adopting system-wide best practices.

Unless they are truly specific to the unique needs of a particular institution, local rules undermine all four objectives. This appears to be the case for a great many local rules adopted by individual CDCR institutions. Local rules applicable to individual California prisons range from trivial prohibitions on the possession of graph paper[21] to essential operational procedures pertaining to prisoner hunger strikes.[22] Indeed, local rules touch all aspects of prison life, including inmate visiting policies,[23] the wearing of religious artifacts,[24] and restricting the types and amounts of personal property a prisoner may possess.[25] Divergence between local rules and CDCR official policy, as provided for in the Code of Regulations and reprinted for prisoners in the Departmental Operations Manual, is commonplace. The rationale for many of these rules can only be to satisfy idiosyncratic decisions from local wardens and other officials wishing to bypass central command and APA requirements, allowing the local rules to be easily implemented as well as be withdrawn at some time in the future.

One troubling example, involving medical services, was uncovered in the now-landmark *Plata v. Schwarzeneggar* (2005) litigation. A significant portion of California inmates require daily medication for physical and psychiatric illnesses. At the time the suit was filed and for a long time thereafter, each inmate's pharmaceutical records were kept within the institution at which they resided when the medication was prescribed. Inmates, however, were frequently moved from prison to prison, and when this occurred medical files did not routinely follow the prisoner, as did his CDCR-held personal property. Despite years of effort to improve the delivery of medical services, the preference for local rules in this area and the failure to adopt a centralized record-keeping database frustrated efforts to make sure that medications moved with inmates. This failure led to a number of inmate deaths, a fact undisputed by the CDCR, but also cost the Department millions of dollars in legal fees, and led the court to place the department into receivership as if it were morally bankrupt.[26] And as we said, the facts leading to these actions are largely undisputed by the Department.

Any number of more mundane local rules reveal unwise risk management practices that breed wide-scale confusion and increase the likelihood of litigation. Take, for example, one local rule pertaining to how an inmate in a dormitory converted from a gym in Corcoran State Prison should position himself while atop a bunk bed: "Bunks: No sitting on the edge of the bunk. All feet and legs must be on the bunk and not hanging over the edge."[27] Inmates in this particular dorm who fail to keep all of their limbs confined to the bunk's edges risk discipline. Or consider the local rule in the form of a memorandum at High Desert State Prison, which prohibits possession of nail clippers, cream-filled pastries, and kneaded erasers, even though such items are acknowledged by the prison as allowable under the prison's Authorized Personal Property Schedule.[28] Such rules are recipes for discontent that escalate into formal complaints.

To be sure, there are many instances in which it is beneficial to have local rules that permit institutions to craft flexible policies to their own individual needs.

Whether it is the uniqueness of population, architecture, or climate, local rules can allow for smart accommodation. However, if they are merely substitutes for a more cumbersome process of developing system-wide rules, or are adopted with an eye to withdrawal once the courts' interests move elsewhere, CDCR loses an effective risk management and supervisory tool. Excessive reliance on local rules cripples CDCR's capacity to accomplish its mandated system-wide goals.

Lessons for Improvement

Over the years it has become clear that these two types of exceptions—emergency regulations and local rules—were vastly overused in the CDCR, and as a consequence weakened CDCR's capacity for oversight, undermined strong statewide leadership, and impaired CDCR's ability to comply with court orders. One of these problems, the overuse of emergency regulations, has been addressed and largely corrected by the state legislature. But the other one, the widespread use of local regulations, remains unchanged.

In 1999, California Senate Majority Leader Richard G. Polanco complained to the California Law Revision Commission (CLRC) that CDCR was overusing its emergency regulation procedure (California Law Review Commission, September 28, 1999, p. 2). Don Spector, who, as director of the Prison Litigation Office, had long seen hard-won legal reforms squandered in the obfuscation of the department's special rulemaking authority, summed up the problem of CDCR's exemption to the APA notice and comment requirements by stating that "the exception is swallowing the rule" (California Law Review Commission, September 28, 1999, Appendix). Similarly, in legislative discussions, the Joint Legislative Committee on Prison Construction and Operations (Joint Committee) expressed concern that "when we gave the Director [the special emergency rulemaking power], the department promised that it would only be used in exceptional circumstances when there was a threat to public safety. Since then, that provision of the Penal Code has been used to justify almost every regulation adopted" (California Law Review Commission, September 28, 1999, p. 3). The Joint Committee noted one recent emergency regulation concerning grooming standards which the state was "now spending millions of dollars to defend in court" (California Law Review Commission, September 28, 1999, Appendix).

Prompted by these concerns, the CLRC reviewed the department's use of emergency regulations (California Law Review Commission, September 28, 1999, pp. 1–5). At the time, OAL had no oversight role; CDCR merely needed to file a statement to the effect that the emergency regulations were necessary due to "operational needs" (California Law Review Commission, September 28, 1999, Exhibit). Finding that "emergency rulemaking is an extraordinary procedure reserved for circumstances where delay could cause serious harm," but admitting its lack of corrections expertise, the CLRC concluded that CDCR's frequent adoption of regulations pursuant to its emergency power does "seem to be a high level of usage" (California Law Review Commission, September 28, 1999, pp. 3–4).

In response, the legislature amended the California Penal Code in 2001 to make it more difficult for CDCR to adopt regulations pursuant to its emergency power. Lawmakers imposed greater oversight by requiring CDCR to include in its submission to OAL "a description of the underlying facts and an explanation of the operational need to use the emergency rulemaking procedure," allowing OAL to review and approve the emergency regulation, and providing that OAL accept and consider public comment on an expedited basis.[29] This additional layer of oversight dramatically reduced the use of emergency rules. The CLRC found that in the years leading up to the amendment, 1996 through 1999, 32 of CDCR's 42 rulemaking actions, or 76 percent, were adopted via emergency rule (California Law Review Commission, September 28, 1999, p. 3). Replicating this analysis for the period 2005 through 2007, the authors of this chapter found that CDCR used its emergency rule making power in only 6 of 30, or 20 percent, of its rulemaking actions.[30] This represents a remarkable drop in CDCR's use of regulatory action through emergency rule. It appears that the statutory proviso that all emergency rules not only be filed with OAL, *but be subject to OAL review*, is responsible for this dramatic decline.

Without more investigation it is impossible to assert with confidence what differences have resulted from this change in the law, but there is no question that it has facilitated more centralized and system-wide rules that make it less likely that California prisons can duck obligations imposed on them by federal judges.

The logic that the CLRC employed to rein in the use of emergency rules is equally applicable to local rules, but as of this writing there has been no reform. As we have seen, making local rules can weaken centralized policymaking and oversight, undermine CDCR system-wide policies, and thwart the intent of remedial orders issued by federal judges. Here, too, a review of local rulemaking should be undertaken with an eye towards using it only when truly required.

More generally, drawing on the spirit of the report issued by the California Law Revision Commission on CDCR's use of emergency regulations, we recommend stronger oversight mechanisms to encourage a tighter structural fit between the department's goals and the means it uses to achieve them. In particular, we recommend that CDCR redefine the definition and scope of local rules. Their use should:

1. be limited to a specific number or classification of inmates, or to a well-specified type of institution-specific need (relating to architectural features or climate)
2. be reviewed by central administrators to determine if local goals conflict with departmental priorities (this review might be entrusted to the CDCR's Office of the Inspector General or a neutral ombudsman)

3. require advance public notice of a pending rule and a meaningful opportunity to comment prior to its taking effect (for example, the Joint Legislative Committee on Prison Construction and Operations could hold a public hearing to evaluate its merits).

Under no circumstances should local rules be used to skirt departmental or judicial oversight.

Of course, no amount of structural realignment is a substitute for capable and committed leadership. But in the hands of a leader with a strong sense of direction and clear lines of authority, fewer emergency regulations and idiosyncratic local rules can only enhance his or her ability to obtain an understanding of CDCR operations, monitor practices, be more proactive, and engage in better risk management. If pursued with finesse and talent, all this should increase institutional effectiveness and efficiency on the one hand, and reduce litigation and the exposure to litigation on the other.

Conclusion

This chapter has examined two developments that relate directly to litigation that has entangled CDCR since the early 1980s: the internal dispute resolution process that affects inmates' access to the courts, and the promulgation of local and emergency rules that weaken strong centralized administration. Both developments are failed efforts to respond to serious problems. Evidence from a variety of sources reveals that internal dispute resolution procedures typically are used to advance institutional interests at the expense of the rights of inmate-complainants, and that their adoption leads to the appearance of legal protection without the reality of protection—form without substance. Accordingly, those who nominally are supposed to benefit from the expanded "access to law" may very well find themselves worse off than they were before.

Similarly, CDCR's decision to rely heavily on the development of emergency and local rules in response to or even in anticipation of the deluge of litigation is misplaced. The CLRC's investigation of "emergency rules" in the 1990s led to a finding of inadequate oversight and a recommendation to reduce reliance on emergency rulemaking. This recommendation was adopted and now they are used sparingly, and adopted only after a deliberative process. There is a central lesson in good public administration to be learned here. Using emergency rules to sidestep the APA requirements of agency rulemaking reveals inadequate management and thwarts central oversight, increasing litigation exposure. The same holds for frequent use of local rules. Although in an era of collaborative decision-making, local rule making has an appeal, it can also mask under-bureaucratization. Certainly, heavy reliance on local rules deprives top leadership of important management information and controls. The response to an underdeveloped, weak, and beleaguered bureaucracy is not to decentralize and decrease the amount of information flowing to central leadership but to improve, enhance, and expand bureaucratic capacity. Heavy reliance on local rules is quite simply poor public administration.

What holds true generally for most bureaucratic organizations is particularly true for correctional administration. The history of prison reform has shown that resistance to change has been greatest at the local level and has come from "street-level bureaucrats." Much of this is inevitable, but from a risk-analysis perspective, the devolution of rulemaking and oversight to local institutions reinforces this inevitability and blinds CDCR leadership to systemic problems. It all but guarantees inadequate oversight.

Accordingly, we have recommended the establishment of a neutral ombudsman system to review inmate appeals, and the reduction of reliance on local rules with a more aggressive use of regulations reviewed and embraced by the OAL.

Institutions that are confident in the administration of their duties are willing to open themselves to outside and stronger internal oversight. It is a sign of mature, competent leadership to adopt this stance. In contrast, reluctance to permit outside evaluation is an indication of timid leadership. In the context of this study, continued reliance on internal dispute resolution mechanisms without independent arbiters not only guarantees endless appeals, it fosters continuing resentment and an inability to use the grievance process to pursue and institutionalize norms. And continued heavy reliance on local rules not only generates ineffective and counterproductive practices, it exposes weak leadership at the top. The continuing litigation, the inability to ameliorate the structural problems it reveals, and widespread acknowledgment of the department's problems—both by the court and within the department—all point to the need for stronger bureaucracy and more confident central leadership.

Stepping back, these cases point to three more general lessons about law and organizations. First, the example of California prisons underscores the dualistic effects of adversarial legalism. It can be, on one side, a costly, unpredictable, and inefficient mode of dispute resolution. Faced with a drumbeat of lawsuits that the CDCR leadership felt had all these pathologies, the CDCR responded like many other large complex organizations: it created a more streamlined alternative. In doing so, though, it lost the other side of adversarial legalism, its responsiveness and capacity to be used against entrenched powerful interests. In the prison system, where complainants have no other remedies, this loss is particularly acute.

Second, there is a lesson here as well about the two sides of bureaucratic legalism. Bureaucratic legalism—"bureaucracy"—has a reputation for rigidity, for lack of flexibility in the face of emergency or in attentiveness to local conditions. But the flip side of this is that bureaucratic legalism is relatively orderly and transparent. By allowing individual prisons to adopt local and emergency rules, the

CDCR made its system more flexible, but also much less orderly, undermining any attempt to respond systematically to outside pressures for reform.

Finally, a methodological point. Using law to change the behavior of complex organizations like prisons is not simply a matter of generating external pressure. As this case vividly demonstrates, it is also a matter of internal governance. Thus, to craft better reforms, we must, as Robert Kagan has done repeatedly in his research, not only consider formal legal structures but examine everyday practices within organizations.

Notes

1 In 2004 the name of the California Department of Corrections was changed to the California Department of Corrections and Rehabilitation. For simplicity, we refer to the agency as "CDCR" or "the department" throughout this chapter.
2 Cal. Code Regs. tit. 15, § 3084.1(a).
3 See 42 U.S.C. § 1997e(a) (2013).
4 See generally, *Plata v. Schwarzenegger*, Docket No. 3:01–01351 (N.D. Cal.).
5 *Coleman v. Schwarzenegger*, 922 F. Supp. 2d 882, 895, 892–97 (E.D. Cal. 2009) (consolidation of the *Plata* and *Coleman* cases).
6 See also ibid. at 912 (explaining that Governor Arnold Schwarzenegger, a primary defendant in both *Plata* and *Coleman*, declared a state of emergency in 2006, warning that "the severe overcrowding in 29 CDCR prisons has caused substantial risk to the health and safety of the men and women who work inside these prisons and the inmates housed in them"; that "the overcrowding crisis gets worse with each passing day, creating an emergency in the California prison system"; and that "immediate action is necessary to prevent death and harm caused by California's severe prison overcrowding.").
7 Comments by J.C. Kelso at the Center for the Study of Law & Society, University of California at Berkeley, October 21, 2008.
8 For a discussion of the PLRA as part of a general retrenchment in access to justice in the United States, *see* Staszak (2015), pp. 207–208, 219–20.
9 "Correctional administrators are largely cognizant of the benefits of effective grievance procedures, including . . . the improvement of the facility's credibility with courts."
10 For an analysis of how courts can use their powers of interpretation to retrench rights, see Barnes (2007a; 2007b, 157).
11 Throughout this chapter, we use "rule" and "regulation" interchangeably.
12 See Cal. Gov't Code §§ 11340 *et seq.*
13 See Cal. Code Regs., tit. 1, § 250.
14 2014 OAL Determination No. 11 (OAL File No. CTU2014–0130–02).
15 Cal. Gov't. Code §11342.545; see, generally, Cal. Gov't. Code at §§ 11346 *et seq.*
16 See Cal. Penal Code § 5058.3.
17 See Cal. Penal Code § 5058(c)(1).
18 This is evidenced from phone calls directly to the division of CDCR responsible for local operations and procedures. Nevertheless, Cal. Penal Code § 5058 requires the secretary to "maintain, publish and make available to the general public, a compendium of the [local] rules."
19 For a history of similar transformations specifically taking place in the Texas Department of Corrections, see Crouch and Marquart (1989).
20 Court-ordered reform was widely perceived as an affront to state sovereignty as well as the autonomy of prison administrators. See Smith (2000): "Correctional institutions could no longer operate quietly, according to the whims and predilections of individual

wardens. States could no longer run prisons and jails according to their own values and for their own convenience."

21 2014 OAL Determination No. 9 (OAL File No. CTU2014–0428–01).

22 2014 OAL Determination No. 2 (OAL File No. CTU2013–0930–01).

23 2007 OAL Determination No. 11 (OAL File No. CTU 07–0709–01).

24 2012 OAL Determination No. 6 (OAL File No. CTU2012–0308–01).

25 2013 OAL Determination No. 5 (OAL File No. CTU2013–0711–01).

26 *Plata v. Schwarzenegger*, 2005 WL 2932243, at *1 (N.D. Cal. May 10, 2005) (concluding that the "State's failure has created a vacuum of leadership, and utter disarray in the management, supervision, and delivery of care in the Department of Corrections' medical system").

27 2000 OAL Determination No. 13 (OAL File No. CTU2012–0308–01).

28 2014 OAL Determination No. 8 (OAL File No. CTU2014–0226–03

29 Cal. Penal Code § 5058.3.

30 Similar to the CLRC study, we excluded editorial changes, changes without regulatory effect, readoption of previously adopted emergency regulations, and actions to make previously adopted emergency regulations permanent.

References

Adlerstein, D.M. (2001). "In Need of Correction: The 'Iron Triangle' of the Prison Litigation Reform Act." *Columbia Law Review*, 101, 1681–1708.

Alarcon, A.L. (2007). "Essay: A Prescription for California's Ailing Inmate Treatment System: An Independent Corrections Ombudsman." *Hastings Law Journal*, 58, 591–621.

Barnes, J. (2007a). *Dust-Up: Asbestos Litigation Reform and the Failure of Commonsense Reform*. Washington, DC: Georgetown University Press.

Barnes, J. (2007b). "Rethinking the Landscape of Tort Reform: Lessons from the Asbestos Case." *The Justice System Journal*, 28(2), 157–181.

Brakel, S.J. (1982). "Administrative Justice in the Penitentiary: A Report on Inmate Grievance Procedures." *Law & Social Inquiry*, 7, 111–140.

Calavita, K., & Jenness, V. (2014). *Appealing to Justice: Prisoner Grievances, Rights, and Carceral Logic*. Berkeley, CA: University of California Press.

California Law Review Commission. Memorandum 99–70. *Administrative Rulemaking: Exemptions From Administrative Procedures Act*, September 28, 1999.

Crouch, B.M., & Marquart, J.W. (1989). *An Appeal to Justice: Litigated Reform of Texas Prisons*. Austin, TX: University of Texas Press.

Edelman, L.B. (2016). *Working Law: Courts, Corporations, and Symbolic Civil Rights*. Chicago, IL: University of Chicago Press.

Edelman, L.B., Erlanger, H.S., & Lande, J. (1993). "Internal Dispute Resolution: The Transformation of Civil Rights in the Workplace." *Law & Society*, 27(3), 497–534.

Edelman, L.B., & Patterson, S.M. (1999). "Symbols and Substance in Organizational Response to Civil Rights Law." *Research in Social Stratification & Mobility*, 17, 107–135.

Edelman, L.B., & Suchman, M.C. (1997). "The Legal Environments of Organizations." *Annual Review of Sociology*, 23, 479–515.

Edelman, L.B., Uggen, C., & Erlanger, H.S. (1999). "The Endogeneity of Legal Regulation: Grievance Procedures as Rational Myth." *American Journal of Sociology, 105*, 406–454.

Epp, C. (2009). *Making Rights Real: Activists, Bureaucrats, and the Creation of the Legalistic State*. Chicago, IL: University of Chicago Press.

Feeley, M.M., & Rubin, E.L. (1998). *Judicial Policy Making and the Modern State: How the Courts Reformed America's Prisons*. New York: Cambridge University Press.

Feeley, M.M., & Swearingen, V. (2004). "The Prison Conditions Cases and the Bureaucratization of American Corrections: Influences, Impacts and Implications." *Pace Law Review*, 24, 433–475.

Fuller, L.L. (1978). "The Forms and Limits of Adjudication." *Harvard Law Review*, 92, 353–409.

Jacobs, A. (2004). "Prison Power Corrupts Absolutely: Exploring the Phenomenon of Prison Guard Brutality and the Need to Develop a System of Accountability." *California Western Law Review*, 41, 277–301.

Kagan, R.A. (2001). *Adversarial Legalism: The American Way of Law*. Cambridge, MA: Harvard University Press.

Krawiec, K.D. (2003). "Cosmetic Compliance and the Failure of Negotiated Governance." *Washington University Law Quarterly*, 81, 487–544.

Lin, A.C. (2000). *Reform in the Making: The Implementation of Social Policy in Prison*. Princeton, NJ: Princeton University Press.

Office of the Inspector General. (2004). *Follow-Up Review of the California Department of Corrections Office of Compliance: Inmate Appeal Branch*. Sacramento: Office of the Inspector General.

Schlanger, M. (2003). "Inmate Litigation." *Harvard Law Review*, 116, 1555–1706.

Silberman, M. (1988). "Dispute Mediation in the American Prison: A New Approach to the Reduction of Violence." *Policy Studies Journal*, 16, 522–532.

Smith, C.E. (2000). "The Governance of Corrections: Implications of the Changing Interface of Courts and Corrections." *Criminal Justice*, 2, 113–116.

Staszak, S. (2015). *No Day in Court*. Oxford, England: Oxford University Press.

Swearingen, V. (2008). "Imprisoning Rights: The Failure of Negotiated Governance in the Prison Inmate Grievance Process." *California Law Review*, 96, 1353–1382.

Talesh, S. (2012). "How Dispute Resolution Design Matters: An Organizational Analysis of Dispute Resolution Structures and Consumer Lemon Laws." *Law & Society Review*, 46, 463–496.

Tibbles, L. (1972). Ombudsman for American Prisons, 48 North Dakota Law Review 48, 383.

United States Ombudsman Association. (2003). *Governmental Ombudsman Standards*. Available at http://www.usombudsman.org/site-usoa/wp-content/uploads/USOA-STANDARDS1.pdf

8

STYLE MATTERS

On the Role of Pattern Analysis in the Study of Regulation

Cary Coglianese

Style pervades society. It features centrally in discussions about and in the appreciation of music, art, fashion, and writing. We also hear claims that style matters for all sorts of social interactions, from parenting to teaching to managing and leading others. With respect to law and its relationship to society, style can matter too. A country's overall legal system is said to exhibit one or another style, with Kagan (2001) famously arguing that the United States exhibits a distinctive style of "adversarial legalism." Actors within the legal system can also exhibit distinct styles too. Among lawyers, for example, some litigators have been said to exhibit a "hardball" style when pressing their clients' cases. Regulatory enforcement officials can choose either to adopt a "by the book" style or a more responsive style in their interactions with the managers of the businesses that they inspect (Bardach & Kagan, 1982). Those businesses and their managers themselves have been said to exhibit one or more particular management styles affecting their posture toward law and legal compliance (Gunningham, Kagan, & Thornton, 2003).

Since style abounds in accounts of law and its relationship with individuals and businesses in society, it is worth pausing to consider what style is, how it comes about, and what it helps to explain. Style itself can operate as both a dependent variable and an independent variable—that is, as something to be explained as well as something to use to explain other phenomena. In this respect, it bears certain affinities with other constructs in the social sciences, such as personality and culture. Perhaps it overlaps with, even duplicates to some degree, these other constructs.

In this chapter, I put style under the proverbial lens, aiming to highlight an important facet of law and society research, in particular the many major contributions reflected in the work of Robert A. Kagan, who has done the most to advance style as key to understanding legal systems, regulatory behavior, and corporate compliance (Coglianese, 2013). More than that, it is my hope to help situate the concept of style in law and society research within a broader social science literature and to encourage critical reflection on what style can contribute to the sociological analysis of the law and what questions about style might deserve to be carefully studied in the future.

Pattern Analysis as Social Science

Style is a type of a pattern, and patterns are all around us, awaiting discovery. Indeed, the world is full of bombarding stimuli that human beings must make sense of in their everyday lives by recognizing them in patterned form. This begins early in life. When an infant's eyes perceive a certain consistent pattern of light, she begins to recognize her parent's face; when she hears a certain consistent range or tone of sound, she recognizes that as her parent's voice. More general patterns emerge as the child encounters more of the world. For example, when she sees patterns of faces with the lips turned down in a frown, she comes to construe sadness in others; when she hears voices time and again that are louder than usual, she interprets anger or disapproval; and so forth. Although pattern analysis is something that humans may instinctively undertake, it is not merely a human capacity; computers, after all, can now undertake pattern analysis to recognize faces and voices, among other things.

In much the same way as children and computers come to recognize patterns, social scientists confront a messy, cluttered, chaotic world, one that is abundant in a steady stream of observable and interpretable phenomena waiting to be understood and explained. The social scientists' job, though, is to make that messy social world comprehensible and predictable by developing reliable generalizations. Social scientists' approach is more self-conscious and systematic—but even so, the first step in explaining the social world is to make sense of it. Only by recognizing patterns, or seeing consistencies and distinguishing inconsistencies, can social scientists begin to explain phenomena or use one set of phenomena to explain another (Zerubavel, 2007). Typically, with social science, these phenomena are more than just lights and sounds or other discrete physical inputs. They are complex conglomerations and dynamic interactions of phenomena internal and external to individual humans. Even characterizing individuals as individuals, and grouping some of them together as similar (based on concepts such as race, class, gender, and more), while distinguishing others, is part of the social scientist's enterprise. Just as a child begins to associate certain physical phenomena with feelings of love, anger, or sadness, so too do social scientists devote considerable effort to interpreting and extracting meaning from various social phenomena, and using that meaning as well as other recognizable patterns to help explain the social world.

Social scientists today may at times seldom see some patterns as patterns at all. For example, when, in their day-to-day work, political scientists study *interest groups*, sociologists study *norms*, anthropologists study *culture*, and psychologists study *personality*, they may not always appreciate that these concepts themselves depend on pattern recognition. What counts as an interest, norm, culture, or personality must be based on some kind of filtering of inputs and accepting of a pattern, even if it is just a pattern of consistent responses to survey questions. Certain patterns may not be noticeable as patterns because social scientists—and others—often agree on what a particular concept means and how it is reflected by or comprises a well-accepted pattern frame. Political scientists, for example, generally understand what counts as an interest group, and how such a "thing" differs from a politician, a government, and a political party—even if interest groups may share something in common with all three of the others.

Foundational to all social sciences is at least some tentative acceptance of basic concepts that draw on pattern recognition. Social scientists use these basic concepts not merely to organize patterns and make sense of the world, but also to try to explain how the world works. Political scientists are not distinguishing interest groups from politicians, governments, and parties simply to describe and distinguish among different entities—no more than the child probably recognizes her parent's face not for its own sake but rather to be able to distinguish between someone who is more likely to feed it and care for it and a stranger who is less likely to do so. Political scientists instead use the concept of "interest group" to try to explain the behavior of politicians or the decisions that governments make. Within the pattern category "interest group," they also further distinguish between different types of groups—say, those that seek to foster short-term or narrow interests (e.g., business groups) versus those that aim to promote long-term or broader interests (e.g., consumer or environmental advocacy groups). Government officials who find themselves in interactions with an imbalance in the number or resources between these two groups, such as when business groups are more numerous or better resourced than consumer groups, may ultimately make decisions that favor narrow private interests over interests of the broader public—a tendency described in the regulatory and public policy literature as "capture," itself a concept used to describe a particular pattern in governmental policies or decisions with skewed outcomes (Bernstein, 1955; Carpenter & Moss, 2013).

Social science is thus an enterprise that seeks to discern patterns among patterns. Its practitioners generate theories—that is, generalized predictions about regularities in patterns—and then seek to see if patterns observed in the world fit the predicted patterns. For example, one widely held theory in the social science study of law holds that the rate at which litigation occurs will vary depending on whether disputes arise between strangers or among neighbors (Macaulay, 1963; Ellickson, 1991). In other words, when there is a pattern of ongoing interactions between the same individuals—say, between neighbors or regular business partners—a dispute is more likely to be resolved directly by those individuals themselves. Axelrod (1984) has developed a still more general theory that encompasses all kinds of interactions—not merely those involving litigation—which holds that when individuals are involved in repeated interactions that they expect to continue over time, they will find ways to work cooperatively with each other, even if their short-term interests seem to be incompatible and cooperation does not seem immediately to their advantage.

In contrast with Macaulay's (1963) study focused on contractual disputes between business representatives in the automobile industry and Ellickson's (1991) study concentrated specifically on land use disputes in Shasta County, California, Axelrod's (1984) theory is much more general, seeking to explain cooperation between individuals as well as organizations across the breadth of social life, defining "cooperation" broadly so that noncooperation (or defection) encompasses everything from unwillingness to help, to suing someone in court, to engaging in war. In this respect, Axelrod is lumping together a broad range of otherwise disparate phenomena—say, whether a prisoner decides to turn state's evidence or a country decides to go to war—into a general pattern of cooperation versus defection. The breadth of Axelrod's work helps to illustrate one of the two basic approaches to pattern analysis, referred to as *lumping* and *splitting* (Zerubavel, 1996). His work, an instance of lumping, tries to make sense of the messy social world by drawing together even seemingly different phenomena that have a core commonality. Lumping involves "finding relevant common characteristics that allow us intelligently and usefully to group apparently distinct phenomena into a single category" (Karkkainen, 2004).

Lumping can be contrasted with splitting—or "finding relevant distinguishing characteristics that allow us intelligently and usefully to separate otherwise similar phenomena into distinct classes" (Karkkainen, 2004). For example, when I developed a "disturbance theory" of disputing in a study of litigation patterns between interest groups and the U.S. Environmental Protection Agency (EPA), I showed that not all litigation is the same and should not be unthinkingly lumped together (Coglianese, 1996). Specifically, I found that, notwithstanding the widely held prediction that individuals involved in ongoing relationships would not resort to litigation to resolve their disputes, the interest group representatives most often involved in interactions with the EPA were the same ones who sued the agency most frequently—precisely the opposite of what the work of scholars like Macaulay, Ellickson, and Axelrod would lead one to predict. But it was not that these scholars were wrong about how repeated interactions and a shadow of the future serve to deter defections; rather, it was that litigation over regulatory matters at the EPA lacked the kinds of features that normally "disturb" a social relationship and make the filing of a lawsuit be viewed as uncooperative. In fact, litigation in the context of environmental regulations was so benign that sometimes EPA regulatory personnel did not even realize that a lawsuit had been filed against the agency.

I mention lumping and splitting not because one is superior to the other. On the contrary, as Karkkainen argues, some of the best social science research "does a good deal of both—lumping seemingly disparate phenomena into original categories that reveal unexpected patterns and lead to novel insights, while employing the chisel of penetrating distinction to sunder conventional, shopworn categories that may conceal more than they reveal" (Karkkainen, 2004). Indeed, any concept that seeks to create patterns can be used both to lump as well as to split, whether the concept may be as seemingly broad as "cooperation" or as seemingly circumscribed as "litigation." The same is true of patterns captured under the banner of "style."

Style in Regulatory Studies

What kind of concept is "style" exactly? As with other social science concepts, style is a way of describing or characterizing patterns in the world. But it also can be a means of explaining other aspects of or patterns in the world, such as different kinds of responses that one style elicits over another. In other words, style can be both a phenomenon to be explained (What are the conditions that lead a particular style to emerge?), and a variable that explains other phenomena (When a particular style holds, what follows?). Perhaps the best way to understand the concept of style is to see how it has been used in various ways throughout the study of regulation, whether to understand regulatory systems, regulatory officials, or regulated entities.

Style of Regulatory Systems

Style has been used perhaps most extensively to try to make sense of different regulatory or legal systems. For example, Kagan has famously characterized the American style of regulation as adversarial and legalistic. What he sees as "the rambunctious, peculiarly American style of law and legal decisionmaking" stems from a pattern in the United States of individuals inside and outside of government relying on detailed rules and the use of courts and litigation to resolve conflicts over those rules (Kagan, 2001). Kagan and Axelrad (2000) offer further evidence of what they characterize as America's distinctive regulatory style by drawing on case studies of different multinational corporations' encounters with regulators in about 10 different developed economies. In the United States, these corporations encounter a regulatory system that generally requires that their managers fill out more detailed paperwork, apply for more extensive permits, and receive permission from a greater number of governmental bodies at the local, state, and federal levels. Reflecting on the findings from this series of 10 case studies, Kagan observes that the fragmented and legalistic U.S. regulatory style can help check governmental abuses and offer other benefits to society; however, he questions whether these benefits fully justify the costly burdens and inefficiencies created by the American regulatory style. Indeed, he notes that "adversarial legalism imposes much higher costs and delays on the American operations of multinational corporations" and that "despite its more threatening character, [it] often does not generate higher levels of protection for the public than do the less legalistic regulatory regimes of other developed countries—at least in the sector of the economy occupied by large corporations" (Kagan & Axelrad, 2000, p. 1).

Kagan's concept of adversarial legalism emerged from the work of Mirjan Damaška, who created a typology of styles of legal procedures around the world. Damaška's typology, itself rooted in Max Weber's creation of "ideal types" of authority (Damaška, 1991, p. 9), explains differences in legal style as arising from differences in governmental structure. A "hierarchical" structure of authority is associated with a more bureaucratized legal style; a "coordinate" structure with a more adversarial style. But style also arises, Damaška argues, from prevailing attitudes about whether government should be an active force in society, a policy implementer, or instead a reactive force, a conflict resolver. No short synopsis can convey the breadth of Damaška's enterprise, but it suffices to say that he seeks explicitly to make a "stupendous diversity" of governmental systems "intelligible" by distilling them "to a manageable set of patterns" (Damaška, 1991, p. 3). Kagan's typology of legal structures owes much to Damaška (Kagan, 2001, p. 10), and is just as ambitious in seeking to categorize through ideal types both the structures of legal authority and their associated legal styles across the globe.

Other scholars have also sought to classify the style of regulatory and legal systems. For example, in his comparative study of risk regulation in the United States and Europe, Vogel (2012) notes how, since the early 1990s, "the EU more stringently regulated a number of health, safety, and environmental risks caused by business than the United States." He notes that "[m]any of the features that formerly characterized the 'American' style of risk regulation . . . have become *more* characteristic of how consumer and environmental regulation is made in the EU and *less* characteristic of how it is made in the United States." He sets out to explain why the EU regulatory system has adopted a much more precautionary style, focusing his explanation on public demands, government officials' preferences, and legal criteria for government decision-making.

Style of Regulatory Officials

Damaška's framework hinges in part on the style of legal officials: careerists in the hierarchical model versus amateurs who are elected into office in the more coordinate model. A much more extensive literature has focused on the particular style of regulatory inspectors and other enforcement personnel (e.g., Bardach & Kagan, 1982; Hawkins, 1984; Reiss, 1984). These inspectors operate at the "street level" to identify potential violations of regulations—and the ways that they respond when they find violations are said to reflect one or the other of two main "enforcement styles" that have dominated academic research on regulatory enforcement for decades: adversarial/legalistic versus cooperative/problem-solving. Bardach and Kagan (1982) provide the classic account of the adversarial legalistic enforcement style, which they describe as "going by the book." That style is characterized by inspectors who see their role as requiring them to identify and punish legal violations, period. Inspectors who go by the book tend to exhibit a "gotcha" mentality and do not concern themselves with excuses offered by regulated firms or even with the reasonableness of the underlying rules and their enforcement. Adversarial enforcement, in other words, is a rote, checklist style of enforcement, doling out punishment almost automatically when violations are discovered.

The cooperative approach sees noncompliance as a problem to be solved more than a moral or legal failing to be punished. Hawkins (1984), for example, offers the classic ethnographic account of water pollution inspectors in the UK who take a more cooperative style by starting out with the assumption that the regulated firm acts in good faith and wants to do the right thing. If a violation is detected, punishment is possible, but it is not the first recourse. Rather, the inspector focuses on problems with how a facility is operating and its effect on water quality; if rules are violated or if other threats to water quality are identified, the inspector works with the regulated firm to solve the underlying problem.

These two styles have demarcated ends of a spectrum that has organized much empirical work on regulatory enforcement. Numerous researchers have tried to determine which style works better in terms of reducing regulatory violations (e.g., May & Winter, 2000). In addition, these two divergent styles can be said to have inspired a third, more hybrid style called "responsive regulation," which has been offered as a better prescription for regulators (Ayres & Braithwaite, 1992). Responsive regulation in effect combines—or, more accurately, sequences—both main styles, with an inspector initiating its engagement with a regulated firm in a cooperative fashion but then following a strategy generally outlined by Axelrod (1984), reciprocating any uncooperative or recalcitrant behavior by the firm with an adversarial, punitive response.

Style of Regulated Organizations

Just as regulators exhibit different styles, so too do the targets of regulation: that is, regulated businesses. Gunningham, Kagan, and Thornton (2003) focus on pulp and paper mills in four countries to understand why some companies go above and beyond compliance in taking steps to protect the environment, while others lag behind. One set of their explanatory variables emphasizes factors external to the companies: regulations, economic pressures, and community demands. As much as Gunningham, Kagan, and Thornton find these pressures to be real, they also report that the key variable lies inside the firm itself, in a "combination of attitudes and executive action" that they consider as the company's "environmental management style." That style ranges across a set of archetypes: "Environmental Laggard . . . Reluctant Complier, Committed Complier, . . . Environmental Strategist . . . [and] True Believer" (Gunningham et al., 2003). Where a firm falls on this spectrum of management styles predicts how well it manages its environmental impacts.

The firm's management style, Gunningham et al. report, helps explain how the external pressures actually translate into firm behavior. It also apparently exerts its own "independent influence on environmental performance" (Gunningham et al., 2003, p. 88). According to the authors, "Environmental management style was a more powerful predictor of mill-level environmental performance than was regulatory regime or corporate size and earnings" (Gunningham et al., 2003, p. 96). These findings fit with findings from other studies that emphasize the importance of internal factors in shaping regulated firms' tendencies to comply with the law or even to go beyond compliance. Other related factors include "management commitment" (Coglianese & Nash, 2001), "organizational identity" (Howard-Grenville, Nash, & Coglianese, 2008), and corporate "culture" (Prakash, 2000; Howard-Grenville, 2009).

The Virtues of Style

In these examples, style helps categorize patterns observed in regulatory institutions and with regulatory behaviors, both by enforcement officials and regulated firms. It is not that every aspect of the U.S. legal system is adversarial, but rather the claim of an adversarial style is that this is a general tendency when viewed across a range of governmental institutions, policy spheres, and time periods. Similarly, it is not the case that UK water inspectors never go by the book nor that U.S. inspectors never try to solve problems, nor is it that no firm with a leadership-driven management style will ever have a compliance problem. The social scientists' purpose is to make the "stupendous diversity" more manageable by observing some dominant tendencies exhibited by various regulatory institutions and actors. It is to identify patterns.

Generalizing about commonalities in regulatory phenomena—whether across different domains of regulation, different inspectors and firms, or over time—amounts to lumping. And yet at the same time, it should also be clear that style is being used by these scholars for splitting too. Kagan and Axelrad (2000) treat the U.S. regulatory system's style as adversarial to contrast it with the more cooperative regulatory styles in other developed economies. They even begin their work by noting that it expressly centers on "differences in national legal and regulatory systems—not merely differences in the law on books but differences in the law in action—and about how much those differences really matter" (Kagan & Axelrad, 2000). Vogel (2012) also splits when he distinguishes Europe's precautionary approach from the U.S. regulatory system's "act-first, regulate-later" posture toward the risks of new technologies—and he too seeks to explain why these differences arise. Adversarial modes of enforcement, again taken to be more prevalent in the U.S., are typically contrasted with what are thought to be the more cooperative styles of enforcement in Europe. And finally, regulated firms' management styles vary to the point that they receive their own typology, from laggards to leaders, again with the purpose of showing how these different styles matter.

But still, with the benefit of several studies in mind, it is important now to pause to ask exactly what "style" is and what work it is doing in regulatory studies. Obviously style helps more sensibly describe the world by identifying patterns and drawing distinctions, but exactly what is style a pattern of? Is style a core construct in the same way that, say, personality might be for psychology or culture might be for sociology or anthropology? Or is it something else?

At first blush, style is similar to personality and culture in that it is capturing a pattern and in that it is both something to be explained as well as something to help explain other phenomena or outcomes. But at least when style is used in the study of regulation, it may not always be meant to be used in quite the same way as a core construct like personality or culture. Personality and culture, in other words, may be more constitutive rather than essential. Personality is constitutive in that it is a part of an individual; culture, too, is a part of an organization or a society. There exist different types of personalities, arranged in terms of "the big five" attributes of personality, while scholars have identified a plethora of different types of cultures. Importantly, these typologies of personality and organizational culture describe patterns with respect to personality and culture, respectively, not the essence of the underlying individuals or the organizations to which they belong. In other words, personality or culture, while obviously central to any individual or organization, respectively, do not define the entirety of the individual or organization. They are not the individual or the organization.

This may be a very subtle point, but it is important to recognize because style, at least when it has sometimes been used to describe a regulatory system or a set of regulatory inspectors, seems much more directly to describe a pattern as one might describe an individual or organization directly—rather than something akin to its constitutive personality or culture. In other words, it is *the regulatory system* that possesses an adversarial legalistic style; the pattern this style represents is not a core construct or constitutive component *of a* regulatory system. Similarly, enforcement style has tended to be little more than a description of a pattern in how inspectors behave, not a pattern in something that might drive or constitute that behavior.

This is not to dismiss or criticize efforts to characterize the style of regulatory systems or enforcement behavior for, in effect, not going more directly to "the source," but it is merely to see that style in regulatory studies may be operating in a slightly different way than core constructs like personality or culture are typically at work in other social science inquiries. It also helps to recognize that while social scientists have spent considerable time theorizing about what core constructs like personality or organizational culture are, the field of regulation lacks the same extensive theorizing about what different types of regulatory style might be and how they do or do not compare or interact with other constructs, like personality or culture. Indeed, although "style" is the word used when describing regulatory systems, enforcement behavior, and regulated firms' management, what it *is* seems to vary across each domain. The style of an entire nation's regulatory system seems akin to the culture of an entire society; it is descriptive of the system as a whole, not of anything intermediate or composite. Unlike the breadth of a system's style, the style of regulatory enforcement behavior is focused on patterns of very specific interactions—but still it is also not getting "inside" the organizations or the individuals involved in this interactive behavior.

Management style may well come the closest to a core construct, especially as it seems quite similar to organizational culture. The definition of management style by Gunningham et al. (2003) in terms of patterns of both relevant attitudes and actions makes it quite close, if not possibly identical to, some definitions of culture (e.g., Schein, 2010). For example, Silbey (2010, p. 471) explains that "at its core culture is an intricate system of claims about how to understand the world and act on it" (quoting Perin, 2005). Howard-Grenville, Bertels, and Boren (2015) offer a definition of organizational culture very similar to management style:

> Organizational culture comprises sets of beliefs held by an organization's members, as well as associated actions that are guided by and sustain these beliefs. Organizational culture underpins day-to-day actions in an organization, but can also be put to use as a tool for adaptation by culturally skillful managers and employees.

Howard-Grenville et al. (2015) explain that they prefer to focus on beliefs rather than values (the term Schein uses) because "beliefs connote patterns or regularities that are associated with action, while values are not necessarily good predictors of action."

At the end of the day, getting good predictions is a key objective of social science. Although style may be functioning differently than core constructs in other fields of social science, and may even be used in different ways across different regulatory studies, it can be embraced as a concept that may be helpful in making predictions in much the same way that quantitative analysis aims to support good predictions. Social scientists frequently rely on multivariable categorization when they engage in quantitative analysis, and style is a type of multivariable categorization. Style, in a sense, could even be said to be like a regression model—albeit a qualitative one. Style flags a limited set of features of a messy world, pulls them out, and identifies them as important in combination.

Of course, if only ever measured and analyzed qualitatively, style may never obtain a high level of precision in its ability to assist with predictions. But it can offer a basis for developing testable theories. It can guide and motivate new research testing these theories, as it has in the regulatory enforcement context in particular. It also generates its own research questions about the conditions under which certain styles affect certain phenomena or outcomes, about what are the key factors in a style that really matter, and about what explains the emergence and sustenance of different styles over time.

Style also promises, at least when well executed, a remarkable additional virtue: verisimilitude. Some years ago, I organized a conference in Washington, D.C., that brought government and industry officials together with scholars to discuss ways to improve corporate environmental management. Bob Kagan was one of the invited speakers, and I will never forget what occurred after he gave a presentation of his research on management style and environmental compliance on the opening panel. The typology he offered—from laggards to leaders—resonated so profoundly with all of the practitioners that morning that they had a hard time talking about anything else for the rest of the day. That kind of deep resonance reveals what may be one of style's most significant virtues: making sense out of the messy world in a way that optimizes between generalizability and verisimilitude.

Cautionary Notes About Style

Style's virtues are, of course, far from guaranteed. Indeed, in some cases it can be "risky," as Kagan and Axelrad put it, "to make sweeping generalizations" especially in the face of "complexity and variation" (Kagan & Axelrad, 2000, p. 2). Social scientists who seek to use style—or other similar generalizations—to explain or predict other social phenomena should be mindful of at least six challenges or cautions.

First, if style is not thought out well, there is a risk of it not really explaining anything at all. If the characterization of the style of a regulatory organization is based on its past actions, then predicting that similar actions will occur in the future may not be explained at all by style—but rather simply by path dependence. Worse still, if social scientists characterize style—say, an organization's management style—based even partly on the very actions to be explained, then it becomes circular to try to use style to explain those actions.

Second, style poses a challenge with precision. As with a multivariate regression, picking the right "variables" or components of a style will be crucial, as will be getting reliable measures of those variables. But because style is not a regression model, it may be difficult to sort out which of its components are most important. If adversarial legalism, for example, is costly to society, are those costs due to its adversarialism or its legalism—or to the interaction of the two? The same kind of question can be asked any time style comprises an amalgamation of discrete and disparate factors. Can we know which of these factors truly matters? Is style at times just used as a "proxy" for everything else that might explain the phenomena seeking to be explained (Coglianese & Nash, 2001, p. 17)?

Third, style must confront questions about how to validate it intersubjectively. If style is used as little more than a gestalt, will everyone see it the same way? Can research based on style withstand the basic tenet of scientific replicability? It is always possible that a particular style describes one part of the proverbial elephant, and thereby seems to fit that part well, but does not necessarily accurately capture the rest of the elephant. Hammitt et al.'s 2005 study comparing risk regulation in the U.S. and Europe suggests that even if a regulatory style might work to explain selective patterns, it may not fit when used with a more comprehensive set of phenomena. Specifically, in contrast with Vogel's (2012) characterization of Europe's risk regulatory system as exhibiting a more precautionary style, Hammitt et al. analyze a much broader array of regulations and conclude that neither the U.S. nor Europe exhibit any distinctly precautionary style. Each regulatory jurisdiction has some risk policies that are consistent with the precautionary principle, while having other policies that are not. Style's lack of a defining scope and the lack of clear criteria about what should be lumped and what should be split makes it crucial that anyone who relies on style think hard about whether the pattern they perceive is based on all of, or the right kind of, evidence.

Fourth, as with any research, discerning style depends on all the other qualities that make for good social science research: everything from care in gathering data to care in analyzing it. My own research on environmental litigation, for example, pointed out how careless scholars had been in studying litigation in that context (Coglianese, 1996). Instead of the conventional wisdom held by scholars that nearly 80 percent of all EPA regulations were challenged in court, a simple review of publicly accessible court records revealed that about 80 percent of EPA regulations were *never* challenged in court. The erroneous datum about EPA litigation had been widely accepted and cited by scholars and used at times to help define a national adversarial legal style. Although finding such a gross error with one particular datum does not necessarily undermine a judgment about a nation's overall style, it should serve as a reminder to style scientists that they need to scrutinize their characterizations of style with care.

Fifth, and relatedly, if style is at least partly perceptual, it may be more susceptible than other scientific concepts to measurement errors based on cognitive biases. With respect to something like a national style of legalism, for example, researchers may "see" more litigation in their home countries simply because they are cognitively more receptive to it (Coglianese, 2013). Determining something like a litigation rate is very hard to calculate in any society, but conceptually it would seem essential to do so with care if one is trying to measure propensity to escalate conflicts to litigation. Potential conflicts that could have but never did erupt can never be observed, and potential lawsuits are exceedingly hard to see (Felstiner, Abel, & Sarat, 1980–1981)—perhaps most especially by researchers studying a society other than their own.

Finally, anyone relying on style as a social science strategy should recognize that style can change. The world is not only messy but it is also changing. What may make sense of patterns that can be observed today may not make sense of patterns that arise in the future. Vogel (2012), recall, found the regulatory styles in Europe and the U.S. to be changing, and his study sought to explain why. Kelemen (2011) argues that Europe overall is becoming more adversarial and legalistic, like the U.S., while Kagan (2007) has offered an explanation for why Europe is remaining, and will remain, less adversarial and legalistic than the U.S. This scholarly debate is informative, and perhaps the most important lesson to draw from it is to see that style can change. That change, when it occurs, is itself a worthy objective for social science research, as scholars like Kagan and Vogel have shown.

Conclusion

In general, society often celebrates style—at least in art, music, and fashion. The role of style in science is, by comparison, greatly overlooked and understudied. That role in advancing the scientific understanding of law and society is even less analyzed as a distinct mode of inquiry. Yet style's role can be an important one if it helps in organizing complex, dynamic realities and in developing explanations and predictions of outcomes or other phenomena of interest. In this chapter, I have tried to make some sense about a concept that itself seeks to make sense of the regulatory world. One thing is clear: if style matters, we ought to do much more to invest in understanding it and what it achieves for scientific inquiry about law and society. Focusing more attention on style should help in finding better or more standard ways of identifying, measuring, and studying the concept, so it can in turn help in making predictions as well as making sense of a cluttered, seemingly chaotic world.

References

Axelrod, R. (1984). *The Evolution of Cooperation*. New York: Basic Books.

Ayres, I., & Braithwaite, J. (1992). *Responsive Regulation*. New York: Oxford University Press.

Bardach, E., & Kagan, R.A. (1982). *Going by the Book: The Problem of Regulatory Unreasonableness*. Philadelphia: Temple University Press.

Bernstein, M.H. (1955). *Regulating Business by Independent Commission*. Princeton, NJ: Princeton University Press.

Carpenter, D., & Moss, D.A. (2013). *Preventing Regulatory Capture: Special Interest Influence and How to Limit It*. Cambridge: Cambridge University Press.

Coglianese, C. (1996). "Litigating Within Relationships: Disputes and Disturbance in the Regulatory Process." *Law & Society Review*, 30(4), 735–66.

Coglianese, C. (2013). "Robert A. Kagan: Man of Style." *Judicature*, 96 (March/April), 236–8.

Coglianese, C., & Nash, J. (2001). *Regulating From the Inside: Can Environmental Management Systems Achieve Policy Goals*. Washington, DC: Resources for the Future Press.

Damaška, M.R. (1991). *The Faces of Justice and State Authority: A Comparative Approach to the Legal Process*. New Haven, CT: Yale University Press.

Ellickson, R.C. (1991). *Order Without Law: How Neighbors Settle Disputes*. Cambridge, MA: Harvard University Press.

Felstiner, W.L.F., Abel, R.L., & Sarat, A. (1980–1981). "The Emergence and Transformation of Disputes: Naming, Blaming, Claiming . . . " *Law & Society Review*, Special Issue on Dispute Processing and Civil Litigation, 15(3/4), 631–54.

Gunningham, N.A., Kagan, R.A., & Thornton, D. (2003). *Shades of Green: Business, Regulation, and Environment*. Palo Alto, CA: Stanford University Press.

Hammitt, J.K., Wiener, J.B., Swedlow, B., Kall, D., Zhou, Z. (2005). "Precautionary Regulation in Europe and the United States: A Quantitative Comparison." *Risk Analysis*, 25(5), 1215–28.
Hawkins, K. (1984). *Environment and Enforcement: Regulation and the Social Definition of Pollution*. New York: Oxford University Press.
Howard-Grenville, J. (2009). *Corporate Culture and Environmental Practice: Making Change at a High-Technology Manufacturer*. Cheltenham, UK: Edward Elgar.
Howard-Grenville, J., Bertels, S., & Boren, B. (2015). "What Regulators Need to Know About Organizational Culture." Penn Program on Regulation Research Paper. Retrieved from www.bestinclassregulator.org.
Howard-Grenville, J., Nash, J., & Coglianese, C. (2008). "Constructing the License to Operate: Internal Factors and Their Influence on Corporate Environmental Decisions." *Law and Policy*, 30(1) (January), 73–107.
Kagan, R.A. (2001). *Adversarial Legalism: The American Way of Law*. Cambridge, MA: Harvard University Press.
Kagan, R.A. (2007). "Globalization and Legal Change: The "Americanization" of European Law?" *Regulation & Governance*, 1(2) (June), 99–120.
Kagan, R.A., & Axelrad, L. (2000). *Regulatory Encounters: Multinational Corporations and American Adversarial Legalism*. Berkeley, CA: University of California Press.
Karkkainen, B.C. (2004). "'New Governance' in Legal Thought and in the World: Some Splitting as Antidote to Overzealous Lumping." *Minnesota Law Review*, 89, 471.
Kelemen, R.D. (2011). *Eurolegalism: The Transformation of Law and Regulation in the European Union*. Cambridge, MA: Harvard University Press.
Macaulay, S. (1963). "Non-Contractual Relations and Business: A Preliminary Study." *American Sociological Review*, 28, 55–69.
May, P.J., & Winter, S. (2000). "Reconsidering Styles of Regulatory Enforcement: Patterns in Danish Agro-Environmental Inspection." *Law and Policy*, 22, 143–73.
Perin, C. (2005). *Shouldering Risks: The Culture of Control in the Nuclear Power Industry*. Princeton, NJ: Princeton University Press.
Prakash, A. (2000). *Greening the Firm: The Politics of Corporate Environmentalism*. New York: Cambridge University Press.
Reiss, A.J., Jr. (1984). "Selecting Strategies of Social Control Over Organizational Life." In K. Hawkins & J. Thomas (Eds.), *Enforcing Regulation*. Boston, MA: Kluwer-Nijhoff, pp. 23–35.
Schein, E.H. (2010). *Organizational Culture and Leadership*. San Francisco, CA: Jossey-Bass.
Silbey, S.S. (2010). "Legal Culture and Cultures of Legality." In J.R. Hall, L. Grindstaff, & Ming-Cheng Lo (Eds.), *Handbook of Cultural Sociology*. New York: Routledge, pp. 470–80.
Vogel, D. (2012). *The Politics of Precaution: Regulating Health, Safety, and Environmental Risks in Europe and the United States*. Princeton, NJ: Princeton University Press.
Zerubavel, E. (1996). "Lumping and Splitting: Notes on Social Classification." *Sociological Forum*, 11, 421–33.
Zerubavel, E. (2007). "Generally Speaking: The Logic and Mechanics of Social Pattern Analysis." *Sociological Forum*, 22, 131–45.

9

THE POLITICS OF LEGALISM

Thomas F. Burke and Jeb Barnes

The chapters in this book attest to the scope and diversity of legalism(s). From California prisons to European bureaucracies, Australian coal mines to Russia's mean streets, from lawsuits against racial discrimination and the carnage caused by tobacco to regulations on data privacy, this book illustrates the vast and befuddling range of phenomena scholars aim to generalize about when they investigate "law." The challenge of such scholarship is, recent accounts suggest, growing by the day; Ran Hirschl contends that the increasing prominence of courts and litigation in politics across nations is "arguably one of the most significant developments in late twentieth and early twenty-first century governance" (2008, p. 69). What are scholars to do when, as Robert Kagan once asked in an article (1995), there is too much law to study? We find answers in the approach pioneered in part by Kagan, and each of the chapters in this book reflects some aspect of this approach. In this conclusion, we look back at the lessons learned from the chapters, and look forward to the ways in which scholars might further advance our understanding of the causes and consequences of the growth of law across the globe.

Overcoming the Law/Politics Divide

A fundamental conceptual stumbling block in this field of study is the law/politics divide. All too often, scholars who study the legal system reinforce rather than challenge the notion that law is a realm apart from politics, that the questions we ask of other political institutions and processes are somehow illegitimate or irrelevant when applied to law and legal institutions. The subtitle of this volume reflects our insistence that scholars of law always keep in mind the basic questions of politics—who is winning and who losing, who is included and who excluded, whose needs are considered and whose ignored, which problems are highlighted and which shadowed.

The law/politics distinction is reflected in the different ways scholars approach adversarial legalism versus bureaucratic legalism. It is taken for granted that the components of public policy structured through bureaucratic legalism—the welfare and regulatory states—are matters of political debate, and that their implementation by executive agencies will often involve political conflict. Those aspects of public policy that are structured through adversarial legalism, though, are often treated either as interruptions of "normal" politics, or as falling outside of politics entirely.

Several of the chapters in this book challenge this view. Much of the "civil rights state" that Shep Melnick describes would not be counted by conventional scholars as "the state" at all, because a core component is adversarial legalism in the form of individual lawsuits brought by nonstate actors. But as Melnick shows, the array of antidiscrimination policies jointly produced by courts, administrative agencies, and Congress has been a consequential and enduring component of American public policy. Some of the politics of the civil rights state takes place in Congress, which has generally supported adversarial legalism, but much of it takes place in the interplay between courts and agencies. McCann and Haltom's chapter on the politics of tobacco shows why interest groups and activists often turn to adversarial legalism even though the results can be a mixed blessing for them—more straightforward bureaucratic legal policies (primarily cigarette taxes) have been successfully fought off by industry. Bignami and Kelemen's dueling perspectives on "Eurolegalism" demonstrate that both concerns about and admiration for adversarial legalism are important aspects of the debate over the shape of European Union institutions and public policy. From the perspective of the chapters in this book, it is a mistake to treat a polity's mix of legal institutions and structure as distinct from politics; instead, the struggle over competing legalisms is deeply embedded within a more general politics of changing norms and institutional choice.

The politics of legalism in these chapters also entails a ferocious politics of implementation that extends far beyond formal legal institutions into society. Whether an unlucky Russian injured in an auto accident sues to recover damages might seem a purely individual decision, but as Kathryn Hendley shows, that decision is shaped by all kinds of social factors the power of insurance companies, the formalism of Russian judges, but perhaps most of all, the corruption and untrustworthiness of Russian institutions, especially the police. Indeed, these institutional, cultural, and political factors are so influential that Hendley's study of a mundane corner of the legal system offers a depressing prism through which to view the whole of Russian society. Similarly, the mine accidents that are the starting point for Gunningham's chapter can be framed merely as failures of management, a matter of proper technique, but his story demonstrates how institutional and political factors—tensions between management and labor, the rise of contracting out, competing norms of efficiency and safety—lay behind the disconnect between central office and site. Feeley and Swearingen's chapter shows first how the California prison system, like many other organizations, has used alternative dispute resolution systems to blunt the impact of adversarial legalism, but also how local prisons have used the idea of emergency and locality to fend off the centralization and rule-boundedness inherent in bureaucratic legalism. The chapters underscore the fact that the translation of law into practice is not a smooth or straightforward process. It's not simply the commonplace that enforcement and implementation of law is variable, but that there is a micropolitics among the targets of law—prisons, mines, errant drivers—that determines how "law on the books" is translated into social practice.

The interplay of law and politics is endemic to modern administrative states. Law cannot be separated from politics because the entire political and policy-making process is shot through with law, both procedural and substantive. In the United States the line between law and politics is particularly confused because the American system of government intentionally disperses policy making power among overlapping branches and levels of government that are diversely representative. As James Madison recognized in Federalist Paper No. 37 (1788[1987], 244) during Ratification, "No skill in the science of government has yet been able to discriminate and define, with sufficient certainty, its three great provinces—the legislative, executive, and judiciary." That is even truer today, as the elected branches often intentionally pass laws that encourage litigation (Barnes, 1997; Burke, 2002; Farhang, 2010) and professional and interest groups combine litigation and lobbying in pursuing their policy agendas (Epp, 2009; Keck, 2014). Under these circumstances, there is no neat division of labor among the branches and levels of government; instead, we have "separated institutions sharing powers" that naturally engender a vigorous political tug-of-war over the institutional form of policy responses and the implementation of policies (Neustadt, 1990, p. 32).

The point is not that the politics of legalism is indistinguishable from other forms of politics, or that all forms of legalism are politically equivalent. While Martin Shapiro famously described the parallel policymaking functions of courts and executive agencies, he also argued that judicial and administrative policy formulation and implementation are likely to differ: Judges tend to be generalists rather than executive agency specialists, they enjoy greater protections from removal than do political appointees in agencies, and they often exercise negative power through judicial review, all characteristics that can make judicial politics quite different from administrative policymaking (1968, p. 44). Similarly, Malcom Feeley and Ed Rubin argue that judicial policymaking is distinguished by the requirement that judges use specialized modes of legal reasoning to convince other judges to adopt their decisions (Feeley & Rubin, 1998, p. 242). Identifying the distinctive aspects of the politics of bureaucratic and adversarial legalism, their sources of power and characteristic consequences, their distinctive strengths and weaknesses, remains a core task for scholars in the field.

Studying Law in Action

A second lesson of the chapters is that to understand how law works, researchers have to dig down beneath formal institutions and official statements to the ordinary places—shops, offices, schools, hospitals, mines, streets, and prisons—where law shapes, or fails to shape, everyday life. A study that merely uses "law on the books" as the independent variable and some measure of outcome as the dependent variable is likely to miss crucial aspects of law in action. A researcher who focused on Russian tort doctrine and the rulings of judges in order to account for outcomes in Russian auto accident litigation would miss most of what's important in understanding this particular corner of law; much more is learned by Hendley's method of talking to the people who decide whether or not to bring lawsuits.

Like many of the scholars in this book, Robert Kagan seems to relish plunging past formal legal doctrine into the messiness of social life, enjoying forays to ports and pulp factories, fast food restaurants and truck stops. Such fieldwork, however, entails all kinds of challenges for the researcher. Moreover it seems to postpone, if not curtail, prospects for a set of elegant, precise, and powerful theories about the impact of law. Studying law seems difficult enough; bringing in more sources of variance and complexity is at first blush discouraging.

Indeed, the chapters find that organizations respond to law in complex ways that can have little to do with law on the books. In their chapter, Feeley and Swearingen show how relations between local prisons and the centralized administration affect the California prison system's response to reform litigation and court orders. Gunningham's chapter on coal mine safety tells a similar story in a regulatory context, as the commitment to "beyond compliance" behavior in response to safety rules within the firm's leadership was blunted by the "safety-second" culture of mining operations. As Kagan's work on organizational response to laws suggests, these are not isolated cases. An organization's management style—a concept examined in the Coglianese chapter—can shape its response to the law, so that firms in the same business facing similar rules may respond very differently to legal commands (Gunningham et al., 2003; see also Barnes & Burke, 2012).

For scholars, the bad news is that there are no shortcuts or proxies for capturing these internal processes by which the politics of legalism shapes policy outcomes—the researcher has to go there. We cannot circumvent the messiness and difficulty of fieldwork by simply positing that entities will respond rationally to the incentives created by enforcement and punishment, even if we can identify the incentive structures of the governing rules (which is no mean feat given the often open-ended nature of formal rules). The good news is that there is lots of work to do, especially in nations and fields in which the law and society approach is new and in which legal scholars have up to now focused almost solely on formal institutions. Careful examination of legal practice is especially good news for qualitative scholars because measuring response to law requires sensitivity to context, creating space for detail-oriented case studies and ethnographies.

Comparison and Conceptualization

The problems and behavior of civil rights leaders, anti-tobacco activists, miners in Australia, prisoners in California, regulatory bureaucrats in Europe, and auto accident victims in Russia are worthy of study on their own, but from a sociolegal perspective, the chapters' detailed case studies raise the question of what unites these tremendously varied examples of law in social life. A skeptic might note that coherence is a generic problem with edited volumes, but we think the diversity of locales and subjects in this book points to something much more significant. As we noted in the introduction, scholars from every corner of the globe are studying the causes and consequences of the increasing role of law and legal institutions in politics and society. What do all these studies add up to? How do they relate to one another? What, if anything, can we make of their confluences and divergences? In Coglianese's more general terms, how can social scientists discern meaningful patterns within all of this bewildering complexity?

Max Weber, arguably the founder of sociolegal studies, was the first to confront this challenge. He sought to understand law and its rising place in society across diverse cultures and governmental systems, everything from tribal tribunals and "khadi justice" to the civil codes of Europe and the eccentricities of British common law. Forms of authority, Weber argued, were changing. Authority based on religion and charisma was fading, and a new form of authority, which he termed "rational-legal," had arisen (Weber & Rheinstein, 1954). Some have interpreted Weber as championing a kind of grand theory of social development in which "rational-legal authority" triumphs and "rationalization" is an inevitable process, with the "iron cage" its tragic endpoint. From this perspective, all the societies Weber studied were simply at different stages on a path with a common destination. Others have argued that this is a misreading of Weber's scholarship. They stress Weber's emphasis on contingency and context, on the complexities of particular traditions and cultures (Kalberg, 1994). In this view, Weber created grand concepts—rational-legal authority, "substantive" versus "rational" law, and formal versus informal systems of authority—as measuring sticks, devices by which to compare different processes, to put them in a global context and so to facilitate comparison. By deploying his concepts in this way, Weber attempted to do justice to the particularities of, say, Chinese law, while at the same time allowing for comparisons to other systems.

Sociolegal scholars today are confronted with challenges analogous to those faced by Weber. Even as they document the wide variation in the forms and practice of legalism in different settings, scholars in debates over the causes and consequences of the juridification of social life are inevitably drawn into broader, more universal comparisons. Here we see a resonance between Weber and Kagan, whose interest in a wide variety of legalisms—acquired through a lifetime of fieldwork—and use of ideal types to categorize the varieties of legal authority puts him squarely within the Weberian tradition. Kagan's typology of forms of rational-legal authority, like the typologies of Mirjan Damaška (1986) and Jerry Mashaw (1983), from whom Kagan drew, can be seen as a continuation of Weber's attempt to make sense of the varieties of legal authority and to facilitate comparisons among them.

TABLE 9.1 Four Modes of Policymaking

Organization of decision-making authority	*Decision-making style*		
	INFORMAL	⟷	FORMAL
HIERARCHICAL	Expert or political judgment		Bureaucratic legalism
↕			
PARTICIPATORY	Negotiation/ mediation		Adversarial legalism

Source: Kagan (2001).

As we described in the introduction, Kagan's typology is divided along two continua. The first is the degree to which authority is centralized and hierarchical, wielded by state officials, versus decentralized and participatory, the outcome of a clash among parties. The second is the extent to which authority is formal, so that decisions are decided according to preexisting rules and procedures, versus informal, so that decisions are made on a case-by-case basis. The result is four ideal types of authority: expert or political judgment (hierarchical/informal); mediation/negotiation (participatory/informal); bureaucratic legalism (hierarchical/formal); and adversarial legalism (participatory/formal).

The "legalization" or "juridification" of social life reflects the move from the informal cells to formal cells, the two forms of legalism. The key concepts employed in this book, adversarial legalism and bureaucratic legalism, are measures that can be used to understand the diverse forms of formal legal authority and how they operate in social life. Each example of legal authority in the chapters, from the Australian agencies that regulate workplace safety to the U.S. federal courts that handled American tobacco lawsuits, can be placed somewhere on the continuum between the ideal types of adversarial legalism and bureaucratic legalism.

It is important to remember that Kagan's terms, like Weber's, represent ideal types. Scholars often use adversarial legalism as a synonym for litigation, but that can be problematic: Forms of litigation across the globe vary in the extent to which they are dominated by parties versus a hierarchical authority—the judge—and so vary in the extent to which they reflect the adversarial legal ideal. The adversarial legal ideal is probably most closely reflected in civil justice systems like those of the United States, in which the judge takes on a secondary role in the framing of the underlying claims and the collection of evidence, in which the scope of the matters parties can dispute (both procedural and substantive) is broad, and especially in which ordinary citizens, for example jurors, have significant decision-making powers. Because adversarial legalism and bureaucratic legalism are ideal types, in the real world, policies and institutions typically fall on a spectrum between them, not at the ends. We believe this is a strength of the typology, particularly for studying something as complex as the growth of law in various settings, because it allows for gradation rather than mere labels.

Contrasting adversarial legalism and bureaucratic legalism may also help correct a tendency that is reflected in much scholarship, to see "rational-legal" authority in developed nations as inevitably centralized and bureaucratic, to treat this as the default. Weber struggled to make sense of common law systems, with their more chaotic, more decentralized, less predictable outcomes (Weber & Rheinstein, 1954, pp. 315–318; Kronman, 1983, pp. 120–125). Adversarial legalism, with its decentralized structure, and fluid, open-ended everyday practice, sometimes seems from a comparative perspective less a form of legal authority than a morass. This may be why adversarial legalism, wherever it arises, seems to some a disruption to "the normal," a process outside of everyday politics and public policymaking.

Adversarial legalism has this disruptive character because it is a form of legal authority, paradoxically, in which state officials take a backseat, and the parties to a dispute drive the process. At its best, adversarial legalism can create law that is, in the sociologists Philip Selznick and Philippe Nonet's terms, "responsive": flexible and open to change in order to rectify social injustice (Nonet & Selznick, 1978). This is because the parties can argue, not just about how a rule of law applies to the facts of their case, but also about the justice of the rule itself and the process used to decide it—arguments that seem difficult to generate within the bureaucratic legalism ideal. That makes adversarial legalism attractive to activists who seek to reshape understandings of rights. It also allows them to create new rights, to bilingual education, for example, in Melnick's chapter on civil rights, or against the sellers of cigarettes, in McCann and Haltom's chapter.

But the structure of adversarial legalism is associated with certain attributes or tendencies that Kagan called "adversarial legalism in practice," which can be unattractive. The decentralization and fluidity characteristic of adversarial legalism can make it problematic both for potential plaintiffs and defendants. Kagan (2001, p. 7) provides a laundry list of common downsides to adversarial legalism, including

1. more complex bodies of rules
2. more formal and contentious procedures for resolving scientific disputes
3. more costly procedures
4. stronger, more punitive legal sanctions
5. more frequent judicial review and intervention into administrative procedures
6. more political controversy over rules and legal institutions
7. less coordinated systems of decision-making
8. more uncertainty and instability.

Thus it should be no surprise that there is a raging debate over the virtues and vices of adversarial legalism, both in the United States and abroad, as attested by the McCann and Haltom chapter on smoking politics and the Eurolegalism chapter by Bignami and Kelemen.

Of course, there is also a debate over the growth of regulation, and a standard list of pathologies associated with bureaucratic legalism; this fuels a parallel antiregulation politics, especially in the United States. Kagan's study with Gene Bardach, *Going by the Book*, is an illustration of these pathologies (Bardach & Kagan, 1982). The everyday practices associated with bureaucratic legalism can be inefficient and rigid, stifling innovation and encouraging the regulated to emphasize formal compliance over pragmatic problem-solving. On the flip side are the standard concerns about underregulation and capture, as regulators internalize industry practices and preferences over time, becoming lapdogs instead of watchdogs.

We worry that the debate over "too much" and "too little" law, and the associated characterizations of the *policy* virtues and vices of both litigation and regulation, will overshadow some of the more productive uses of Kagan's comparative typology for scholars interested in the *politics* of legalism. In the last few paragraphs of this volume, we sketch out some ways in which we think elements of Kagan's approach can be used to strengthen scholarship on a variety of fundamental questions about law and politics. Our sketch is necessarily tilted toward the particular research questions and locales with which we are most familiar, and so we invite readers to think through implications for the topics and places in which they are interested.

One fundamental set of questions, in an era in which "judicialization," "juristocracy," and "the global expansion of judicial power" are heralded, concerns the political consequences of a shift from the other forms of authority in Kagan's box—negotiation/mediation, expert/political judgment, and bureaucratic legalism, to adversarial legalism. What groups and interests does a shift to adversarial legalism tend to empower? Whom does it weaken? By locating authority outside a centralized state apparatus, adversarial legalism would seem to shift political power away from legislatures and the executive, but to whom?

Scholars offer a number of intriguing hypotheses. In *Juristocracy*, Ran Hirschl contends that judicialization offers a mechanism by which political and economic elites preserve their power, particularly as legislatures become more democratic (Hirschl, 2004). Hirschl's study of the judicialization of "megapolitics" in Canada, New Zealand, South Africa, and Israel runs against the view in the United States that litigation is a haven for otherwise disfavored groups, a means by which to bypass legislatures and executive agencies that have been captured by the powerful, as it did famously in the case of the NAACP and civil rights (Peretti, 1999). Then there is the famous Marc Galanter hypothesis (1974), often supported by empirical research (see, for example, Kritzer & Silbey, 2003) that courts tend to advantage organized groups (repeat players) at the expense of individuals (one-shotters), disproportionately favoring the same powerful interests that flourish elsewhere. Consistent with this idea, Lisa Vanhala, in a recent article on the use of litigation in environmental policy in France (2016), finds that the groups that most actively challenge the French environmental ministry in court tend to be the same groups most powerful in environmental policymaking, a finding that echoes Cary Coglianese's conclusions about judicial review of environmental rulemaking in the United States (Coglianese, 1996).

This brief recitation of just a few studies suggests, unsurprisingly, that the politics of adversarial legalism is complex and contingent. So we might reframe the question: Under what conditions does a move to adversarial legalism shift power, when does it leave power undisturbed, and when does it serve to preserve the (threatened) power of elite groups? Kagan's framework seems useful in answering these questions for a simple reason: it focuses researchers on the counterfactual, the comparison point for the judicialized political process they are studying. That to study judicialization inevitably requires a comparison point seems a banal observation, and yet it is often lost in research on the politics of rights, courts, and litigation (Burke & Barnes, 2009; Barnes & Burke, 2015). To say anything meaningful about how and why different legalisms shape politics, we have to compare the social and political consequences of the alternative forms of authority—expert, legislative, executive—that they replace. The existing literature obscures this point because it tends to lump together forms of legalism under umbrella terms such as "judicialization" and also to treat all nonjudicial forms of authority as equivalent. All forms of legalism become "law," all forms of authority other than legalism become "politics," and so the simple law/politics distinction reappears.

We can see the promise of Kagan's approach when considering how others have addressed growing legalism in a variety of settings. In *Courting Social Justice* (2008), for instance, Varun Gauri and Daniel Brinks and their collaborators grapple with core questions related to the social impact of judicial enforcement of social and economic rights in the developing world. Like the authors in this volume, they eschew the simplistic distinctions between legislative and judicial processes and call for a comparative analysis of the effects of legalization. They treat legalization as a continuum between various institutional arrangements. Their framework allows them to aggregate insights from case studies of legalization in diverse settings, including South Africa, Brazil, India, Nigeria, and Indonesia, and hypothesize about some of the conditions under which formal rights matter.

Gauri and Brinks' volume offers many insights, and is a model of exploring legalism in settings outside of industrialized democracies. Yet Kagan's approach might enhance their analysis on at least two levels. First, as the authors themselves acknowledge, the case studies in their volume focus on formal rights and, in their words, not all of the "pathways" of "social and economic rights can affect the availability and quality of social and economic goods" (Gauri and Brinks, 2008, p. 7). Drilling down below the surface of formal rights and into the everyday world of legalism on the ground, the kind of fieldwork pursued by Kagan and many authors in this volume, would surely provide a much more nuanced account of the effects of legalization.

Second, Gauri and Brinks treat legalization as a single continuum, which creates several kinds of difficulties because, as Kagan's framework suggests, the variety of legalisms they encounter in the volume have properties that in some cases cannot adequately be aggregated into a single dimension. Gauri and Brinks acknowledge that while their case studies focus primarily on courts, they also include "quasi-judicial forums" (2008, p. 28), and processes more akin to "mediation or arbitration than . . . judicial, adversarial litigation" (2008, p. 28). By providing a more dimensional understanding of "legalization," the Kagan framework, we think, could be used to distinguish more carefully these cases and so sharpen their analysis. For example, in their discussion of South Africa, Gauri and Brinks note that despite relatively strong constitutional language, the South African courts have been largely deferential towards the government and the cases have been "defensive," or narrow, focusing on particular disputes as opposed to setting broad policy. Rather than thinking of this as a case of ineffective legalization, it might be treated instead as an instance in which law is made by organizations other than courts, and analyzed as a case study in the varying political consequences of adversarial versus bureaucratic legalism. The general point is that Kagan's multidimensional typology should provide a better basis for comparison than the single dimension of legalization the authors employ.

This, of course, is only one example. Having a more refined language of comparison can sharpen research on a wide range of questions related to the rise of rights, courts, and litigation. For example, there is no shortage of hypotheses in the literature about the political risks of turning away from "normal" politics to judicial policy making (Barnes & Burke, 2015). In his famous critique of using courts to make social policy, Gerald Rosenberg (2008) argues that litigation not only represents an ineffective means to make policy—a "hollow hope"—but also, given its costs, forces groups to abandon other, allegedly more consequential forms of advocacy as they divert their limited resources to do battle in court. In a parallel argument, Gordon Silverstein (2009) worries that litigation ossifies politics by framing issues in terms of rights that become "givens" and limit discourse and reform options down the road. We have contended that these and other prominent studies insufficiently consider whether alternative forms of authority, for example bureaucratic legalism or legislative politics, have the very same tendencies. Studies of the effects of judicialization, and of legal rights, necessarily invoke an other, some kind of comparison point, but in much research this remains shadowy and underexplored (Burke & Barnes, 2009; Barnes & Burke, 2015). Kagan's framework, an attempt to typologize all forms of rational-legal authority, can help researchers refine their comparisons.

Kagan's typology also offers useful concepts for studies of how and why forms of legalism emerge and change over time, urgent questions in an era in which both old and new democracies—and some authoritarian polities—seem to be empowering their judiciaries. Kagan (1994) himself has written about the sources of political appeal of adversarial legalism in the U.S. context, along with a number of scholars who study law and public policy (e.g., Melnick, 1994; Barnes, 1997; Burke, 2002; Farhang, 2010). Others have written about the creation of strong courts in new democracies, the way authoritarian governments have sought to strengthen courts in some realms, and the development of transnational courts and their effect on domestic politics—an issue discussed in the Eurolegalism colloquy between Bignami and Kelemen in this volume. Here again, rather than lumping together all forms of legalism in such studies, we urge scholars to think carefully about the sources of variance implicit in Kagan's framework. To what extent are newly empowered courts, in his terms, participatory, open to novel claims about both substantive and procedural justice, versus hierarchical, merely applying governmental rules as in a bureaucracy? As seen in the Bignami and Kelemen colloquy, even when scholars disagree over the exact form of legalism in a particular setting, having a common set of terms sharpens the dialogue and yields better questions.

Although adversarial legalism is probably Kagan's most famous formulation, in fact he spent the bulk of his career examining the politics of bureaucratic legalism. There is, of course, a vast literature on the politics of bureaucracy in political science, but much of Kagan's writing on regulation, like that of his comrades in sociolegal studies, points us instead to the politics of bureaucratic legalism *in regulated organizations*. Because we live in a "society of organizations" (Perrow, 1991), the failure or success of both regulation and litigation in fostering social change largely depends on how organizations implement legal commands, a point made vividly by the Gunningham and the Swearingen and Feeley chapters in this volume. Large, complex organizations that, say, implement rules governing safety in coal mines, the rights of prisoners, or sexual harassment in the workplace, must develop a kind of interior bureaucratic legalism.

In contrast to neo-institutionalist research, which probes patterns of organizational response to law within a given field, usually through surveys of the organizations, regulatory scholarship often attempts to understand response to law by looking more deeply within organizations. Kagan and his colleagues developed the concept of "management style" to typologize patterns of organizational response to law. The challenge, as Coglianese writes in his chapter for this volume, is to find a way of talking about internal organizational dynamics that does not turn these internal dynamics into a general catch-all, so that "management style" becomes synonymous with open-ended concepts like "culture" or "style." Part of the problem may be that management style was originally formulated as an ideal type that encompasses a number of dimensions simultaneously, including the commitment of the organization to the goals of the law, the degree to which the organization created formal structures in response to the law, and whether consideration of the law was embedded in the standard operating procedures of the organization. As Coglianese argues, future research in this area should strive to make the concept of management style more concrete and amenable to measurement across a wide range of organizations, perhaps by parsing the components of style into separate dimensions.

Whichever of these avenues of inquiry scholars find themselves drawn to—the political consequences of shifts in legalism, the causes of evolving styles and combinations of legalism, the politics of organizational response to legal commands—we believe that Kagan's characteristic blend of fieldwork and comparison offers a useful model. Kagan's approach is based on the recognition that legalism is much more than a set of formal rules and institutions, that it is constituted by everyday practices far from courthouses and regulatory agencies. Yet despite its emphasis on local practices, it provides a set of concepts for organizing findings and framing broad questions. We recognize that Kagan's methodological middle path is somewhat out of step with powerful tendencies in social science. Faced with the complexity of social life, many scholars have decided to simplify and specialize, focusing on narrow questions related to formal structures of authority and incentives, or even eschewing observational research altogether in an attempt to capture abstract dynamics through laboratory experiments. Others have taken the opposite tack and embraced contingency and complexity, stressing thick description over the discovery of patterns and comparisons. Kagan's approach is in tension with both of these tendencies because it seeks to balance context and comparison, structure and agency, formal rules and social practices, lumping and splitting. Yet as Kagan's long and distinguished body of scholarship attests, for those who seek to better understand the growth of law and its implications for polities around the globe, it offers a promising way forward.

References

Bardach, E., & Kagan, R.A. (1982). *Going by the Book: The Problem of Regulatory Unreasonableness*. Philadelphia: Temple University Press.

Barnes, J. (1997). "Bankrupt Bargain? Bankruptcy Reform and the Politics of Adversarial Legalism." *Journal of Law and Politics*, 13(4), 893–934.

Barnes, J., & Burke, T.F. (2012). "Making Way: Legal Mobilization, Organizational Response, and Wheelchair Access." *Law & Society Review*, 46(1), 167–98.

Barnes, J., & Burke, T.F. (2015). *How Policy Shapes Politics: Rights, Courts, Litigation, and the Struggle Over Injury Compensation*. New York: Oxford University Press.

Burke, T.F. (2002). *Lawyers, Lawsuits, and Legal Rights: The Battle Over Litigation in American Society*. Berkeley: University of California Press.

Burke, T.F., & Barnes, J. (2009). "Is There an Empirical Literature on Rights?" *Special Issue Revisiting Rights Studies in Law, Politics and Society*, 69–91.

Coglianese, C. (1996). "Litigating Within Relationships: Disputes and Disturbance in the Regulatory Process." *Law & Society Review*, 30(4), 735.

Damaška, M.R. (1986). *The Faces of Justice and State Authority: A Comparative Approach to the Legal Process*. New Haven: Yale University Press.

Epp, C.R. (2009). *Making Rights Real: Activists, Bureaucrats, and the Creation of the Legalistic State*. Chicago: University of Chicago Press.

Farhang, S. (2010). *The Litigation State: Public Regulation and Private Lawsuits in the U.S.* Princeton, NJ: Princeton University Press.

Feeley, M., & Rubin, E.L. (1998). *Judicial Policy Making and the Modern State: How the Courts Reformed America's Prisons*. New York: Cambridge University Press.

Galanter, M. (1974). "Why the 'Haves' Come Out Ahead: Speculations on the Limits of Legal Change." *Law & Society Review*, 9(1), 95.

Gauri, V., & Brinks, D.M. (Eds.) (2008). *Courting Social Justice: Judicial Enforcement of Social and Economic Rights in the Developing World*. New York: Cambridge University Press.

Gunningham, N., Kagan, R.A., & Thornton, D. (2003). *Shades of Green: Business, Regulation, and Environment*. Stanford, CA: Stanford Law and Politics.

Hirschl, R. (2004). *Towards Juristocracy: The Origins and Consequences of the New Constitutionalism*. Cambridge, MA: Harvard University Press.

Hirschl, R. (2008). "The Judicialization of Mega-Politics and the Rise of Political Courts." *Annual Review of Political Science*, 11(1), 93–118.

Kagan, R.A. (1994). "Do Lawyers Cause Adversarial Legalism? A Preliminary Inquiry." *Law & Social Inquiry*, 19(1), 1.

Kagan, R.A. (1995). "What Socio-Legal Scholars Should Do When There Is Too Much Law to Study." *Journal of Law and Society*, 22(1), 140.

Kagan, R.A. (2001). *Adversarial Legalism: The American Way of Law*. Cambridge, MA: Harvard University Press.

Kalberg, S. (1994). *Max Weber's Comparative-Historical Sociology*. Chicago: University of Chicago Press.

Keck, T.M. (2014). *Judicial Politics in Polarized Times*. Chicago: The University of Chicago Press.

Kritzer, H.M., & Silbey, S.S. (2003). *In Litigation: Do the Haves Still Come Out Ahead?* Stanford, CA: Stanford Law and Politics.

Kronman, A.T. (1983). *Max Weber*. Stanford, CA: Stanford University Press.

Madison, J. (1788). Federalist Paper No. 37. Reprinted in *The Federalist Papers* (1987). New York: Penguin Classics.

Mashaw, J.L. (1983). *Bureaucratic Justice: Managing Social Security Disability Claims*. New Haven: Yale University Press.

Melnick, R.S. (1994). *Between the Lines: Interpreting Welfare Rights*. Washington, DC: Brookings Institution.

Neustadt, R.E. (1990). *Presidential Power and the Modern Presidents: The Politics of Leadership from Roosevelt to Reagan*. New York: The Free Press.

Nonet, P., & Selznick, P. (1978). *Law and Society in Transition: Toward Responsive Law*. New York: Harper & Row.

Peretti, T.J. (1999). *In Defense of a Political Court*. Princeton, NJ: Princeton University Press.

Perrow, C. (1991). "A Society of Organizations." *Theory and Society*, 20(6), 725–62.

Rosenberg, G.N. (2008). *The Hollow Hope: Can Courts Bring About Social Change?* Chicago: University of Chicago Press.

Shapiro, M.M. (1968). *The Supreme Court and Administrative Agencies*. New York: The Free Press.

Silverstein, G. (2009). *Law's Allure: How Law Shapes, Constrains, Saves and Kills Politics*. New York: Cambridge University Press.

Vanhala, L. (2016). "Legal Mobilization Under Neo-Corporatist Governance: Environmental NGOs Before the Conseil d'Etat in France, 1975–2010." *Journal of Law and Courts*, 4(1), 103–30.

Weber, M., & Rheinstein, M. (1954). *Max Weber on Law in Economy and Society*. Cambridge, MA: Harvard University Press.

INDEX